Canada Among Nations 1996

Canada Among Nations 1996

Big Enough to be Heard

EDITED BY

FEN OSLER HAMPSON

&

MAUREEN APPEL MOLOT

Carleton University Press

© Carleton University Press, Inc. 1996
Carleton Public Policy Series # 19

Printed and bound in Canada

National Library of Canada cataloguing

Canada Among Nations

1984–
Annual.
1996 ed.: Big enough to be heard.
Each vol. also has a distinctive title.
Produced by the Norman Paterson School of
    International Affairs of Carleton University.
Includes bibliographical references.
ISSN 0832-0683
ISBN 0-88629-282-4 (1996 ed.)

    1. Canada—Foreign relations—1945- —Periodicals.
2. Canada—Politics and government—1984- —Periodicals.
3. Canada—Politics and government—1980-1984—Periodicals.
I. Norman Paterson School of International Affairs.

FC242.C345   327.71   C86-031285-2
F1034.2.C36

Cover design: Your Aunt Nellie

Cover photo: AP/Wide World Photos, Richard Drew

Carleton University Press gratefully acknowledges the support extended to its publishing program by the Canada Council and the Ontario Arts Council.

The Press would also like to thank the Department of Canadian Heritage, Government of Canada, and the Government of Ontario through the Ministry of Culture, Tourism and Recreation, for their assistance.

CONTENTS

List of Contributors   vii

Preface   ix

Introduction

  I Being Heard and the Role of Leadership   3
     Fen Osler Hampson and Maureen Appel Molot

The Policy Process

  II Redesigning Canadian Diplomacy in an Age of
     Fiscal Austerity   23
     Evan H. Potter

  III Future Defence Policy in an *Époque de vaches maigres*   57
     Hal P. Klepak

New Challenges in an Era of Globalization

  IV Canada and the Halifax Summit   83
     Gordon S. Smith

  V Is There Life After Deathstars? Communications
     Technology and Cultural Relations   95
     Keith Acheson and Christopher J. Maule

  VI Canada and the United States: Still Calm
     in the "Remarkable Relationship"   111
     Joseph T. Jockel

The UN System: 50th Anniversary Review

Reflections: Ambassadors' Round Table
  VII   *Robert R. Fowler*   135
  VIII *Louise Fréchette*   149
  IX   *Geoffrey A.H. Pearson*   163

The UN System

X The Security Council: Trial and Error in Moving to a
Post-Westphalian International System 175
Harald von Riekhoff

XI Canadian Public and Governmental Perceptions
of United Nations Reform 201
Gregory Wirick

XII Rethinking Peacekeeping: The Bosnia and Somalia
Experience 221
David B. Carment

XIII NGOs and the International System:
Building Peace in a World at War 251
Kenneth D. Bush

XIV International Financial Institutions: Beginning of the
End or End of the Beginning? 273
Roy Culpeper

XV Canada and the OAS: *Terra Incognita* 301
John W. Graham

List of Acronyms 319

CONTRIBUTORS

Keith Acheson is a professor in the Department of Economics, Carleton University.

Kenneth D. Bush is an adjunct assistant professor in the Department of Political Science, Queen's University.

David B. Carment is an assistant professor in The Norman Paterson School of International Affairs, Carleton University.

Roy Culpeper is President of the North-South Institute.

Robert R. Fowler is Ambassador, Permanent Mission of Canada to the United Nations.

Louise Fréchette is Deputy Minister, Department of National Defence.

John W. Graham is a senior advisor, The Americas, International Foundation for Electoral Systems (IFES).

Fen Osler Hampson is a professor in The Norman Paterson School of International Affairs, Carleton University.

Joseph T. Jockel is a professor in the Canadian Studies Program, St. Lawrence University.

Hal P. Klepak is a professor in the Department of History, Royal Military College.

Christopher J. Maule is a professor in the Department of Economics, Carleton University.

Maureen Appel Molot is a professor in the Department of Political Science and professor and Director of The Norman Paterson School of International Affairs, Carleton University.

Geoffrey A.H. Pearson is former Head of the UN Bureau, Department of Foreign Affairs and International Trade.

Evan H. Potter is the Senior Fellow at the Harrowston Program on Conflict Management and Negotiation, University of Toronto and the founding editor of the Canadian Foreign Policy Journal.

Gordon S. Smith is Deputy Minister, Department of Foreign Affairs and International Trade.

Harald von Riekhoff is a professor in the Department of Political Science, Carleton University.

Gregory Wirick is an international affairs consultant and an associate with the Parliamentary Centre.

Preface

Big Enough to be Heard is the twelfth volume in The Norman Paterson School of International Affairs series on Canada in international affairs. The chapters in this edition examine a range of issues in Canadian foreign policy that were current during calendar 1995, a year which saw a referendum on Canadian unity and which celebrated the fiftieth anniversary of the United Nations.

The theme of this year's volume is the need for choices in Canadian foreign policy. In an environment of fiscal constraint, there is some urgency to reviewing the range of Canada's international commitments and to establishing priorities for the rest of the decade and beyond. The necessity of choice is also related to the multitude of international organizations to which Canada belongs. If we can no longer afford to be a member of a large number of international institutions, which memberships will we continue and on what grounds will we decide? These questions, and others, are among those addressed by chapters which consider Canadian foreign and defence policy in an era of austerity, Canada-U.S. relations, Canadian participation in the June 1995 G-7 conference in Halifax, Canadian peacekeeping activities and the role of Canadian non-governmental organizations in peace-making, and Canada's five decades of participation in the United Nations.

Financial support for *Big Enough to be Heard* has come from the Military and Strategic Studies Program of the Department of National Defence and from The Norman Paterson School of International Affairs.

This volume could not have been put together without the assistance of a number of people whose contributions we are happy to acknowledge. Brenda Sutherland has once again supervised the initial editing of the manuscript and has been patient with the editors' many corrections. Janet Doherty organized the authors' workshop and reminded the contributors to be punctual with their submissions. Vivian Cummins and the School of International Affairs Resource Centre assisted the editors in gathering materials for use in the Introduction. Don Montrichard prepared the glossary and assisted with the editing of the volume. Noel Gates, Pauline McKillop and John Flood all helped with various stages of the production process.

Big Enough to be Heard has been an enjoyable project on which to work. We hope that it contributes to the ongoing debate on Canadian foreign policy.

Fen Osler Hampson
Maureen Appel Molot
Ottawa, March 1996

Canada Among Nations 1996

Introduction   I

Being Heard and
the Role of Leadership

FEN OSLER HAMPSON

AND MAUREEN APPEL MOLOT

When Brian Tobin, Canada's former Fisheries Minister, stood on a barge in New York harbour in front of the United Nations with the captured fishing nets of a Spanish trawler, he dramatically catapulted Canadian concerns about overfishing off the Grand Banks of Newfoundland into the forefront of world headlines. In a single, brilliant publicity manoeuvre, Canada was able to make its voice heard. But an effective voice in foreign policy depends upon more than just good public relations and sound bites. The title of the 1996 edition of *Canada Among Nations*, "Big Enough to be Heard," can be read in two ways, with a question mark at the end raising uncertainty about whether Canada has enough clout to continue to play a significant role in international affairs, or with an exclamation mark suggesting that, domestic stresses and challenges aside, Canada remains a credible, major player on the international scene.

The contributors to this volume believe that Canada continues to be an international actor of consequence, as our membership in the G-7 and a host of other international organizations exemplifies. Cautionary notes are sounded about the repercussions of debates on national unity and fiscal constraints on Canada's capacity to remain a serious international player.[1] But the real message is that our importance and relevance in the international sphere increasingly depend on sound leadership, clear priorities, and direction from our political leaders at home. Although the Chrétien government has conducted extensive consultations with Canadians from almost every walk and branch of Canadian life, it has given little sense of direction about what Canadian foreign and defence policies should be at a time of severe fiscal stringency, mounting debt, and domestic political troubles. Though the election of that government to power on October 25, 1993 marked a professed return to the verities of Pearsonian internationalism, what Canadians have in fact got is a tepid brew of "Pearson lite"—policies that are big on rhetoric and symbolism, but weak on substance and political direction. Instead of asking "where's the fish?" Canadians are increasingly wont to ask "where's the beef?"

This volume of *Canada Among Nations* is intended to provide both a review of Canadian foreign policy achievements over the past year and a half and an assessment of the challenges that lie ahead. We are privileged to include contributions by scholars and distinguished practitioners in this year's volume.

As in the past, each article in *Canada Among Nations* is a freestanding contribution and no effort has been made to reach a consensus among the authors. Indeed, as the chapters make clear, contributors have their own distinct viewpoints and perspectives on where Canada stands in the community of nations and where the country's foreign policy priorities should lie.

QUEBEC REFERENDUM

The October 30 sovereignty referendum in Quebec was unquestionably the domestic event which had the greatest impact on Canada's international profile in 1995. The Chrétien government utilized every opportunity presented by international meetings or trade missions to demonstrate to all Canadians the benefits of a strong and united Canada. Whether it was the June 1995 Halifax Summit of G-7 nations (see Chapter 4 by Gordon Smith), the Team Canada trips to Asia and

Latin America led by the Prime Minister, or the meeting of La Francophonie, the message was the same: Canada remains strong and committed to fulfilling its international obligations; Canada plays a unique and valued role internationally as a result of its membership in a range of global and regional organizations; Canadians reap enormous advantages from the country's international reputation for stability, democracy and commitment to active diplomacy.

The message was intended for both domestic and foreign audiences. Whether it was credible to either is a matter for conjecture. There is no empirical evidence to suggest that Canadian voters (especially "soft" separatist Québécois or the separatist elites) are predisposed to supporting federalism on the basis of Canada's involvement in peacekeeping, Team Canada trade visits, or other international activities. At home, polls demonstrated the concern of Canadians with issues of economic well-being, primarily jobs and unemployment. Few Canadians see a clear link between Canada's international profile and their own immediate futures. Only for those in the business and financial sectors did Canada's international image and the importance of stability resonate as an issue of consequence in the debate over Canada's future.

This being said, it is important to note that foreign policy is one area where there has been a surprising degree of national consensus over the last fifty years. Such cohesiveness has not always prevailed in the past. Recall that for the first half of this century foreign policy was a source of great divisiveness in national debates; Québécois and other Canadians were at loggerheads over Canada's involvement in the Boer War and both world wars. On issues of trade, peacekeeping, democratic development and human rights, as well as Canada's role in the international organizations, there are no national divisions. Where there are divisions they relate to our manner of projecting our internal differences to Wall Street and our largest trading partner.

The overwhelming economic importance of the U.S. (slightly over 80 percent of Canada's exports go to that country) meant that both Quebec and Canada expended considerable resources trying to get their respective messages across to their southern neighbour. Members of the PQ government addressed a range of American audiences to argue that an independent Quebec would adhere to all Canada's economic obligations, including membership in the World Trade Organization and the North American Free Trade Agreement (NAFTA), and that business would continue without interruption. As

J.T. Jockel notes in Chapter 6, the United States has long adhered to the mantra that "the future of Canada is for Canadians to decide." President Clinton employed a variant of this phraseology during his February, 1995, visit to Ottawa, saying to a joint session of the House of Commons and Senate that "[in] a world darkened by ethnic conflicts that tear nations apart, Canada stands as a model of how people of different cultures can live and work together in peace, prosperity and mutual respect."[2] However, as the referendum date drew nearer, representatives of the Clinton Administration spoke in less neutral terms. Secretary of State Warren Christopher, for example, noted that an independent Quebec should not assume that it would have exactly the same sort of ties with the United States as Canada did, a not so veiled threat that Quebec might not automatically enjoy membership in NAFTA and other beneficial arrangements.[3] Just five days before the referendum, in carefully worded remarks that were welcomed in Ottawa, President Clinton referred to Canada as "a great model for the rest of the world and a great partner for the United States" and expressed the hope that this "can continue."[4]

The debate over national unity in a country that had been designated by the United Nations as the most attractive in the world in which to live sparked astonishment, if not apprehension, in many countries. Those with ethnic minorities could not help but ponder the impact on their own futures of a pro-sovereignty referendum outcome. What gave the Quebec question extra salience in Europe was that region's recent experiences with integration and disintegration, ranging from the evolving European Union to the breakup of the former Yugoslavia. Canada, rarely covered in the foreign press, was suddenly front-page news in many parts of the world and reporters converged on Montreal to cover the referendum. Although the narrowness of the result surprised international audiences, many interpreted the slim "no" victory with less concern than was felt in Canada. Some Third World countries feared that if Quebec did separate and, as a result, Canada became more inward-looking, the country might not continue to be able to play the important role it had historically assumed with respect to Third World concerns.

In the short term the referendum debate does not appear to have had a negative impact on Canada's international image. At international meetings immediately following the October 31, 1995 vote—the Commonwealth Summit in New Zealand and the Asia Pacific Economic Cooperation Summit (APEC) in Osaka, Japan—the referendum received polite mention from our allies. There was some jousting between Canada and Quebec at the Summit of La Francophonie in Benin, but that, too, was not taken too seriously by other participants. However, there is a long-term cost to divisiveness and disunity at home. The view that Canada cannot run its own show may gain ground. We may get the reputation of a nation that does not practice what it preaches.

As we look to the future and the connection between national unity and foreign policy, Quebecers and the rest of Canada should realize that negotiations directed at renewed federalism, sovereignty-association or outright independence will not take place solely on the terms that Quebec and the rest of Canada want. Globalization and the growing internationalization of financial markets have greatly reduced the autonomy of governments and other political actors. Canada's debt issues have deep-seated causes and foreign actors will only support Canadian and Quebec interests at a price. We had a taste of this in the weeks prior to the referendum when the Canadian dollar fell and there were concerns about federal and provincial bond ratings.

FISCAL CONSTRAINTS

As Evan Potter notes in Chapter 2 and Hal Klepak in Chapter 3, the second issue that will affect Canada's capacity to be heard in international fora is that of resources—what we can afford to spend on the ever-expanding range of foreign policy and defence concerns. The demands for Canadian participation in international activities and the expectations arising from that participation are increasing at the same time as the monies available for these ventures are being curtailed by the need to reduce the country's annual deficit. The budget of the Department of Foreign Affairs and International Trade (DFAIT) declined slightly from the 1994-95 to the 1995-96 fiscal year while that of the Canadian International Development Agency (CIDA) has been reduced steadily over the last few years. The Canadian government is now spending a smaller proportion of its total budget on foreign affairs and aid than it did at the beginning of the decade (see Table 1 of Chapter 2). Under the government-wide Program Review launched in 1994 DFAIT will experience budgetary reductions of 15 percent in the current (i.e., 1995-96) and the next two fiscal years.

The federal government is trying to reduce both the debt and the deficit. Financial constraints and budget cuts translate into the need to make choices. The issues then become the process by which Canadian foreign policy priorities are established and the considerations attendant upon decisions to continue or withdraw from particular commitments, or to embark on new ones.

The process of determining Canadian foreign policy priorities under the Chrétien government has been two-track, a consultative, public process and an internal DFAIT review. How the two relate to each other and whether they will come together in a manner that will facilitate the articulation of a new foreign policy direction and the establishment of a structure appropriate to its implementation remain to be seen. Whatever happens, continuing consultation with Canadians about foreign policy goals and priorities should not be allowed to become an excuse for inaction or failure to exercise decisive leadership by making some tough choices.

The public side of the foreign policy review process stemmed from a commitment made by the Liberal Party in its Foreign Policy Handbook and electoral platform to "an open process for foreign policy-making."[5] The details of the review process have been analyzed elsewhere and therefore do not require repetition here.[6] Suffice it to say that the 1994 National Forum and the parliamentary review process provided a segment of the Canadian public with the opportunity to express their opinions on foreign policy (and defence) issues. Despite, or perhaps because of, the number of briefs received, the Report of the Special Joint Committee of the Senate and the House of Commons Reviewing Canadian Foreign Policy[7] was comprehensive in its coverage of the issues and cautious in its recommendations. In only one chapter, that on "Projecting Canadian Culture and Learning Abroad," did the Committee demonstrate some new thinking. If the government was looking for guidance in establishing new directions for Canadian foreign policy or assistance in determining which responsibilities it might shed, the Special Joint Committee's product was of little help. That the government's Response to the Special Joint Committee's report agreed fully with 61 of the 80 recommendations and accepted another 15 or 16 "in substance"[8] suggests that either the Committee's deliberations captured the essence of government priorities or that the government, and by implication the Department of Foreign Affairs and International Trade, were not yet prepared to face the need for choices.

Consultation on foreign policy issues continued in 1995 with the Second Annual National Forum. Unlike the First Forum, in which the participants considered a very broad range of topics, the second focused more narrowly on international institutions: participants examined four categories of institutions—those involved in peace and security, trade and economic relations, sustainable human development, and culture and communications—and made recommendations on steps Canada should take to promote greater efficiency, coherence, accountability and transparency in these organizations.[9] At the forum, the government announced the creation of an Advisory Board (created in November 1995) to advise the Foreign Minister on Canada's policy priorities. This advice will then affect the type of outreach and consultations—or democratization—that is pursued by the new Foreign Policy Mechanism located in the Policy Branch of DFAIT. The creation of the Mechanism and the Advisory Board in some ways represents a second-best fulfilment of the Liberal government's promise of a Foreign Policy Development Institute, included in the Handbook and mentioned in the Parliamentary Final Report.

That the government is carrying through with its commitment to democratize the foreign policy process is commendable, however. Whether democratization can make any contribution, let alone a significant one, to the delineation of foreign policy priorities is another matter. At one level, activities that promote a more informed public and give the impression of a more transparent policy process may help to generate good will for the government in the current environment of popular disenchantment with political leaders. At another, there is the more cynical view that the consultative process is simply one of cooptation[10] of interests and the outcome of concern that the frustration of groups with their lack of influence on policy choices might in the longer run simply increase the disenchantment with the government and its consultative undertakings. In the end, the articulation of Canada's foreign policy priorities will not emerge from consultation, admirable though that is, but from leadership at the top which is prepared to examine Canada's current global undertakings and determine which will be critical in the years ahead.

Concomitant with the public side of the foreign policy review has been the DFAIT internal review process. Thus far this latter procedure has had two phases: the preparation of *Canada in the World*, the government's response to the Special Joint Committee Report,[11] and an internal review of the Department's role and operations, initiated in early 1996.

As was stated in the introduction to *Democracy and Foreign Policy*—the 1995 edition of *Canada Among Nations*—*Canada in the World* is a very general statement of Canadian foreign policy interests. It identifies three objectives that were to guide Canadian foreign policy over the next few years: "the promotion of prosperity and employment; the protection of our security within a stable global framework; and the projection [abroad] of Canadian values and culture."[12] The first two purposes are so broad that virtually any activity can be deemed to fit within them. The third was the government's response to the new direction for Canadian foreign policy enunciated by the Special Joint Committee.

Canada in the World did not consider what the role of a foreign ministry should be. Although the Government Statement recognized the constraints on Canada's fiscal capacity and, therefore, the need to make choices, it neither proposed any nor discussed the parameters which might guide the fashioning of priorities. Indeed, in the face of fiscal limitations, the document proposed and subsequently established a new branch in the Department entitled Global Issues and Culture, headed by an assistant deputy minister. While this new unit can be justified as essential for the administration of one of the three pillars of Canadian foreign policy, there may have been other means that could have been used to accomplish this goal within DFAIT or in collaboration with other departments. What is noteworthy is that cultural affairs, a responsibility which the Mulroney government, a few years earlier, had attempted to eliminate from the responsibilities of DFAIT,[13] had been refurbished and given greater prominence; yet when the time came to provide the funds that would translate the priority into a reality, there were only modest resources in the 1995-96 and 1996-97 Departmental Estimates for cultural activities.[14] The result was an impression of confusion and lack of direction regarding DFAIT's role and priorities and the wherewithal to implement them.

The internal review now under way in DFAIT is yet another attempt to come to grips with the realities of diminished resources. Its impetus is not solely internal to the Department but also stems from a perspective current in the central agencies of government, the Privy Council Office (PCO), the Treasury Board and the Department of Finance, which views DFAIT as having difficulty in establishing its priorities and as not forming part of the domestic political agenda. In 1995 PCO had initiated its own review of Canada's overseas representation with the clear intention of achieving efficiencies and savings.[15]

The message from the Clerk of the Privy Council to the Deputy Minister of DFAIT was apparently succinct: the Department is doing too much and must decide upon which activities it intends to focus.

Four distinct but interrelated topics comprise the internal review: the Department's role and responsibilities; headquarters structure and management processes within the Department; improving the efficiency and effectiveness of Departmental operations; and expenditures and overseas representation. A small task force under the direction of an assistant deputy minister is examining each of these subject areas. The review process is expected to take three to four months, with the expectation that there will be recommendations for the Ministers in June, 1996 and implementation of decisions thereafter.

This review will not be easy either to organize or to integrate at the end. It makes most sense for the examination of DFAIT's role and responsibilities to be undertaken first, since decisions on these aspects could be expected to influence the other areas under review. However, because it has taken longer than originally anticipated for the review to receive the internal support necessary for its initiation and because the time frame allowed for the overall process has been short, all four topics are being examined simultaneously. Whatever the recommendations of the internal review, their implementation will require determination and skill on the part of the most senior DFAIT officials. When proposals are made for reductions in DFAIT commitments or changes in structure, a range of opinion, both domestic and, as Roy Culpeper notes in Chapter 14, foreign, can be marshalled to advocate the maintenance of the status quo. In Chapter 2, Evan Potter analyzes many of Canada's current foreign policy obligations and makes recommendations as to which might be less critical at the end of the 1990s.

Achieving a consensus on where cuts should be made and how the government can marshal increasingly scarce resources to meet new priorities is going to prove a difficult task. Never before has Canada had so many ministers with responsibilities for foreign affairs. The new Foreign Minister, Lloyd Axworthy, presides over a herd of colleagues: Art Eggleton, Minister of International Trade, Raymond Chan, Minister of State for Asia-Pacific, Christine Stewart, Minister of State for Latin America and Africa, and Pierre Pettigrew, Minister for International Cooperation and Minister Responsible for La Francophonie. All but the two ministers of state were appointed to their positions in the February, 1996 cabinet shuffle. The diffusion of leadership and responsibility at the very time when it should be con-solidated in the interests of coherence and accountability is troubling. The challenge for Foreign Minister Lloyd Axworthy, is to take the lead and bring new ideas, focus and a clear sense of direction to his portfolio, particularly on the political side, where priorities are less well defined than they are on trade matters.

CANADA AND INTERNATIONAL INSTITUTIONS

A major part of the debate over Canada's capacity to remain a highly engaged international actor will centre around our continued partic-ipation in a multitude of international organizations. Canada was an important player in the founding of the United Nations and Bretton Woods system some fifty years earlier. As Geoffrey Pearson reminds us in his chapter in this volume, Canada was one of the few coun-tries to place international interests ahead of its own national interests in supporting the creation of the United Nations. Although the UN made little progress in achieving the security purposes of the Charter, it did carve out a unique role for itself in conflict prevention and ter-mination—a role that was developed jointly through the efforts of Secretary-General Dag Hammarskjold and Lester B. Pearson.

The United Nations' 50th anniversary was a cause for both cele-bration and concern. The UN has played a major role in ending civil wars and promoting international peace and stability through its wide range of peacekeeping activities at the end of the Cold War. Superpower divisions in the Security Council hobbled the UN during much of the Cold War. These divisions dissipated with the sudden col-lapse of the Soviet empire, the rise of democratic governments in the former Soviet Union, Latin America, and Asia, and a new, worldwide commitment to human rights and democratic development in fledg-ling democracies. Louise Fréchette discusses the major role played by the UN at the end of the Cold War in bringing peace to Namibia, Mozambique, El Salvador, and Cambodia and in helping to establish new international norms and standards in the areas of human rights, the environment, and sustainable development. She reminds us that the end of the Cold War was marked a new sense of optimism about the possibilities of international cooperation which breathed fresh life into efforts to reform the UN.

This new spirit of optimism, however, proved to be surprisingly short-lived. In spite of the fact that some 20 new UN missions were established in the period 1990-94, the UN's peacekeeping "failures" in Somalia, Rwanda and the former Yugoslavia in the 1990s, coupled with a growing public perception that its bureaucracy was bloated and inefficient, damaged its reputation and undermined its credibility, as is noted by David Carment in his chapter. Although much of the blame for the Organization's seeming inability to deal with ethnic conflict and humanitarian crises lies with the permanent members of the Security Council, the UN as a whole has taken the brunt of public criticism and blame for inaction. Matters have not been helped by growing Congressional hostility to the United Nations and the fact that the U.S., along with several other major contributors, remains in arrears in its regular budget contributions to the Organization. The UN's financial crisis is a continuing major cause for concern, particularly to countries like Canada which are strong supporters of the Organization and believe that it has an important role to play in the maintenance of international peace and security. Robert Fowler argues in Chapter 7 that the UN's financial and political crisis must be resolved soon because "the UN is our best hope for maintaining order in our ever more complex world."

Canadians celebrated the UN's 50th anniversary by offering constructive proposals for reform directed at enhancing the Organization's effectiveness and making it more coherent and more accountable to its members. Greg Wirick underscores in Chapter 11 that the 50th anniversary was marked by flurry of activity and numerous consultative groups and commissions—some government-initiated, some private—all of which led to numerous suggestions as to how the UN might be strengthened. At the official level, Canada's main contribution was a proposal for the creation of a rapid reaction capability in the Organization. The plan would be for the UN to assemble a multifunctional force of up to 5,000 military and civilian personnel that could be deployed quickly, with the authorization of the Security Council, to an area of crisis.

Canada also suggested ways of strengthening advance planning by the Secretariat and among those countries contributing forces to international peacekeeping operations. This initiative focused international attention on the need for stronger instruments of crisis management and prevention in international organization. Harald von Riekhoff indicates in Chapter 10 that Canada continues to maintain a strong interest in reform of the Security Council, as part of its larger effort to reform the UN system. Canada is keen to make the

UN more accountable to its members and ensure that those countries which contribute to international peacekeeping and other UN operations have a voice in decision-making and perhaps even a vote. Canada has already agreed to expanding the permanent membership of the Security Council and supporting, in principle, the inclusion of Germany and Japan. In addition to strengthening regional representation on the Council Canada must, however, also work with other middle powers in looking for ways to strengthen its own involvement and participation in the Security Council and the General Assembly.

As noted above, the Second Annual Forum reaffirmed "the central importance of international institutions, particularly the United Nations, to Canada's security and well-being," but also recommended that "Canada should pay increasing attention to regional organizations in Asia through ASEAN [Association of Southeast Asian Nations] and in the Americas through the OAS [Organization of American States] and related inter-American institutions." The Forum suggested that Canada should play a lead role in "promoting greater efficiency and transparency among international institutions" and also work towards the elimination of duplication and for greater policy coherence and reform, particularly among the Bretton Woods Institutions and the World Trade Organization.[16]

These themes are developed by John Graham in his chapter on the OAS and by Roy Culpeper in his chapter on international financial institutions (IFIs). Graham points out that there is a gap between the rhetoric and the performance of regional organizations like the OAS. In the areas of democracy and human rights in the hemisphere, there is gathering momentum and convergence on key norms and principles, reflected in various OAS documents and agreements and culminating in the commitment by hemisphere chiefs of state at the December 1994 Summit of the Americas in Miami to advance democracy, human rights, and the rule of law in the region. However, OAS instruments which have been responsible for taking action in these areas, in particular the Unit for the Promotion of Democracy and the Inter-American Commission on Human Rights, continue to be hampered by a lack of resources and inconsistent operational strategies. Reform of the OAS to make it more transparent, professional and accountable should be a Canadian priority if the intention is to make the OAS a more effective instrument of regional cooperation.

Roy Culpeper argues that reform of IFIs has moved to the forefront of the international economic agenda. Although IFIs have contributed in important ways to the growth of today's global economy, the accelerating forces of globalization have created new problems and called the very existence of some of these institutions such as the World Bank, into question. The Bank, however, under its new president James Wolfensohn, has initiated far-reaching reforms which are addressing some of the concerns of its critics. The same cannot be said of the IMF, which is resistant to change. The Mexican peso crisis ushered in a period of new turmoil in international currency markets and put the spotlight on the IMF at the Halifax summit. Culpeper believes that the world economy is at a crossroads and needs competent international financial institutions to help exercise governance over global markets. The issue of IFI reform has reappeared on the agenda of the 1996 G-7 summit in Lyon, France, together with questions of international development assistance replenishment, the treatment of multilateral debt, the IMF quota review and SDR (Special Drawing Rights) allocation.

The challenges of reform extend across the entire spectrum of international institutions, from the UN to its various agencies, from international financial institutions to regional organizations like the OAS. If there is a clear message that comes out of these chapters it is that international institutional reform is an urgent priority, but that Canada will have to focus its efforts on those institutions which are most relevant to Canadian interests. Not only should Canada review its list of memberships in international institutions, but it should also base its support on performance and limit it to those bodies which are effective, transparent, and responsive to reform.

In focusing on international institutions, it is important not to lose sight of the growing involvement and importance of Canadian non-governmental organizations (NGOs) in international affairs and Canadian foreign policy. Ken Bush, in his chapter, discusses how the Canadian government is increasingly turning to NGOs to carry out tasks previously performed by governments, such as the delivery of humanitarian aid and assistance to war-torn societies. He also points out that international financial institutions, like the World Bank and the IMF, are also turning to NGOs to help offset the dislocations brought on by structural adjustment programs. The government's cuts to the Official Development Assistance (ODA) budget, in 1995 and again in 1996, are, however, weakening NGO capacity to carry out the very tasks and functions the government would like this sector to perform, forcing NGOs into humanitarian and relief areas of activity

at the cost of longer-term development objectives. Like the government, the NGO community is finding it increasingly necessary to
focus and concentrate resources on countries and regions where the
need is the greatest and development assistance can be put to the
best use.

CANADA-U.S. RELATIONS

Whatever decisions Canada takes with respect to its overall foreign
policy priorities, its main preoccupation will continue to be the management of its relationship with the United States. Different
interpretations have been advanced over the years to explain how
smaller countries handle their dominant relationships, among them
the argument that smaller partners are frequently able to obtain their
preferred outcome in bilateral disputes because they are able to marshal more resources to focus on the relationship. While this has been
largely the case in Canada-U.S. relations, the assessment has to be
qualified because of the threats of aggressive U.S. protectionism in
recent years and the impact of the U.S. electoral cycle.

A number of chapters in this volume address different aspects of
Canada-U.S. relations. Hal Klepak, in Chapter 3, comments on the
Canada-U.S. defence relationship in the context of his broader review
of Canadian defence policy in an age of diminished resources and
changing needs. In Chapter 5, Keith Acheson and Christopher Maule
raise questions about Canada's policy of protecting its cultural industries in the face of changing technology which renders borders totally
permeable. They also chronicle a number of bilateral cultural disputes during 1995 which had as their basis a different definition of
culture in each of the two countries. For the United States culture is
seen as entertainment, which translates into investment and export
opportunities for Americans; for Canada, culture is part of the definition of the country which may, from time to time, require
government protection to remain vibrant.

Reviewing Canada-U.S. relations over 1995, J.J. Jockel suggests
that disputes over cultural industries and softwood lumber notwithstanding, the Canada-U.S. relationship during that year was
remarkably calm. He also notes changes in the way the relationship
is managed; gone, under Chrétien, are regular meetings between the
Prime Minister and the U.S. President that were such an important
feature of the Mulroney era, and gone is the commitment of the two

countries' foreign ministers to meet four times a year. The relationship is now managed in a more traditional way, through occasional meetings of ministers and senior officials and the two countries' ambassadors.

If 1995 was a reasonably calm year in the bilateral relationship, 1996, which is an election year, may be different. The Clinton Administration, cognizant of the need generated by electoral pressures, particularly those from the Republican right, to be seen as defending domestic interests, has taken an aggressive stance on a number of bilateral issues. As a result of the downing by the Cuban regime, on February 24, 1996, of two planes flown by Cuban-Americans, the American Congress passed a piece of legislation, the Cuban Liberty and Democratic Solidarity Act, which had been on the legislative agenda for much of 1995, but which had lain dormant.[17] The Act, signed by President Clinton on March 12, 1996, is a throwback to U.S. extraterritorial legislation of the 1950s and 1960s which subjects non-U.S. companies to American law. In this instance, Canadian (and all other non-U.S.) firms doing business in Cuba could be prosecuted and their executives denied entry into the United States. Canada argues that the legislation contravenes provisions of the North American Free Trade Agreement and, like Mexico, is considering a challenge of the legislation under NAFTA.[18] A second acrimonious bilateral dispute—over the tariffication of agricultural subsidies[19]—is under review by a NAFTA panel; and differences over Canadian softwood lumber exports to the U.S., which have been the subject of a number of panel processes under both the Canada-U.S. Free Trade Agreement and NAFTA, and which were thought to have been resolved in January, 1996, remain outstanding, despite the expectation that a five-year agreement limiting Canadian exports will go into effect on April 1, 1996.

CONCLUSION

Canada is a relatively small player on the world scene, but is still big enough to be heard. Much of our foreign policy is reactive to events beyond our control. On few matters do we alone determine how issues will be debated and decided. New challenges in the areas of globalization, trade, culture and communications are rapidly changing our country from within and posing new hurdles for our policies without. At one level, administrative restructuring will have to be sensitive to these changes as resources dwindle. At another level, the government's move to democratize foreign policy decision-making, in order to create new channels of communication and consultation and to break through DFAIT's rather inward-looking culture is desirable. Issues and choices are too complex and affect too many segments of Canadian society to be left in the hands of bureaucrats, however capable they may be. At some point, however, the process of consultation and debate about options must end. Ultimately, the government's record will be judged not by the number of people it consults but by the way in which it defines its priorities and makes choices.

NOTES

1   The authors benefited from conversations with officials of the Department of Foreign Affairs and International Trade on some of the issues discussed in this chapter.
2   The White House, Office of the Press Secretary, "Remarks by the President to the Canadian Parliament," February 23, 1995.
3   Jeff Sallot, "Clinton cites Canada as world model," *The Globe and Mail,* October 26, 1995, A7. In this regard readers might also note the study by Charles Roh, "The Implications for U.S. Trade Policy of an Independent Quebec," (Washington and Ottawa: Center for Strategic and International Studies and Centre for Trade Policy and Law, 1995), cited by Jockel. Roh, a former member of the office of the U.S. Trade Representative, analyzes the challenges an independent Quebec would face in attempting to join a number of international trade agreements and in trying to secure preferential trade benefits from the United States.
4   Cited in Sallot, "Clinton cites Canada as world model."
5   Liberal Party of Canada, *Creating Opportunity: The Liberal Plan for Canada* (Ottawa: September, 1993), 109, and Liberal Party of Canada, *Foreign Policy Handbook* (Ottawa: May, 1993).
6   See for example, Maxwell Cameron and Maureen Appel Molot, "Does Democracy Make a Difference?" and Kim Richard Nossal, "The Democratization of Canadian Foreign Policy: The Elusive Ideal," in Maxwell Cameron and Maureen Appel Molot, eds., *Canada Among Nations 1995: Democracy and Foreign Policy* (Ottawa: Carleton University Press, 1995), 1-25 and 29-43; Janice Gross Stein, "Ideas, even good ideas are not enough: changing Canada's foreign and defence policies," *International Journal* L, no.1 (Winter 1994/5), 40-70; Denis Stairs, "The Public Politics of the Canadian Defence and Foreign Policy Reviews," *Canadian Foreign Policy* 3, no. 1 (Spring 1995), 91-116; and Heather Smith, "Seeking Certainty and Finding None: Reflections on the 1994 Canadian Foreign Policy Review," *Canadian Foreign Policy* 3, no. 1 (Spring 1995), 117-24. For a

discussion on the inclusion of Canadian culture and values in the reviews see John Hay, "Projecting Canadian Values and Culture: An Episode in the Making of Canadian Foreign Policy," *Canadian Foreign Policy* 3, no. 2 (Fall 1995), 21-32.

7   Report of the Special Joint Committee of the Senate and House of Commons Reviewing Canadian Foreign Policy, *Canada's Foreign Policy: Principles and Priorities for the Future* (Ottawa: Publications Service, Parliamentary Publications Directorate, 1994).

8   Canada, *Government Response to the Recommendation of the Special Joint Parliamentary Committee Reviewing Canadian Foreign Policy* (Ottawa: Canada Communication Group, 1995) and Stairs, "The Public Politics," 113.

9   Report of the Second Annual Forum, "International Institutions in the Twenty-First Century: Can Canada Help to Meet the Challenges?" Government of Canada, Media Relations Office, Department of Foreign Affairs and International Trade, Ottawa, December 27, 1995, and a paper prepared by Evan Potter for the Forum, "Canada and the Reform of International Institutions," *Canadian Foreign Policy* 3, no. 2 (Fall 1995), 83-102.

10   See Evan Potter, "Widening the Foreign Policy Circle: Democratization or Co-optation," *bout de papier* 13, no. 1 (Spring 1996) 14-16.

11   Canada, Department of Foreign Affairs and International Trade, *Canada in the World: Government Statement* (Ottawa: Canada Communication Group, 1995).

12   *Canada in the World,* i and 10.

13   Responsibility for cultural affairs and projecting Canadian culture abroad was to be given to a revamped Canada Council in accordance with the view held by Reid Morden, then Assistant Undersecretary of State, envisaging a "back to basics" Department of External Affairs and International Trade. See Potter, Chapter 2 in this volume, as well as Evan Potter, "Canada's Foreign Policy and Foreign Service in the 1990s," in Fen Osler Hampson and Christopher J. Maule, eds., *Canada Among Nations 1993: Global Jeopardy* (Ottawa: Carleton University Press, 1993), 48-51.

14   Hay, "Projecting Canadian Values and Culture," 24 and 32.

15   See in this regard the problem Evan Potter notes, that while DFAIT has been prepared to close missions, the Departmental recommendations have been overruled by the Minister and the Prime Minister.

16   Report of the Second Annual National Forum, "International Institutions in the Twenty-First Century: Can Canada Help to Meet the Challenge?" Government of Canada, Media Relations Office, Department of Foreign Affairs and International Trade, Ottawa, December 27, 1995, 3, 5, 10.

17   This piece of legislation was also known as the Helms-Burton Bill after its Congressional sponsors, Senator Jesse Helms of South Carolina and Representative Dan Burton of Indiana.

18   Drew Fagan, "Canada steps up trade fight," *The Globe and Mail,* March 13, 1996, A1, A2. Canada is also considering joining the

European Union in a World Trade Organization (WTO) challenge to
the U.S. legislation.

19   There is a clash here between the expectations arising from NAFTA
and those created by the World Trade Organization (WTO). NAFTA
protected Canadian marketing boards which are the core of Canada's
supply management system for poultry, eggs and milk. Under the
WTO, marketing boards must be replaced by tariffs, which will eventually be reduced. Canada, which introduced tariffs on poultry, eggs
and milk at the beginning of 1995, argues that these are acceptable
under the NAFTA because the agreement permits tariffs to replace
quotas on supply-managed goods; the tariffs are import restrictions
imposed pursuant to a "successor agreement" to GATT Article XI and,
as such, are justified under NAFTA. Canada maintains, furthermore,
that the possibility of tariffication was discussed at the NAFTA talks
and both sides agreed on it. The U.S. takes the opposite approach,
i.e., that the NAFTA requires the phasing out of all tariffs within a ten-
year period and precludes the imposition of new ones, and that there
was no agreement on tariffication during the NAFTA talks. Interests
are arrayed in both countries on this issue because huge amounts of
money and markets (the Canadian one) are at stake. A five-person
binational panel has been struck, with Elihu Lauterpacht of Britain as
the chair.

The Policy Process

II

Redesigning Canadian Diplomacy in an Age of Fiscal Austerity

EVAN H. POTTER

Apart from national unity the most important determinant of Canadian foreign policy in the mid-1990s is the precarious state of national finances. Simply put, federal and provincial debts drive Canadian public policy choices.

Few observers of Canadian foreign policy would deny that the number and complexity of foreign policy issues are increasing, yet the resources available to manage them in the pursuit of Canada's national interest are decreasing. If we assume that the "old" foreign policy concerns of non-proliferation, economic diplomacy, alliance politics, and multilateralism will continue to be important, we are left with three alternatives. We can either increase our foreign policy budget to reflect this expanding agenda, we can do more things less well, or we can accept that some international issue-areas now have lower priority for the Canadian government. This last choice implies that Ottawa will shift focus away from some traditional functional concerns and geographic sectors so that Canada's international policy decisions and programs can have *maximum impact* in those areas where there is a clear and identifiable Canadian interest.

The growing domestic fiscal pressures highlight a fundamental tension in the conduct of Canada's international relations—that between a more engaged global player in an age of globalization and interdependence [1] and that of a more disengaged, largely regional,[2] actor. On the one hand, some have questioned how long Canada can afford to continue to enhance its prestige in a number of expensive spheres of influence simultaneously, for example, in the United Nations (UN), the North Atlantic Treaty Organization (NATO), the Commonwealth, La Francophonie, the Asia Pacific Economic Cooperation forum (APEC) and in the Group of Seven (G-7).[3] Yet, at the same time, a powerful countervailing force strengthens this internationalism. It is characterized first by Canada's growing economic dependence on the rest of the world: in 1995 exports accounted for 37 per cent of national income, up from 17 percent in 1960; each billion of the $250 billion in total exports represented 11,000 domestic jobs, and overall foreign direct investment in Canada was $150 billion. Second, changing demographic patterns have increased the heterogeneity of Canada's population, with five million Canadians being foreign-born and, it is anticipated, one million more to come who will be residing in Canada by the turn of the century. (Chinese will soon become the third most commonly used language after English and French.) Finally, there is the searing collective experience of Canadian participation in two world wars on European soil, a continent which, despite the hype about the Asia Pacific region in government and business circles, should not yet be seen as merely a residual part of Ottawa's foreign policy calculus.

This chapter will examine the impact of growing fiscal pressures on Canada's ability to maintain both the rhetoric and the reality of a "liberal internationalist" foreign policy, a legacy of successive postwar Canadian governments from Louis St. Laurent to Brian Mulroney. The following three criteria will be used to evaluate Ottawa's policy choices under more austere fiscal conditions: (1) the Liberal government's 1995 statement, which laid out the three overriding foreign policy objectives of promoting prosperity and employment, protecting national security within a stable global framework, and projecting Canadian values and culture abroad;[4] (2) operational concerns of efficiency, effectiveness, and accountability; and (3) the interests of non-governmental organizations (NGOs), business, the provinces and labour.

WHEN FACING A REAL CRISIS, MAKING CHOICES IS NO LONGER TABOO

The last two years have witnessed the largest concentration of reviews on how Canada conducts its international relations since the Trudeau government's reviews between 1968 and 1970 that culminated in *Foreign Policy for Canadians*.[5] The current crop of overlapping reviews, following the Liberal Party's own highly detailed *Handbook* on foreign policy[6] and its subsequent synthesis a few months later in the so-called Liberal Red Book,[7] comprises: a privately supported research program on Canada's foreign and defence policy priorities for the next century that produced the so-called Canada 21 Report (March 1994);[8] the first National Forum on Canada's International Relations (March 1994);[9] a full re-assessment of Canada's foreign and defence policies by two parliamentary Special Joint Committees (April-November 1994) that culminated in two reports,[10] prompting a response through the *Defence White Paper* (December 1994)[11] and the Government's foreign policy Statement, along with a detailed response to the parliamentary foreign policy report (February 1995);[12] a private sector review headed by L.R. Wilson, Chairman of Bell Canada Enterprises, of the federal government's export market development programs;[13] a review by a former Liberal cabinet minister, Serge Joyal, of the federal government's role and operations in the field of international cultural and academic relations;[14] a parliamentary review of international financial institutions (May 1995) that preceded the Halifax G-7 Summit where the agenda was the same;[15] and a public review of Canada's commitment to international organizations at the second National Forum on Canada's International Relations (September 1995).[16] What distinguished this series of reflections and analysis from their antecedents was that they took place in the absence of the Cold War and in the presence of the twin domestic crises of maintaining national unity and preventing fiscal collapse. Not surprisingly, the two common threads running through the reviews were the merits of greater "selectivity" and the need to eliminate the duplication and overlapping of programs and institutions and, second, that Canada's success internationally would reinforce Canadian identity and unity at home.[17]

The majority of the reviews were much better at laying out the criteria for selection than in actually making choices. The notable exceptions were the Canada 21 Report, which bluntly stated that the Canadian Forces should be shorn of its traditional military capabilities;[18] the Reform Party's dissenting opinion on the Special Joint Committee's report reviewing Canadian foreign policy, which castigated the other political parties for making recommendations that would in Reform's eyes increase rather than decrease foreign policy spending;[19] and the Wilson report, which called for over $100 million in cuts to the Government's international business development budget.[20] The parliamentary review had hedged its recommendations,[21] the Government's response to those recommendations had tended towards the non-committal, resulting in an expensive series of consultations that, while arguably having "democratized" the policy-making process,[22] to date have not produced any fundamental changes in the conduct of Canadian foreign policy. In fact, it has been the government-wide Program Review (now in its second phase), spearheaded by Paul Martin and the Department of Finance, whose mandate it is to reduce the federal deficit by making government more efficient, that has and will continue to force Ottawa's foreign policy planners to make hard choices with regard to their policies and programs.

This chapter's premise is that Canada can no longer afford to be a nation equally of the "Americas," the "Pacific," the "Atlantic," and the "Arctic." Just as Australia did in the 1980s, Canada must come out from behind the liberal internationalist veil and start deciding which regions and functional areas in our foreign policy will be given priority in the next decade.

LIVING WITH UNCERTAINTY—ABROAD AND AT HOME

The proposals for realigning Canada's foreign policy in light of new fiscal realities must be seen in the context of new coalitions of important players and important shifts in the political and economic spheres both abroad and at home.

Players in the international system are shifting their views on national and international objectives. With the decline in growth rates in the industrialized world, governments are increasingly concerned with meeting their citizens' expectations by variously reducing domestic expenditures, emphasizing export-led growth and, if necessary, increasing protectionism. With regard to alliances, in the absence of the Soviet threat there is no longer a central common purpose within NATO. A portion of the North-South cleavage is being reshaped as some of the former developing countries begin to overtake Northern nations. At the same time, the gap between the Least Developing Countries and the rest of the world is growing. Meanwhile, China, an emerging economic and military giant with little interest in being constrained by multilateral institutions, is causing greater militarization of the Asia Pacific region. Transnational issues such as the environment (e.g., fisheries, forests), migration, refugees and terrorism are increasingly the focus of foreign ministries. Cutting across these structural changes are the challenges to Western values posed by so-called "failed states," such as Haiti and Somalia, and fundamentalism in all its stripes; as well, advances in Information Technologies (ITs) are transforming the conduct of international relations through the effects of globalization, democratization, and fragmentation.

Canada is more vulnerable to the above trends than many other nations given its high dependency on trade, its severe domestic economic problems (characterized by unsustainable debt, low annual growth rates and high unemployment), and the ongoing political instability caused by the threat of Quebec's secession from Confederation. However, the single most important change in the international system for Canada is that the United States, as the world's sole superpower, is more self-absorbed and less multilateralist. Domestically, the Canadian public sector is undergoing the most profound structural changes in a generation. With a massive combined federal and provincial debt of more than $830 billion that threatens to surpass Canada's gross domestic product (a debt-to-GDP ratio that is higher than every other G-7 member's except Italy), federal and provincial governments are in the midst of radically downsizing the apparatus of the state.

This "rationalization" of the Canadian state, in tandem with the call in the foreign policy reviews for a more strategic approach to Canada's international relations, has important implications for the priorities, directions and resources of those state institutions with a statutory mandate to manage Canada's international political, trade, security, defence, aid, and cultural relations. Since the chapter in this volume by Hal Klepak examines the impact of reduced resources on Canada's Department of National Defence (DND),[23] the discussion here will focus on the impact on the Department of Foreign Affairs and International Trade (DFAIT, hereafter also referred to as the "Department" or "Foreign Affairs") and the Canadian International Development Agency (CIDA). Indeed, in the fiscal year 1994-95 the Department was subject to the most extensive reappraisal of its mandate in at least a decade. As result of the successive private- and public-sector foreign policy reviews, DFAIT saw the transfer to CIDA of its program for the delivery of technical assistance to the countries of Central and Eastern Europe and the former Soviet Union; a substantial change to its international business and consular programs; the reduction of staff in Canada and at missions abroad; and the reduction of voluntary grants and contributions to domestic organizations and associations, NGOs, and certain international organizations by approximately 20 percent.[24]

INSTITUTIONAL RE-ENGINEERING

Two years ago, in an analysis of the policy process at DFAIT, I noted that Reid Morden, the then Under-Secretary of State (now called Deputy Minister), had responded to charges that his Department had become increasingly irrelevant to the business of government by embarking on a "back to basics" campaign. His initiative turned out to be only partially successful in bringing about sweeping changes to the coordination, oversight and programming of DFAIT activities.[25] As I noted, the fundamental question was whether the "imperatives of foreign policy, in which international relations and domestic policy [were] increasingly fused, [could] be reconciled effectively with the Department's streamlining approach."[26]

The Department was at that time—as it is today—under the budgetary gun. On the one hand, the philosophy of downsizing was perfectly reconcilable with the strategy of specialization, the aim being to maximize the Department's strengths in the face of government-wide cutbacks. The thinking was that by going "back to basics," DFAIT was in fact launching a preemptive strike to eliminate the rationale adopted by central agencies such as Finance and Treasury Board for even deeper and, in its eyes, more damaging cuts to its budget. Yet, on the other, by giving priority to "traditional" diplomatic activity such as military and economic relations over non-traditional—but expanding—foreign policy agenda items such as culture, epidemic diseases, advancement of women, and the environment, the management of Canada's foreign policy appeared, in the view of observers both inside and outside of the Pearson building to have taken an anachronistic turn. What at first glance seemed entirely logical, given budgetary pressures, was turning out to be fundamentally flawed. Just as other foreign ministries were devising new institutional mechanisms to respond to an expanding definition of security, the growing importance of cultural diplomacy, and the advantage of close collaboration with civil society actors, Canada's foreign ministry was divesting itself of precisely those issue-areas that were due to increase in number, were the most complicated and interconnected, and usually revolved around actors outside government.

Gordon Smith, Reid Morden's successor, who is facing an even harsher fiscal climate in Ottawa, has taken a somewhat different approach to the challenge of doing more with less. He is a fervent proponent of the use of ITs to make Departmental operations more efficient and is probably the first deputy minister of foreign affairs to regularly "surf" the Internet. The showpiece of the Department's drive towards the greater use of information and communications technologies is SIGNET, a protected communications system that connects all of the Department's computers and allows instantaneous communication between members of the Canadian foreign service in Canada and abroad. In addition to the expected productivity increases engendered by the new technology, there is also a human cost, with an estimated 300 Departmental staff in Ottawa and another 100 abroad expected to lose their jobs.[27] A second major component of the Department's cost-cutting program is the increasing replacement of foreign service officers abroad with locally engaged staff—particularly at high-cost locations in Western Europe and Asia—given that it costs Ottawa on average $100,000 per year (excluding salary) to maintain a DFAIT employee abroad.[28]

One interesting phenomenon of middle power diplomacy in an age of austerity is the sharing of resources with other like-minded countries. For example, Canada and Australia already have consular sharing agreements for about 26 countries, common diplomatic bag facilities, staff exchanges, and support for each other's candidates and positions in international organizations. In 1993 Canada and Australia began to co-locate missions abroad, beginning with Phnom Penh and Bridgetown, to achieve financial economies and greater efficiencies.[29] However, as the foreign policies of the industrialized states become more trade-oriented and thus competitive, there is a question about how close even like-minded countries can and should get in sharing facilities.

Ottawa currently operates 129 missions abroad, and 33 satellite offices (e.g. offshoots of embassies, high commissions and consulates), with 39 in Europe, 35 in Africa and the Middle East, 32 in the Asia Pacific, 27 in Latin America, 21 in the United States, and eight designated for international organizations.[30] The combination of advanced communication technology and the high cost of keeping Canadian staff abroad will translate into more numerous micro-Canadian foreign missions and a high ratio of locally engaged to Canada-based staff, with the result that for the first time in the history of the Department of Foreign Affairs a number of missions will be run entirely by non-Canadian staff.[31] It is noteworthy that, while senior officials at DFAIT have advocated the closure of certain embassies and high commissions for economic reasons, their advice has been overturned by ministers who insist that no embassy or high commission can be closed. Indeed, six new missions have been opened in the last two years alone. The lesson here is that the political imperatives of a highly visible and symbolic Canadian presence abroad (especially one spurred on by domestic constituencies) will often outweigh the economic restraint that is preached by these same political leaders.[32]

Table 1 shows that DFAIT's total budget since 1987 as a percentage of total government expenditure has remained steady and certainly has not declined as precipitously as those of DND or of CIDA. In fact, until 1994, DFAIT's budget had continued to grow because of compensation for overseas inflation, currency losses, salary increases for employees, additional funds for non-discretionary costs such as peacekeeping, and funding for new initiative sources from the government's priority reserve. Starting in 1995 the Department's budget, however, has begun to decline and it is now planned to decline steadily to the end of the century because of spending reductions arising from Program Review I and II, and the sunsetting of funding for specific programs (e.g., Green Plan, Access North America Program). There are no longer any central reserves (at the Treasury Board or elsewhere outside the Department) to finance new policies or programs. Thus any new initiative such as providing assistance to peace-building following a conflict will have to be financed from existing resources by reallocation either within the Department or inter departmentally.[33] The Department does have a small operating reserve, but it is acknowledged that it is inadequate to finance future so-called "pressures" on Canada emanating from the

Table 1
DFAIT/CIDA/DND Share of the Federal Dollar Over a
9-Year Period, 1987-88 TO 1995-96 (in $ millions)

Years	1987-88	1988-89	1989-90	1990-91	1991-92	1992-93	1993-94	1994-95	1995-96
DFAIT budget	898	940	1,078	1,106	1,238	1,247	1,334	1,408	1,304
DFAIT's percentage of federal budget	.82	.78	.82	.75	.78	.77	.83	.87	.79
CIDA budget	2,103	2,226	2,005	2,167	2,220	2,278	2,107	2,037	1,730
CIDA's percentage of federal budget	1.91	1.86	1.53	1.46	1.41	1.41	1.31	1.26	1.05
Total External Affairs[a] as percentage of federal budget	2.9	2.9	2.6	2.6	2.5	2.5	2.4	2.4	2.2
Total DND budget as percentage of federal budget[b]	9.4	9.4	8.7	8.1	8.1	7.7	7.4	7.1	6.7

Source: Government of Canada, *Main Estimates*, 1987-1995.

a   In addition to DFAIT and CIDA this expenditure includes Canadian Commercial Corporation (until 1992-93), Export Development Corporation, International Centre for Ocean Development (until 1992-93), Canadian Institute for International Peace and Security (until 1992-93), International Development Research Centre, Canadian Secretariat (from 1990-91), and the International Joint Commission.

b   Source: *Canadian Defence Information* as cited in *The Globe and Mail*, December 26, 1995, A4.

international system. The budgetary decline is sure to produce an operational complexion for the Department that is considerably changed from that of only five years ago.

These circumstances have prompted internal reviews of how the Department manages its resources, with a view to uncovering cost savings. Canada's representation abroad, for example, is currently relatively modest in comparison to that of other G-7 countries or many smaller members of the Organization for Economic Cooperation and Development (OECD). Nevertheless, costs can only be cut so far since the dispersion of foreign operations requires the Department to maintain substantial administrative support infrastructure for telecommunications, accounting systems (DFAIT deals with over 95 currencies), and real property. And since DFAIT

personnel represent only 48 percent of the total Canadian government officials working abroad, the demands presented by other
Canadian government employees constitute one of the principal
obstacles to the reduction of the Department's foreign expenses.

With regard to the overall orientation of DFAIT, under Smith's
guidance non-traditional security issues (e.g., migration, the environment, refugees) that were formerly buried within the Department's
security and trade branches are now showcased in a new Global
Issues and International Culture Branch. The new security agenda is
a veritable growth industry within the federal government, with
Foreign Affairs, CIDA, the Canadian Security and Intelligence Service,
the Department of Citizenship and Immigration and DND all
embarked on research programs.

Curiously, the same enthusiasm is not shown for advancing
Canada's cultural diplomacy, although it was elevated in the
Government's 1995 Statement to the status of a foreign policy objective, "equivalent in priority (apparently) to the very security and
economic success of the country."[34] Where, for example, the Special
Joint Committee reviewing Canada's foreign policy called for DFAIT
to exercise a lead role in developing international cultural, scientific,
and educational policy at the federal level, the Government
responded by agreeing that DFAIT should take the lead in this regard
but uttered a diplomatic "no" to committing more program money, or
investing more authority in the Department's cultural affairs bureau.[35]
Indeed, the Department's Main Estimates for 1995-96, after reciting
recent initiatives in the field such as a Canada-U.S.-Mexico creative
artists' residencies program and a memorandum on cultural cooperation with Hong Kong, indicates no major initiatives in the area of
international cultural relations for the coming year, cataloguing
instead a series of program reductions; the word "culture" does not
even appear in the index to the Estimates. As Hay concludes, this
"was a plainly truncated policy that the government was initiating—
short of budgetary or organizational commitment...."[36]

Major Program Changes
Senior officials responsible for trade at DFAIT are actively seeking to
keep the Department relevant to the interests of Canadian exporters
and investors. There have been persistent criticisms about how the federal government has been spending its estimated $600 million trade
promotion budget (concentrated at DFAIT but spread over 22 federal

government departments). Canadian business has, in recent years, repeatedly told Ottawa that it does not subscribe to the universalist philosophy that has traditionally underpinned the federally run international market development services. It has urged Ottawa to reallocate resources, reducing the focus on OECD countries (with the exceptions of Japan and the U.S.) and concentrating more on growth markets in Asia Pacific.[37] In effect, it has advocated far less government spending on what it considers to be mature markets in Western Europe. The Canadian Chamber of Commerce even went so far as to suggest that the private sector could take over the business promotional services now provided by DFAIT through its embassy and consulates in the United States.[38] The most radical solution has been the call for the wholesale privatization of the Trade Commissioner Service, with DFAIT's trade promotion function set up as either a separate crown corporation (along the lines of the Export Development Corporation). Alternatively, it has been suggested that Canada could adopt the New Zealand model, in which the Trade Development Board is operationally driven by the private sector but takes direction from the Minister for Trade Negotiations (97 percent of the funding from this Board comes from the government).

Neither the former Minister for International Trade, Roy MacLaren, nor his senior officials were enthusiastic about such radical institutional changes, especially the prospect of privatization. Instead, the Departmental response to private sector criticism was: to focus on productivity enhancements (a World Wide Web site on the Internet, fax links etc.); to provide strategic business intelligence rather than more general market information; to shift Trade Commissioners and resources to emerging markets in Latin America and Asia Pacific; to invite greater participation by the provinces; to reduce duplication in programs; to concentrate support on companies with annual sales of $10 million or less; to move towards full cost recovery on international trade fairs and missions; and to reduce direct subsidies to Canadian business by cutting $7.5 million from the Program for Export Market Development.[39]

While the federal government shows no signs of relinquishing its monopoly over Canada's international business promotion programs, it has been quite willing to spin the Passport Office off as a Special Operating Agency (which remains responsible to the Minister of Foreign Affairs) and to propose that the Consular Services program[40] (which cost DFAIT more than $30 million in 1994) be restructured so that it will become a full cost recovery program. Canadians would thus be expected to start paying user fees when using Canadian government services abroad, much in the same way that some analysts have advocated that user fees be charged for certain health care services under Canada's socialized medical care system.

COLLABORATION WITH CIVIL SOCIETY: SOLUTION OR COMPLICATION?

As foreign ministries face more issues at greater depth with less money, there is an increased need for closer collaboration between Canada's foreign policy practitioners and civil society actors (e.g., NGOs, private voluntary organizations, universities) both in terms of policy advice and of implementation. As Draimin and Plewes point out, the increased use of civil society actors and the "democratization" of Canadian foreign policy go hand in hand since "the realm of foreign policy is no longer the exclusive domain of the state,"[41] a message that was delivered in the final report of the 1994 National Forum.

For a variety of structural reasons (e.g., the underdevelopment of Canada's policy think-tank community and the "walls" created by a professional public service) Canada's federal bureaucracy has had particular difficulty in tapping non-governmental expert views and incorporating them into the policy-making process and in using non-governmental actors to implement strategies. This problem has been most acute in the foreign policy arena where the confidentiality of state-to-state relations has impeded the systematic use of non-government actors in the pursuit of Canada's international interests. This will likely have to change, however. The dual trends of (1) a global "associational revolution" that has been facilitated by advances in information technology such as the Internet, and (2) the broadening and deepening of foreign policy issue areas, has meant that non-state actors may often be as well or better informed than government officials with regard to the details of, say, a non-traditional security problem (e.g., famine, refugee crisis) or crimes committed on cross-border electronic networks.

The professional foreign policy practitioners, usually generalists in a rotational foreign service such as Canada's, are stretched ever more thinly as a result of budget cuts across a wider variety of specialist areas. This situation presents Ottawa with the choice to get out of certain foreign policy areas—for example, monitoring elections in South Africa and Central America—and leaving the implementation entirely in the hands of the non-governmental sector, with government retaining the right to set policy direction. In fact, this has already started in an ad hoc way inasmuch as Canada's official delegations to some international forums, such as the negotiations for an Arctic Council, have a significant number of non-governmental delegates.[42]

Within the Canadian foreign policy bureaucracy there are different approaches to the use and perceived value of civil society. For instance, the use of NGOs to give advice on, and to help implement, Canada's foreign aid objectives is a long-standing practice of CIDA (through the Non-governmental Organizations Division of its Canadian Partnership Branch). DFAIT's approach has been much more piecemeal and haphazard. The Department appears much better at coordinating its activities with the business sector through the SAGIT and ITAC structures. It remains notably weak with regard to the mechanisms in place for outreach to the Canadian academic community.[43]

Foreign policy practitioners will be disappointed if they think that there will be substantial savings in staff costs from using non-diplomats—especially from the academic community—to help the Department analyze policy problems. The reason for this is the glaring lack of policy capacity outside of Ottawa (especially in the security and international trade fields). Indeed, based on current trends, the national capacity for producing policy-relevant research on international issues will reach a point of irreversible decline in the next few years.[44] Instead of saving money, the federal government should envisage spending more money on developing extra-governmental research capacity, since with few exceptions the business and private foundational sectors have shown no inclination to do so. Therefore, the use of Canadian scholarly expertise in the short term should not be viewed as a panacea for DFAIT's own lack of capacity to "cover off" a growing number of international issue areas.

CANADA AND INTERNATIONAL ORGANIZATIONS[45]

The discussion thus far emphasizes that, with fewer and fewer government dollars available for Canada's external relations in the years ahead, the existing reforms in the management of Canadian foreign policy are necessary but not sufficient for the effective maintenance of Canada's foreign interests. Other measures will have to be considered.

Since the Second World War, Canadian foreign policy has developed in and around multilateral associations—primarily the UN, NATO and the GATT. Membership in international organizations (IOs) permitted Canada a greater degree of influence than could be achieved unilaterally or bilaterally. Today, however, the expectations and demands placed on international institutions have far outpaced their capacity to react effectively. At the same time, diminishing public treasuries have forced member governments to search for more creative and less expensive solutions to enduring and to new problems.

Even before the end of the Cold War critics complained that Canada was not properly leveraging its international memberships and that Canadians could no longer afford to be inveterate joiners of every international club. The shift in the centre of economic gravity from Europe to the Asia Pacific region, the economic blossoming of Latin America, and the shift from global geopolitics to geoeconomics was, in the critics' view, not adequately reflected in Canada's memberships in IOs.

How to Choose International Institutions

Choosing which specific international institutions Canada should support and to what degree is extremely complicated. First, due to the substantial links between trade and aid, trade and the environment, security and sustainable development, establishing priorities for membership in IOs under such conditions of mutual dependency becomes extremely difficult. Second, some institutions may be better at preventing or managing conflicts than at resolving them. Others will have a comparative advantage in resolving, but perhaps not managing, conflicts once they have begun. Third, some IOs will be mandated for long term goals such as sustainable development, while others will tackle short term tasks such as famine relief. Fourth, some of them are normative or standard-setting and some are operational. Fifth, international organizations of all sizes to which Canada has significant commitments will have either a domestic or foreign constituency or both. Finally, the exponential growth of international activities throughout the post-war period has spawned an extraordinarily broad range of multilateral organizations, many of which are in the NGO sector. With such a complex cross-section of variables it becomes difficult to make broad generalizations, such as whether we should favour the UN system over the Atlantic IOs on security matters, or whether we should support the World Trade Organization (WTO), the

G-7, and key International Financial Institutions (IFIs) in preference to UN Specialized Agencies on economic matters.

What further undermines an informed discussion of the management of Canada's multilateral commitments in a period of cutbacks is a set of popular fallacies concerning Canada's investment in international institutions. First, the question of the net cost of IOs to Canada is in many ways a red herring; the real question is the efficient use of our contributions, which may lead to savings. In fact, our assessed contributions to all IOs is $217 million, with the single largest fee— $49 million—going to the UN Organization (membership in UN agencies requires separate fees), and the smallest—$10,000—going to the Canadian Council on International Law.[46] In addition, the multilateral share of total Canadian aid has remained at around 33 percent or $812 million, which puts us at the average for the OECD. We actually pay a relatively small price—less than 1 percent of the federal government's $170 billion in annual expenditures—for handling our vital interests in an international system that is highly competitive and under new pressures.

Second, some suggest that we should only participate in IOs that demonstrate an immediate net benefit for our national interests. But the value of many contributions will not be evident for years; thus removing ourselves from, or drastically cutting our commitment to, institutions because there is no immediate benefit would likely mean that much of our participation in IOs would consist of emergency aid, something that some members of the Canadian political class would be only too happy to support. Those interests that appear indirect and remote today have a nasty habit of becoming direct national interests— the potential for nuclear war, for example, or the arrival of refugees.

Third, with so many overlapping international institutions, some suggest that the multilateral system is highly inefficient. It is paradoxical that the overlapping security system in Europe (NATO, Organization for Security and Cooperation in Europe—OSCE, Council of Europe, West European Union—WEU) is also an institutional version of flexible response since it addresses problems at the individual, state, regional, subregional, and international levels. These complex and overlapping institutional structures have mitigated the anomalies created by changing political circumstances and temporary difficulties over institutional membership.

Finally, not only is a significant amount of Canada's international business accomplished through multilateralism, but Canada actually makes money from certain organizations. It is worth mentioning that these multilateral obligations frequently derive from treaties that Canada has signed.[47]

The above discussion points to the inherent difficulty and irresponsibility of a "quick fix" approach to rendering Canada's multilateral commitments more efficient by withdrawing from, or significantly diminishing our role in, certain institutions. Such an approach frequently leads to a choice between, for example, staying in the Pan-American Health Organization or providing financial support to the Test Ban Treaty. The following section seeks to differentiate between high and low priority international institutions.

Reforming International Economic Institutions

In the area of international trade, the overarching challenge in the years ahead will be to establish an interlocking set of multilateral and regional agreements to carry forward the momentum of the Uruguay Round of trade liberalization. It is unlikely that multilateralism through the WTO will be the primary driver of international economic order between 1995 and the turn of the century. Instead, regional or plurilateral groupings such as APEC and the OECD will be useful, if imperfect, catalytic tools for deepening international cooperation by codifying and locking in new practices faster than would be possible under multilateral commitments. Institutions such as the Commonwealth and La Francophonie, that embody many of Canada's values and objectives, will be important complements to these regional arrangements. At the very least the other types of IOs will, in the absence of multilateral action, play a major role in keeping everyone at the table and limiting the scope for the major powers to act unilaterally.

While trading and production relationships may be problematic they are nevertheless closely governed; international financial relationships, on the other hand, are not. It is in this domain that Ottawa must invest its scarce resources.[48] The free fall of the Mexican peso showed how relatively random shocks in a middle-sized country could reverberate throughout the world's financial markets, creating economic and political instability and threatening the common global social interest. The problem is that the public goods supplied by national governments such as central banks and regulatory authorities are absent at the global level. Between the G-7 Finance Ministers, the Bank for International Settlements (BIS) and the International

Monetary Fund (IMF), there is not yet an agreed system for the management of financial crises or potential crises, let alone for ongoing macroeconomic management.

One of the major choices to be made here is whether Ottawa should continue to invest in the International Labour Organization, an institution that many consider to be moribund. In 1993-94 the contriution was $9.5 million. Yet labour and social policy will be one of the most important international trade agenda items in the coming years. Does it make sense to withdraw from the only international institution that attempts to bring together government, labour and the business community, rather than trying to endow it with some enforcement capabilities? With regard to the management of international financial crises, Canada should consider innovative ways of creating an oversight capacity through cooperation among the G-7 finance ministers, the BIS and the IMF, instead of making new investments in a proposed Global Economic Council that would mirror the UN Security Council.

Reforming Security Institutions

In the area of peace and security the question is how Canada can best harness the potential of the UN and regional security organizations to enhance collective security. The UN has been and remains a cornerstone of Canada's overall security policy. Yet the crisis of the UN system as a whole—precipitated by its failures in Rwanda, Somalia and the former Yugoslavia—and the growing problem of its budget means that it has been stretched to its breaking point.

Preventive diplomacy is emerging as a key function of the UN Secretariat. But as the linkages between social, economic, and political development and peace become better appreciated, the UN is also becoming more engaged in the other areas because of their significance for stability. Some development work in support of peace building is now being done by peacekeepers; some by specialized agencies. Thus there are not just more UN missions in the post-Cold War world; there is a greater variety. Although the exponential increase in total costs for UN peacekeeping missions (arrears on peacekeeping contributions totalled U.S.$3.2 billion in 1994) raises the questions of affordability for the international community, there is a potentially larger issue: the quality and preparedness of missions. Is it efficient to use peacekeepers to build civil society? To create a more efficient division of labour, more could be done by using the

Bretton Woods institutions, working with the UN and bilateral donors, not just to reconstruct peace, but also to help to avert the creation of conditions for future conflict—the pre-preventive diplomacy.

Canada is adapting to these changes in multilateral peacekeeping. The withdrawal of Canadian peacekeepers from Cyprus in 1992 and Ottawa's subsequent decision not to commit personnel to a number of other UN peacekeeping missions, and its more recent decision to earmark only 1,000 troops for one year to the NATO peacekeeping force in the former Yugoslavia, all point to a shift away from its traditional approach to managing international conflict. Ottawa is taking steps to make more use of Canada's comparative advantages, such as its expertise in logistics and in peace building, especially now that the Great Powers are increasingly active in peace enforcement and peacekeeping.

The search for new institutional means to cope with changing levels and kinds of threats has led to a renewed interest in subglobal and regional organizations. Clearly the UN should retain a global responsibility for peace and security. It has the prestige and resources to carry out certain operations such as peacekeeping; but regional organizations, with more detailed knowledge of local conditions, may be better placed to aid in early warning, preventive diplomacy and the reconstruction of civil society. The task in the next several years is to find the right match of mandates, that is, the complementarities that would allow regional groups to support the UN and vice versa, and to avoid gaps among and between them. For instance, NATO has significant mobilizing capacity but is weak on the preventive side, while institutions such as La Francophonie and the Commonwealth may be better able to play larger preventive and peace building roles. To enhance *confidence building*, regional organizations around the world are collaborating with former rivals through a range of joint activities. Finally, with regard to *capacity-building*, there is now greater interest in making regional organizations more effective bodies and consequently there is greater political support for them.

Nevertheless, questions persist as to the usefulness of regional bodies in general and the future of specific organizations. For instance, should the international community use regional institutions to develop new approaches to the prevention, management and resolution of conflict when other, perhaps more informal and less expensive, approaches (contact groups, "citizen diplomacy" of eminent persons) might achieve the same objectives? Alternatively, should the UN be reformed and strengthened first, to see what, if any, role there is for regional forums?

In conclusion, the debate in Canada focuses on whether it is better to belong to as many peace and security organizations as possible, so as to maximize our experience, or to restrict ourselves to the UN (or even particular niches within the UN) and a smaller number of organizations which are most important to our national objectives. It would seem that Canada's functional transition from peacekeeping and peace enforcement work to peace building implies that we should not again spend tens of millions of dollars on operations such as those in Somalia and the former Yugoslavia, where there is no peace to keep.[49] Such monies would bring a greater return if invested in preventing the root causes of conflict or in preventing conflict through mediation and negotiation.

Reforming Development Assistance Institutions

With a foreign policy driven by the need for Canada to promote domestic economic growth, the challenge in the area of sustainable development is twofold: to strengthen the capacity of developing countries and to identify the appropriate means by which IFIs and international development agencies can better meet human security and basic needs.

A number of trends provide the context in which Canada's choices in aid policy will be made. First, the satisfaction of basic needs (food, water, shelter, health, education) will continue to be a priority of international development assistance since it is expected that by 2010 the absolute poor will number about 1.2 billion. Second, there is now a much greater awareness of the deterioration of the global physical environment and the way in which the depletion of non-renewable resources can lead to social, political and economic conflict. Third, economic progress means little, and may be unsustainable, without peace and personal security. Fourth, there is no longer one monolithic Third World. The levels of economic growth are very uneven, with the poorest of the poor (especially in Africa) having low or even negative per capita growth rates, and in danger of de-linking from the world economy altogether. At the same time, the outstanding economic performances of many East Asia nations suggests that it may no longer be appropriate to classify them as "developing."

While the challenges facing developing countries are substantial, the recent foreign policy debates in Canada have brought up hard questions about Canada's continuing active engagement. Many Canadians see our involvement in developing countries as complementary to our pursuit of equity and social justice domestically. But others ask whether Canada can afford to transfer the same amounts of assistance to the South, provide development assistance to over 100 countries, and be active in so many institutions, particularly some of the UN specialized agencies, which have histories of financial mismanagement. Still others, in the business community, worry that a shift away from bilateral to multilateral aid will hurt the Canadian economy because of the reduced opportunity for tied aid. Meanwhile, there is a large debate around the acceptable trade-offs between short term economic growth and good governance. That is, to what extent should multilateral development financing be conditional on a country's social or military spending? Finally, perhaps the most contentious issue within the NGO and government communities is the appropriate division of labour among the plethora of overlapping development institutions.

The elimination of poverty, improved social standards, more participatory forms of government and reduced military spending in the South will not only reinforce Canadian values, but also reduce the social, economic, and security costs which Canada incurs through peacekeeping expenses, the resettlement of refugees, and action on illegal drugs and infectious diseases. The lack of support for sustainable development in Somalia, for example, clearly magnified the eventual costs to Canada and other countries. Do we pay now or later? The challenge is to leverage our aid dollars through a more efficient use of international institutions, which may lead in some cases to the elimination of the least useful organizations. The process has already begun. Canada withdrew from the UN Industrial Development Organization (UNIDO) in 1993.

In order to pursue a more efficient international development policy and yet also reflect the various interests at play in the debates summarized above, it is necessary to reduce government-to-government aid to the more developed countries of the developing world (e.g., Indonesia, Malaysia); to question whether the rebuilding of the former countries of the Soviet bloc should be spearheaded by Canadian taxpayers' dollars through CIDA or by private interests; and, increasingly, to use regional development banks for the financing of long term development. We should be careful to ensure that in the quest for efficiency we do not eliminate some useful duplication such as that between the World Bank, which now is more cognizant of human rights and the environment, and some of the UN specialized agencies.

That being said, it must be pointed out that in recent years concern has mounted among donors, including Canada, that the performance of the UN's development and assistance wing, which includes the United Nations Development Programme (UNDP), United Nations Children's Fund (UNICEF), World Food Programme (WFP), and United Nations Environment Programme (UNEP), has not been up to expectations. In particular, Canada's participation in the WFP and our commitment to UNEP should be revisited. There may be merit in amalgamating the UNDP with UNEP to create a global environmental institution.

Reforming Cultural Institutions
With regard to culture, the task is to identify the appropriate balance in projecting and protecting Canadian values, skills, and cultural industries through international institutions. It is not clear that Ottawa's ongoing investment in UNESCO ($13.7 million in 1993-94) could not be more usefully directed at such organizations as the Commonwealth and La Francophonie, which promote distinctly Canadian values in a more continuous and cost-effective manner, with greater visibility and impact. Organizations such as the Commonwealth, with its history of activism in the area of human rights (e.g. South Africa), may be a more effective forum than the UN for promoting "good governance" among member-states such as Nigeria. La Francophonie, of more recent vintage, offers parallel possibilities across a broad spectrum of French-speaking cultures in Africa and around the world. *TV5*, a French television network, projects Canadian perspectives and talent throughout the French-speaking world, whilst offering unprecedented new outlets for expanding domestic cultural industries. Is this the model forum and strategy for Canada to follow in promoting its values? Both the Commonwealth and La Francophonie have key roles to play in developing civil society through activities like legal and parliamentary reform, and through promotion of and adherence to norms of conservation and human rights. Finally, despite Canada's occupation of 30 percent of the Arctic land mass, the North has until recently been neglected in our foreign

policy. The Arctic Council, currently in gestation, offers ground-breaking institutional mechanisms bringing together the eight Arctic nations for dealing with environmental threats (e.g., oil spills), as well as input from aboriginal, environmental, and scientific communities.

MAINTAINING THE RELEVANCE OF CANADIAN FOREIGN POLICY

How can Canada's foreign service and its foreign policy be expected to remain relevant in the 1990s? The past three years have seen a delayed reaction to the need to become more discriminating in our international commitments. In 1994, DFAIT and the Prime Minister's Office decided to enunciate a clear corporate aim: a "Team Canada" approach to conquering foreign markets. An equally apt expression for the political side of the Department's functions has not yet been expressed, however.

With Canada seen by some as a "declining middle power,"[50] DFAIT will have to fight skilfully and entrepreneurially to control the forces of change instead of being buffeted by them. This has two dimensions: Canada's historical tendency to engage in "diffuse internationalism" rather than to focus its strategies solely on its high priority interests; and the fact that in a post-Cold War era, where structural power is less important, there is an even greater incentive for intellectual leadership on the part of Canada's foreign-policy makers. On the first aspect, observers frequently suggest that Canada could perhaps learn from the Australian experience. Australia now considers the Asia Pacific region as its natural sphere of influence and has, as a consequence, radically reduced its diplomatic commitments to the Americas and Europe. It is, however, unfair to attempt to "regionalize" Canada's foreign policy—despite the fact that some have said the country is inexorably destined to be a "nation of the Americas"—given its status as a G-7 member, its membership in more international institutions than any other middle power, and the oft-quoted characterization of it as a "regional power without a region."

With regard to an "entrepreneurial" (but not necessarily high-cost) foreign policy that seeks to have a maximum impact in those areas where there is a clear and identifiable Canadian interest, one has to ask where are the likes of Lester Pearson, Norman Robertson, Marcel Cadieux and Escott Reid, all of whom had international reputations? Will Canadians be called upon by the international community to provide intellectual leadership on the current crop of international policy dilemmas, such as humanitarian intervention, peace building, and the new trade policy issues of labour, environment and intellectual property? After all, outside the circle of the Permanent Five members of the UN Security Council, there is not a strong correlation between geographic/military size and the ability to "make a difference" in promoting peace, equity and justice in the international system. Indeed, as the history of Canadian diplomacy shows, it often helps to be in the next tier of nations. And to take another example, how much did it cost the Norwegian government to play a key role in helping to build bridges between Israel and the PLO?

Finally, the fundamental change that is required for DFAIT to approach the world strategically is that it should shift from its traditional "maintaining good bilateral relations" posture to managing bilateral relations primarily as leverage for achieving specific bilateral and multilateral goals which are of highest priority to Canada. This has real cost implications. For instance, Canada may find that maintaining fully staffed embassies in Denmark, Norway, Sweden, Finland—and now in each of the Baltic republics—while certainly promoting Canadian priorities, does not necessarily meet the standard of "highest" priority. Moreover, the amount of Canadian aid in some of the world's developing countries is symbolic when compared to that of some large donors of development assistance such as Japan; would it therefore not make sense to terminate Canadian aid programs in these countries altogether and focus only on those developing countries, say, those in the sub-Saharan region where Canada's aid can make the largest difference?

Bilateral relationships with old friends such as the United States will remain key. However, Canada will increasingly choose both partners and institutions, perhaps with sunset clauses, to obtain specific shorter-term objectives or to reflect longer-term prospects. Ottawa will not maximize its influence in global affairs by confining itself to "prestige" institutions such as the G-7 at the expense of playing a leadership role in other emerging alliances, whether in La Francophonie or in an Arctic Council.

CONCLUSION

As this chapter has shown the foreign policy reviews of the last two years have re-emphasized that Canada's national interests require it to have a global rather than a regional foreign policy, and hence a widespread and effective diplomatic presence. At the same time, the debates and the final parliamentary foreign policy and defence reports, along with the Program Reviews, resonated with insistence on the need to "make hard choices."

The challenge for DFAIT in the coming years is to provide services to a growing, more multicultural population, while also maintaining top-quality research and policy advice on an expanding and more complex international policy agenda, and to do all this with fewer dollars. Goals of "efficiency," "cost-effectiveness," and "accountability" are not necessarily incompatible with the management of a more complex, expanding international agenda. It has been pointed out above that control over an expanding foreign policy agenda and a shrinking budget can be achieved through organizational changes (e.g., the creation of a Global Issues Bureau), the application of ITs, co-location agreements, more cost recovery in international business promotion programs, the closure of consulates, and a shift in emphasis towards social and economic multilateral institutions and away from military ones. Without a doubt, the responses to date by Ottawa's foreign policy planners to fiscal realities have been imaginative, needed and flexible. They are, however, not enough.

Implicit in the parliamentary foreign policy review, the Government's response, and DFAIT's response to Program Review, was that savings in Departmental operations would reduce the likelihood of compromising the liberal international impulse in Canada's foreign policy. The problem, as pointed out, is that the budgetary cutbacks in Canada's external affairs will be ongoing and deeper than those which could be offset by existing and potential future operational savings. As shown in the Appendix, for Canadian diplomacy to retain its credibility and relevance the following hard *political* choices will have to be made:

- selective closing of embassies and high commissions in countries that are not of high priority and where Canadian economic and political interests are not paramount, in addition to those consulates that have already been closed;
- reduction of official Canadian representation abroad (especially the high proportion of officials from federal departments other than DFAIT) and their replacement by non-official representatives;

- governmental withdrawal from, or major reductions in, certain functional areas such as international business promotion and some traditional peacekeeping operations;
- reduction in foreign aid to developing countries on the threshold of joining the First World; and
- a reduction in Canada's commitment to specific international organizations such as NATO, ILO and some other UN specialized agencies, with a complete withdrawal warranted in certain cases.

The options are not new. They have been discussed and debated within government circles and publicly as ways of conducting Canada's diplomacy in a period of fiscal austerity. The Canadian response to date has been decidedly piecemeal, characterized by cabinet ministers succumbing to pressure from interest groups, fierce resistance from within DFAIT to the privatization of the Trade Commissioner Service, and a preference for tinkering rather than embarking on radical institutional change that are the hallmarks of the Australian and New Zealand responses to financial cutbacks and the changing geopolitical realities of the post-Cold War world.

Another issue raised by this chapter's emphasis on the fiscal constraints is the fact that Canada has tried to take the lead role in far too many international policy initiatives, a legacy of the golden age (1947-1957) of Canadian diplomacy. Canadian diplomats expressed to the author both their pride and sadness at no longer being able to live up to the high expectations of their foreign colleagues. Not since the time of Prime Minister R.B. Bennett has Canadian foreign policy been so dominated by trade, yet the view from abroad of Canada's international role continues to be that of a country highly valued for its diplomacy of ideas on promotion of international justice, fairness and the rule of law. The problem is that Canada no longer has the governmental capacity to be so broadly engaged at the official level. It is not that Canada should not be globally engaged; rather, the means of this global engagement will have to change. Less and less will our international face be presented by diplomats, soldiers and aid officials; more and more we will be visible through the staff of Canadian-based NGOs and academic, philanthropic, and business organizations. The financing needed to support this non-official Canadian presence in international affairs will in the short term come mostly from public coffers, but such expenditures over time will be phased out, in effect, forcing the Canadian private and philanthropic sectors either to support this Canadian presence abroad or to let it die. It is unlikely that the Canadian state through its institutions (CIDA, DND, and DFAIT) will be able move back into such domains once it is out of them.

To return to the three choices outlined in the introduction to this chapter, in light of the certainty of declining budgets for international programs and foreign policy interests: we cannot be an effective global player unless we focus on our actual vital interests—bilateral (United States), multilateral (UN, G-7, WTO), and functional (peace building, international business development)—and dispense with a history of overemphasis on role and influence in our diplomacy. Ottawa must become expert in niche diplomacy and a "good dancer" on the international policy stage, picking and choosing those issue areas (e.g., Arctic Council, proposal for a UN rapid-reaction force), and bilateral and multilateral partnerships that maximize Canadian interests.

APPENDIX

Degrees of Change in Ottawa's Foreign Policy Capacity and Outlook

OLD	NEW
The federal government is the chief source of funding for, and implementer (through 22 agencies and departments) of, Canada's international business development program. It is based on a philosophy of universal coverage.	Canada's Trade Commissioner Service in the Department of Foreign Affairs and International Trade concentrates its resources on hard-to-access markets in Asia and Latin America, and leaves the Canadian private sector, acting through horizontal industry associations (Canadian Exporters' Association, Canadian Chamber of Commerce, Canadian Manufacturers' Association), to promote its products and services in the more familiar markets of Western Europe (including Russia) and the United States. This latter activity can be funded either through an export tax or by a transfer of funds from the federal government's trade promotion budget to these associations.

The Departments of Foreign Affairs and International Trade and National Defence have monopolies on mediation in foreign conflicts (and their aftermaths), the promotion of international education and the promotion of Canadian values and cultural industries abroad.

Non-governmental organizations, Canadian universities, and Canada's philanthropic organizations play a larger role in the projection of Canadian values and interests abroad in areas such as election monitoring, peace-building, academic links and culture.

Canada has foreign policy in which all regions are "priorities".

Canada's foreign policy remains global but there is realization that our interests are now concentrated more and more in the Americas and the Asia Pacific regions and less and less in Europe and the Middle East/Maghreb.

Canada has its own embassies and high commissions around the world.

There is greater use of co-location agreements with like-minded states to save costs. In addition, a select number of high commissions and embassies are closed in those regions of the world (Scandinavia, Africa) in which Ottawa's bilateral relationships are no longer a priority, given the availability of multilateral fora in which to achieve our desired objectives.

Canada is known to be inveterate joiner of international organizations in order to leverage its influence.

In the interest of defining our comparative advantage in the post-Cold War world and increasing the effectiveness of our international contributions, Canada will shift its resources away from international security institutions to economic and social institutions. There will also be a strong desire, given the experience with certain UN agencies, to join international organizations with sunset clauses and new, smaller more issue-specific international organizations (e.g., Arctic Council) in which Canada can play a lead role.

Canada's aid program is dispersed among 128 countries (although 70 percent of country-to-country disbursements go to 28 countries).

There will be a concentration of Canada's diminishing pool of aid. In making the choice of countries of concentration, CIDA will be guided by first and foremost its mandate of helping the poorest of the poor and meeting basic human needs. The largest 28 recipients (many in sub-Saharan Africa) will receive a higher and higher percentage of Canada's Official Development Assistance. As a consequence Canada will have to pull out entirely from certain Latin American, Caribbean, Pacific and Southeast Asian countries despite the strong historic ties with some of the countries affected.

Canada's international security interests are focused on the major institutions such as NATO and the UN. Canada expends considerable resources on nuclear non-proliferation issues.

Although nuclear weapons proliferation is still a concern, Ottawa recognizes that it may have more influence helping to shift the international security framework forward so as to include greater policy emphasis on the effects of global trends in social policy, labour, migration, and poverty on international stability. This has implications for the types of multilateral affiliations that Canada now seeks in order to respond to this new security agenda. Canada moves away from expensive peacekeeping assignments to less expensive conflict prevention and post-conflict reconstruction initiatives, in which the private sector shares in the costs and benefits

---

Previously, the geographic Branches (Asia Pacific, Latin America, Africa and the Middle East) have been split between DFAIT and CIDA.

Synergies are made possible by having one geographic Branch responsible for aid, trade, political and security relations. It will also have resource implications since fewer Assistant Deputy Ministers and staff will be needed once these Branches in CIDA and DFAIT are amalgamated. .

NOTES

The author would like to thank Maureen Appel Molot and Fen Osler Hampson for their helpful comments on an earlier draft of this chapter.

1   See, for example, the conclusions of the Report of the Special Joint Committee of the Senate and the House of Commons Reviewing Canadian Foreign Policy, *Canada's Foreign Policy: Principles and Priorities for the Future*, (Ottawa: Publications Service, Parliamentary Publications Directorate, 1994). Hereafter cited as Special Joint Committee, Foreign Policy.

2   This is the thrust of the Reform Party's dissenting voice on the future directions of Canadian foreign policy. See Report of the Special Joint Committee of the Senate and the House of Commons Reviewing Canada's Foreign Policy, *Canada's Foreign Policy: Dissenting Opinions and Appendices* (Ottawa: Publications Service, Parliamentary Publications Directorate, 1994). Hereafter cited as Dissenting Opinions.

3   The British government, for example, by the end of the 1970s had reconciled itself to the fact that it would no longer be able to continue to play a leading role simultaneously in three circles of influence: the Commonwealth, Europe, and the international community. See chapter on British foreign policy in Roy C. Macridis, *Foreign Policy in World Politics*, (Prentice Hall: Englewood Cliffs, N.J., 8th edition, 1992). For a contrasting Canadian perspective on spheres of influence, see endnote 32.

4   Canada, *Canada in the World: Government Statement* (Ottawa: Canada Communication Group, 1995). Hereafter cited as Government Statement.

5   Canada, *Foreign Policy for Canadians* (Ottawa: Information Canada, 1970).

6   Liberal Party of Canada, *Foreign Policy Handbook*, (Ottawa: May 1993), Mimeo. This was authored by two Liberal MPs, Lloyd Axworthy and Christine Stewart.

7   Liberal Party of Canada, *Creating Opportunity: The Liberal Plan for Canada*, (Ottawa, October 1993), esp. Chapter 8. This document became known as the Red Book.

8   Canada 21 Council, *Canada and Common Security in the Twenty-First Century*, (Toronto: Centre for International Studies, University of Toronto, 1994). Hereafter cited as the Canada 21 Report.

9   Janice Gross Stein and Pierre Pettigrew, "Report on the National Forum on Canada's International Relations," *Canadian Foreign Policy* 2, no. 2 (Spring 1994).

10   See Special Joint Committee, Report; Senate and House of Commons, The Report of the Special Joint Committee on Canada's Defence

Policy, *Security in a Changing World*, (Ottawa: Publications Service, Parliamentary Publications Directorate, 1994).

11   Canada, Department of National Defence, *1994 Defence White Paper*, (Ottawa: Minister of Supply and Services, December 1994).

12   See *Government Statement; and Canada, Government Response to the Recommendations of the Special Joint Parliamentary Committee Reviewing Canadian Foreign Policy* (Ottawa: Canada Communications Group, 1995)—hereafter cited as *Government Response*, which was the companion document to the Government Statement.

13   "International Business Development Review Report," Submitted to the Honourable Roy MacLaren, Minister for International Trade, September 30, 1994. Hereafter cited as the Wilson Report.

14   Serge Joyal, *Affaires Culturelles Internationales, Enseignement Supérieur et Coopération Scientifique*, unpublished report for the Department of Foreign Affairs and International Trade, August 1994. In fact Joyal had prepared two similar reports, one for Foreign Affairs and the other for the Department of Canadian Heritage.

15   Canada, Parliament, Report of the House of Commons Standing Committee on Foreign Affairs and International Trade on the Issues of International Financial Institutions Reforms for the Agenda of the June 1995 G-7 Halifax Summit, *From Bretton Woods to Halifax and Beyond: Towards a 21st Summit for the 21st Century Challenge*, (Ottawa: Publications Service, Parliamentary Publications Directorate, May 1995).

16   The public review was the Second Annual National Forum on Canada's International Relations held in Toronto, 10-11 September 1995. See forum report "International Institutions in the Twenty-First Century, Can Canada Help to Meet the Challenge? Report of the Second Annual National Forum," *Canadian Foreign Policy* 3, 2 (Fall 1995). An internal review was undertaken for the government by the Department of Foreign Affairs and International Trade in the late autumn of 1995.

17   See "Overview," *Special Joint Committee, Foreign Policy*; and Maxwell A. Cameron & Maureen Appel Molot, "Does Democracy Make a Difference," in Maxwell A. Cameron and Maureen.Appel Molot, eds., *Canada Among Nations 1995: Democracy and Foreign Policy*, (Ottawa: Carleton University Press, 1995), 7-17.

18   Canada 21 Report, 69.

19   Only the Reform Party's members on the joint House of Commons-Senate Committee studying Canada's foreign policy felt that fiscal responsibility should be the main determinant of Canada's future international relations. They bemoaned the parliamentary report's lack of recommendations for specific cuts and suggested that Canada should make cuts to its bilateral aid and to international grants and non-mandatory contributions, and should drop its membership in "non-essential" international organizations. See *Dissenting Opinions*, 29.

20   Wilson Report, i. According to the Report, the implementation of its 20 recommendations would result in a reduction of $55 million to the

Department of Foreign Affairs and International Trades budget, and an overall reduction of $115 million to the Government's international business development support. These savings, the Report admitted, could not be achieved without reducing the size of the public service.

21   This author was told that the reason that the special joint parliamentary committee reviewing Canada's foreign policy did not advocate any major reductions in foreign policy programs and international affiliations in its final report was that it believed that the House of Commons Standing Committee on Foreign Affairs and International Trade would in future make such recommendations.

22   On the process and expense of the Canada 21 and parliamentary foreign policy consultations, see Denis Stairs, "The Public Politics of the Canadian Defence and Foreign Policy Reviews," *Canadian Foreign Policy*, 3, no. 1 (Spring 1995), 91-116. For a distinctly less enthusiastic appraisal of the Liberal Government's attempt to democratize Canadian foreign policy, see Kim R. Nossal, "The Democratization of Canadian Foreign Policy," *Canadian Foreign Policy*, 1, no. 1 (Fall 1993), 95-104; and Nossal, "The Democratization of Canadian Foreign Policy: The Elusive Ideal," in Maxwell A. Cameron and Maureen Appel Molot, eds., *Canada Among Nations 1995: Democracy and Foreign Policy*, (Ottawa: Carleton University Press, 1995), 29-43.

23   See Chapter 3 in this volume.

24   The assessed, as distinguished from the *voluntary*, contributions to international organizations have not been reduced yet.

25   "Back to basics" referred to the abandonment of what were no longer considered "core" Departmental activities, and was to entail the transfer of DFAIT's immigration role to the department then called Employment and Immigration Canada (now Citizenship and Immigration Canada), the cultural and academic relations program to the Canada Council, international expositions to Communications Canada, and the international sports program to Fitness and Amateur Sport (now Canadian Heritage). Such was the resistance to the transfer of the academic relations from DFAIT to the Canada Council that the Senate, with its majority of Conservative senators, did not pass the parliamentary bill. See Evan H. Potter, "Canada's Foreign Policy and Foreign Service in the 1990s," in Fen Osler Hampson and Christopher J. Maule, eds., *Canada Among Nations 1993-94: Global Jeopardy*, (Ottawa: Carleton University Press, 1993), 48-51.

26   Potter, "Canada's Foreign Policy," 56.

27   These will be mostly in secretarial and clerical positions.

28   This is based on the total cost of $170 million to keep 1,700 DFAIT staff abroad. These December 1995 figures were provided to the author by DFAIT's Human Resources Development Bureau. The Auditor General's 1995 report cites a lower total expense of $144.5 for 1994-95. See *Report of the Auditor General of Canada to the House of Commons* (Ottawa: Office of the Auditor General, May 1995), 8-14.

29   Peter MacArthur, "Benchmark for Middle Power Diplomacy: The Australian Model," *bout de papier*, 11, no. 2 (Summer 1994), 29.

30   Based on data provided to this author by the Corporate Services
      Branch of the Department of Foreign Affairs and International Trade.
31   Department of Foreign Affairs and International Trade, *Outlook on
      Program Priorities and Expenditures*, 5. Of DFAIT's 149 points of ser-
      vice staffed by Canadian nationals, 103 (70 percent) have fewer than
      five Canada-based staff and 58 (40 percent) have only one or two
      staff.
32   During a "townhall meeting" following the very narrow "No" victory
      on the Quebec referendum in 1995, Prime Minister Chrétien stated
      that Canadians should feel proud to be able to play leading roles in
      both La Francophonie and the Commonwealth. The inference here, at
      the highest political level, was that while Ottawa could make
      unprecedented deep cuts in its domestic programs, the prestige asso-
      ciated with an active, internationalist foreign policy (usefully invoked
      during national unity crises) militated against a proportional amount
      of retrenchment in Canada's international policies and programs.
      "National Townhall," CBC Television News, Monday, December 11,
      1995.
33   "DFAIT's Medium Term Financial Outlook," *Panorama*, no. 1, January
      2, 1996, (Ottawa: Department of Foreign Affairs and International
      Trade), 2-3.
34   For a discussion of the role of culture in the Chrétien Government's
      foreign policy agenda in 1994-95, see John Hay, "Projecting Canadian
      Values and Culture: An Episode in the Making of Canadian Foreign
      Policy," *Canadian Foreign Policy* 3, no. 2 (Fall 1995), 21-32.
35   *Government Response*, 75-91.
36   Hay, "Projecting Canadian Values," 24.
37   See Jock A. Finlayson, "Canadian Trade Policy: A Private Sector
      View," *Canadian Foreign Policy* 1, no. 3 (Fall 1993).
38   Tim Reid, "Challenging Canada's International Business Paradox: A
      Private Sector Perspective," *Canadian Foreign Policy* 1, no.1 (Winter
      1992/93), 98, 101. The seminal document on renewing Canada's trade
      development system—which, ironically enough, was produced within
      DFAIT and made public—remains Andrew Griffith, "Straight Talk on
      Why Canada Needs to Reform its Trade Development System,"
      Canadian Foreign Policy 1, no. 1 (Winter 1992/93), 61-86.
39   See Department of Foreign Affairs and International Trade, "Outlook
      on Program Priorities and Expenditures—1995-96 to 1997-98," mimeo.
40   These are the services provided to any Canadian citizen abroad
      through 180 points of service.
41   Tim Draimin and Betty Plewes, "Civil Society and the Democratization
      of Foreign Policy," in Cameron and Molot, eds., *Canada Among
      Nations 1995* previously referred to in endnote 22, 1995), 67 and end-
      note 8. While Draimin and Plewes focus on the role of NGOs, the
      same point could be made about all other for-profit and not-for-profit
      voluntary organizations that are part of the growing network of expert
      communities in the private sector and the growing voluntary, or third,
      sector. See also Chapter 13 in this volume, by Ken Bush.

42   This is apparently still the exception, judging from the composition of Canadian delegations as compared with those of other countries.

43   The historical emphasis, ironically enough, has been to invest in the creation of Canadian studies associations abroad rather than to invest in the creation of mechanisms to tap into the diverse domestic scholarly community. This is beginning to change with the creation of a Foreign Policy Mechanism to help the Department to reach the expert communities in a more comprehensive and systematic way.

44   The crumbling of Canada's foreign policy research capacity can be traced to the closing down of the CIIPS, the Economic Council of Canada and the Science Council of Canada in 1992. Other research organizations such as in the university community—facing their own budgetary cutbacks—have not been able to fill the gap.

45   This section is adapted from my "Canada and the Reform of International Organizations: Visions for the Future," a paper presented at the Second National Forum on Canada's International Relations, held in Toronto, Canada, 10-11 September 1995. The paper was subsequently published in *Canadian Foreign Policy* 3, no. 2 (Fall 1995), 73-92.

46   These figures cover the membership fees alone and do not include the operational cost for Canadian participation in, for example, UN peacekeeping and NATO missions, which would be assessed to the Department of National Defence, nor do they include the costs to government departments such as DFAIT (including CIDA) that manage Canada's participation in these organizations.

47   I am indebted to Alan Morgan, Senior Policy Advisor at the Department of Foreign Affairs and International Trade, for pointing this out to me.

48   See also Chapter 14 in this volume, by Roy Culpeper.

49   The cost of Canadian involvement in Somalia and the former Yugoslavia in 1993-94 was $46.2 million and $44.4 million respectively. Canada. Department of Finance, *Estimates 1995-96*, DFAIT Part III, (Ottawa: Supply and Services Canada 1995), 125.

50   See Arthur Andrew, *The Rise and Fall of a Middle Power: Diplomacy from King to Mulroney* (Halifax: James Lorimer, 1994).

III

Future Defence Policy in an *Époque de vaches maigres*

HAL P. KLEPAK

For Canada as a whole, but particularly for its defence forces, recent times have ceased to be merely the famous *années de vaches maigres* everyone must occasionally face, and have turned into a true era of these increasingly thin livestock. Strategic analysts would be hard put to suggest a scenario in which defence policy would gain priority from the government and people of Canada, at least one which could be a realistic basis for planning in this country.

In this period it seems clear that, barring a hopefully unlikely national convulsion accompanied by violence, or a great international disaster from which Canada could not afford to stand aside, security priorities for the Canadian state will continue to decline. While it may indeed be true that international crime, the drug trade, local crime in the streets, illegal immigration, the spread of epidemics and other non-traditional threats will become more pressing issues for the country, it is doubtful that defence policy and its armed servants will offer either the cadre or the means for dealing with them, at least in the sense of assuming direct responsibility for combatting them.

Under these circumstances, it must be expected that defence budgets will continue to fall, that the armed forces will either level off where they are now or even decline further, not only in personnel strength but also in combat and other capabilities. This is not an ideal scenario in a world with the uncertainties of today but it does appear to be a more than likely one. Indeed, as has been the case before in defence policy, future Canadians may well again be asked to pay the price for financially based decisions taken in peacetime on optimistic readings of the international and domestic scenes. There is a fear that current cuts will leave the country weak in the presence of some future crisis.

It is therefore worth asking, in line with the discussions of other aspects of Canadian policy to be found elsewhere in this volume, what kind of choices this era offers defence decision makers in this country and what might be the most helpful, though no doubt still painful, options they should consider accepting. In order to attempt such an enquiry, this chapter will look at the recent context of public discussion of decision making on defence matters in this country, will then suggest an analysis of what factors will probably continue to impinge on such decision making, and finally will ask where one might go in order to get the most out of reduced interest in, and money for, national security.

THE PUBLIC CONTEXT OF THE CURRENT DEBATE

Perhaps the most noticeable change in the national debate on defence issues in recent years is its highly public nature. Some of this is no doubt the result of the very favourable light in which the Armed Forces were seen both in the Gulf War and during the very taxing circumstances of the Oka Crisis. But just as important have been negative events such as the Somalia affair and its sequels, videos of unsavoury aspects of military service, especially in the Airborne Regiment, and widespread closing of defence installations, including the veritable storm over the demise of the bilingual Collège militaire royal de Saint-Jean.

More serious discussion has centred, however, in the defence and foreign policy review processes set in motion by the Liberal government shortly after it took power in 1993. Prime Minister Chrétien made it clear that he intended these reviews to reflect the new government's commitment to wide consultation of the public in the process of governmental decision making in the future. And there can be little doubt that the result was an exceptional discussion by Canadians of issues of concern for them in both the foreign and the defence policy realms, and an unprecedented coverage of defence and wider security matters in the press.

Coming out of the reviews were two major reports which were followed, for defence, by the *1994 Defence White Paper*, and for foreign policy, first the government response and shortly thereafter the issuing of *Canada in the World*. It should be emphasized that defence affairs were central to all these publications and not just those related directly to defence policy.

Behind this interest, however, there has been a drive to re-examine defence policy in the light of the greatly changed context of national security in the 1990s, unrecognizable when compared with that of the Cold War which had dominated Canadian thinking on defence for well over four decades. There has also been an even more determined effort to find ways to cut defence budgets in order to address the pressing need to reduce the deficit and regain domestic and international confidence in Canada. Indeed, there is little doubt that the "peace dividend" was widely considered by Canadians as their due.[1]

While specialists and committees clamour about the importance of our defence efforts for world peace and national security, budgets plummet and little public interest in maintaining formerly respectable levels for such expenditures can be garnered. The foreign policy committee report, for example, states that

... While the new global environment appears to be less directly threatening to Canada in a military sense, the demands on Canada to contribute to international security have increased, rather than diminished, just at a time when fiscal restraint makes it more difficult to respond ...[2]

The defence policy report suggests, in terms which it is difficult to contest,

... To withdraw militarily from the world community carries an automatic loss of influence and access in the very councils where our own economic and security interests are at stake ... if we are prepared to acknowledge that we cannot predict the future, then we must be ready to invest in a degree of military preparation whose justification is, in part, the medium and longer term ... it is folly to base defence policy upon the assumption that because the present appears comparatively safe, so too will be the future.[3]

The same report acknowledged early on, however, "many other urgent calls on the federal purse."[4] And the *Defence White Paper* could hardly hide that "the defence funding assumptions contained in the 1994 budget envisaged a level of defence spending in the year 2000 that, in real terms, would be less than 60 percent of that assumed in the 1987 Defence White Paper."[5]

In fact, what is happening is that the defence budget is suffering larger losses in the current era of restraint than any other portion of the federal government's activities. And this can only be happening because the government feels, as previous governments have felt many times before in this country's history, that cuts in this area will have less dramatic political effects than those in other fields. In the ongoing battle between what John Tredennick has called the "military culture" and the "fiscal culture," it is clearly the latter which is winning out at virtually every turn.[6]

This was already the case in the last 25 years of the Cold War, and there was little likelihood that it would not become even more prominent as the dominating tendency in the years following. And while the nature of the first half-decade of the new world context has been far from peaceful, and therefore the call for Canadian military activity in support of the long-popular peacekeeping role has risen in frequency rather than fallen, it is also true that even this kind of operation has seen its terms of reference change and its popularity fall. As is well known, peacekeeping operations have broadened and deepened to involve what many now term, at times with maddening looseness, *peacemaking, peace enforcement, peace building*, etc. These operations have often become more dangerous, less likely to result in thanks, larger, more costly, and more intrusive into national sovereignty.[7]

It must also be said that, despite an early near-unanimity on the value of such operations, critical voices are now much more often heard, even in Canada.[8] It is worth remembering that peacekeeping in its historic post-1956 context was sustained by two sets of reasoning: one humanitarian and the other strategic. The first argued that peacekeeping gained time for the parties to a conflict to think again, take stock of the situation, and negotiate. Therefore it was a *good thing* in and of itself in a world of conflict.

The strategic thinking behind support of peacekeeping during the Cold War also had a powerful logic, especially for Canadians. This suggested that a country like Canada, placed on the main route of attack for most missiles and aircraft flying from one superpower to attack the other, must ensure that small "brush fire" wars did not invite superpower intervention and thus escalate such conflicts into a confrontation where a nuclear exchange could be contemplated. John Holmes quotes the British historian Denis Brogan to good effect when he says "the basic Canadian relationship is not either with the United States or with the United Kingdom but with the world of the hydrogen bomb.... Neutrality has become not so much unattainable as irrelevant."[9]

Needless to say, in the post-Cold War era pro-peacekeeping arguments may still hold on the humanitarian side of the discussion. But in the absence of a credible scenario for a nuclear exchange between Russia and the United States, the military argument becomes less convincing. And in an era of vastly reduced defence budgets even peacekeeping may not prove a completely sacred cow.[10] In addition, it must be said that the capabilities of armed forces tailored to the Cold War are to some degree limited in peacekeeping operations (defined widely) despite the excellent performance of Canadian Forces peacekeepers over the last four decades.

The navy is of course an essentially anti-submarine force, a situation which is perfectly logical, given the threats it has had to face in the decades since the Royal Canadian Navy's formation. The Air Force has also had an overwhelmingly high performance interception and tactical support role for decades, even though the air transport tasking has been taken seriously too. Even the Army, steeped in peacekeeping since 1956, has had as its main role the supply of heavy—though decreasingly heavy with time—armoured and mechanized forces prepared for the main central front in Europe. Thus even the land force is not primarily geared to peacekeeping, and therefore the forces as a whole and individually make do at peacekeeping; they do so very well indeed, but they are not equipped, armed, configured, or especially trained with reference to this role.[11]

It must thus be said that the context for defence budgets and the policy which is driven by them is vastly altered today from that of

a few short years ago. The changes involved impose the consideration of even radically revised policies as ways to balance the
demands of budgets and legitimate security needs. Before addressing possible answers, however, it is necessary to spend some time on
the changes themselves, for it is they which will determine what priorities will be.

EXTERNAL FACTORS

The first overwhelmingly important factor of recent years, and one of
vast significance for services still organized and armed in accordance
with their previous terms of reference, is the end of the Cold War.
The comfortable North Atlantic-based world of half a century, successor to the imperial and Commonwealth experience of well over
three centuries linking us with Europe as a bedrock of our national
existence, is gone. The disappearance of the main focus of Western
defence efforts of several decades threw confusion into the armed
forces of all NATO nations, even though there was generalized plea-
sure that the Cold War had been won, that communism was no
longer a threat, and that Western values had triumphed.

In direct terms, however, the events of 1989-91 meant that the
roles of the Canadian Armed Forces, and the defence policy (and to
a great extent the foreign policy) which employed them, were largely
a thing of the past. There was no immediate threat to the sea lanes
which linked Canada and North America to Europe and the rest of
the world. Gone was the possibility, remote at the best of times, of a
major Soviet assault on Western Europe, the raison d'être not only for
Canada's mechanized forces in Europe and at home but also for its
fighter-ground attack squadrons. Also well behind us was any real
possibility of a bomber strike on Canada, the main reason for the Air
Force's high performance interceptors cooperating closely with the
USAF in the air defence of North America.

Under the new circumstances, it was obvious that the Canadian
Forces would soon be looking for new roles within a defence policy
which would redefine national interests and priorities with security
dimensions. But this consideration of the new context has taken
place in a world so changed as to challenge much more than the
Cold War elements of our national security thinking.

The shocks to the central North Atlantic foundation of our relationships were not to end with the close of the Cold War. The largely

Eurocentric basis of so much of Canadian defence policy was shaken much more fundamentally. For the Europe which came out of the end of the East-West competition was far from anything this country had ever known. NATO had in many senses come just in time in 1949. In a world where the edifice of British military, economic and cultural influence was falling into a void and where the asymmetries of North American life were becoming only too obvious to Canadian decision-makers, counterpoises to the weight of our great neighbour, or even means to multilateralize essential elements of the bilateral relationship, were notable for their absence.[12]

As the United Nations displayed ever more clearly its impotence in the late 1940s, Canada found in NATO an almost ideal alliance, which allowed as it did for the multilateralizing of the security relationship with the U.S., included as members both mother countries, and provided a forum for economic and cultural, as well as defence discussions among the countries of the evolving North Atlantic community. In this grouping the Europeans also found their central pillar of foreign and defence policy. There was great commonality of interests, of which one part no doubt was security, but another was the feeling of belonging to this very special part of the world.

In the 1990s, Canada has found a Europe distinctly absorbed in its own problems, especially in the security area. The remaking of the map of Europe, and the fighting which has accompanied it from the Balkans to the former Soviet Union, has revealed a level of instability in the old continent which the Cold War had hidden. Canada's linkages with its mother countries, and their European partners, had shown their limitations well before in the failed 1970s discussions of Mr. Trudeau's "Third Option." But by now Canada had ceased to have very much relevance to Europe at all, and with the direct threat gone, Canadians soon lost the interest in Europe's security which had caused them to station forces there permanently for decades. Europe had also lost interest in Canada, although our troops were still welcome as peacekeepers in the continent's trouble spots.

If Canadian trade was hardly vital for Europe any longer, European trade was also decreasingly key to Canada's well-being. And while investment interest remained quite high, this was not the stuff by which communities were sustained. All these tendencies frittered away the mutual connections and interests and paved the way for the current state of affairs, where much lip service is paid to the traditional linkages but little concrete action is taken to maintain them. The withdrawal of the Canadian Forces from their bases in Baden and Lahr has only been the most visible sign of this growing distance.

Equally new, although also dating, of course, from before the end of the Cold War, has been the explosion of interest in, and the contact with, the Asia-Pacific region. The second area of trading importance for Canada, this vast section of the world long ago replaced Europe as a commercial partner. In connections as varied as investment and immigration, the European connection has been displaced in importance by Asia-Pacific. And recent public policy statements, while often trying to downplay the extent of this change, have been unable to hide it entirely from the Canadian public.[13]

In the security field, there have been both direct and indirect results of this growth in linkages. Ottawa has begun to be active in Asia-Pacific security matters well beyond anything ever known in the past. Several more fleet units have been transferred to the West coast from the East. And British Columbia's military installations have been relatively safe from the severe chopping going on farther east. The fall in relative priority for Europe could hardly be more visible than in this shift of resources and interest. Indeed, it could be argued that Canada's security interest would have even been greater here if it were not for the reluctance of key players in the Pacific Basin to accept it, or to see too much progress made generally in the area of regional defence cooperation.

In addition, there has been the growth of the Latin American connection, one resisted by foreign policy makers in this country for well over a century and by defence planners for even longer. From being the forgotten region of the world for Canada, Latin America has come to have growing priority in Ottawa. Having joined the OAS in 1990 and NAFTA in 1994, and taken both steps in the context of a troubling drift towards "blockism", the nightmare of policy makers for decades, Canada has found itself not only welcome in the inter-American community but acknowledged them as a valuable partner whose place in the hemisphere is one it has by right and geography. No other potential bloc accords this status to Canada.[14]

While trade with Latin America remains at below 3 percent of total Canadian world commerce, it is growing rapidly and the region represents the only area of the world where the percentage of Canadian total exports represented by high technology products is rising.[15] This is of great importance for a country such as ours, which does not wish to return to the status of a mere resource supplier.

The security relationship has grown apace, to the surprise of all observers of Canadian-Latin American relations before 1989. Abandoning its former posture of refusing to sign the Rio Pact, to honour the security provisions of the Charter of the Organization of American States, or to have anything to do with inter-American security matters south of the Rio Grande as of that year, Ottawa has come to be one of the main movers in security matters in the hemisphere.[16]

Canadian Forces units and personnel have been sent on operations to all the five Central American states and to Haiti on several occasions over the last six years. Canada is active, indeed a leader, in the reform of the inter-American security system as well as in the new security activities of the OAS. Ottawa sends officers to all manner of inter-American security meetings, emphasizing arms control and disarmament, peaceful solution of disputes, peacekeeping, human rights and civil-military relations issues. Canada now also receives a limited number of Latin American officers for training. And while Canada has so far eschewed membership of the Inter-American Defence Board, formerly the key coordinating body of the inter-American security system, it has done so because of the reduced relevance of that board when compared to the dynamism of the OAS Security Committee of which Canada is a very active member.

Thus it is not too much to say that Canadian security policy in the Americas has been definitely transformed over the last few years. And here again there is a reflection of the clear shift in priorities going on in Ottawa in the defence field, a shift farther and farther away from Europe and closer and closer to less traditional regions.

All of this, however, pales in significance when compared with the extraordinary change in the nature and depth of the U.S.-Canadian relationship over the last decade. The Canada-U.S. Free Trade accords, the "open for business" policies of the Mulroney government, "open skies," (which gives joint access to air routes) the steady rise of the U.S. percentage of total Canadian trade to the 80 percent level: the list of breakthroughs in this connection is a long one. In effect, a century-old policy of standing as aloof as thought possible from North Americanism as a concept and a reality has been abandoned in favour of a decision to move dramatically closer to the southern giant. If Trudeau's three options were a continuation of the status quo, closer integration with the U.S., or a broadened relationship with Europe and other areas of the world, there is no doubt in what direction the Mulroney and Chrétien governments decided to move. While the latter was initially, or at least electorally, reluctant to take the path chosen, it too, after a few short weeks in power, saw no other choice.

Here in North America, wartime and Cold War cooperation had of course already been great between the two continental neighbours.[17] But instead of the end of the Cold War leading to less interconnection, the trend has been entirely in the opposite direction. The great battle over free trade was for many the last gasp of Canadian nationalism as it had been known for a century. Once that battle was over, and it had been accepted that Canada's future was inextricably bound to that of the U.S., the logic of ever greater linkages steadily grew more powerful. NAFTA, for Canada, was never a big issue as it was in Mexico because the key fight had already taken place.

In the security field the situation was more nuanced. As Joel Sokolsky has argued, the United States has not had less need of Canada for many decades.[18] With the end of the Soviet threat, the value of Canada's air and sea space, indeed even its land, declined for the United States. That country could now choose whether it wanted to have Canada as a close partner in defence terms, while Canada's freedom of choice was more circumscribed by power considerations and other elements of geopolitics and sheer *realpolitik.*

The withdrawal of Canada from Europe, despite its heightened peacekeeping role worldwide, could not but drive the Canadian Forces into a still stronger relationship with the U.S. In everything, from the acceptance of NORAD as an organization increasingly concerned with narcotics—despite Canadian perceptions of the drug problem as a non-security isssue—to the relative massive growth in the number of personnel sent to the U.S. for training and to the decline of the Commonwealth in Canadian defence arrangements, everywhere the United States became relatively more important to the Canadian military, presenting a real danger of transforming them into a continentalized force with few important non-U.S. connections.[19]

All of this must of course be seen in the context of the revolution in the power balance at the global level. The defeat of the Russian empire and its ensuing disintegration have left the United States in a position where, in political, strategic, and cultural terms, it is the undoubted leader of the world community. Current potential competitors for that position, Japan, Germany, and the European Union, have, for largely historic and domestic political reasons, eschewed any real consideration of challenging the United States for that leadership.

Canada's geography does not allow it to escape the full consequences of this massive shift in relative military power and
ideological clout. Even in the area of cultural affairs, the power of the
United States seems uncheckable. And no country is more exposed
to it than is Canada.[20]

One could go on at much greater length on these massive
changes to the international context of Canada in the 1990s. But it is
clear from the foregoing that the external situation faced by this
country has been transformed from what it was a few short years ago.
In the security field this has already occasioned major changes in
defence policy. It remains to be seen if these changes are the best for
this new international environment.

INTERNAL FACTORS

It is possible to argue, of course, that the internal context of Canada
is as much changed as is the external. Although they may constitute
the problem that only rarely speaks its name, it is understood by most
analysts that the deep divisions experienced by this country in recent
years have security dimensions. Even if most specialists agree that
Canadian traditions augur well for a peaceful transition to a new era
if Quebec should leave Canada, few would continue to suggest that
there is no danger at all of violence at some level.

In a confederation such as Canada that of course does not mean
open conflict between an independent Quebec and the rest of the
country. It would be more likely to mean heavy strains on those peaceful traditions imposed by disorders in a Quebec which, as Claude Ryan
has said, is as divided within itself as Canada has been as a whole.

The Oka affair and other incidents of recent years, increasingly
severe social tensions caused by structural adjustment to the new
world economy, and desperate attempts by governments at all levels
to reduce deficits through cuts in public expenditure, all make it difficult not to be somewhat troubled about the prospects for continued
social peace at the levels known for the last several decades. National
unity difficulties aggravate those tensions and, in so doing, may subject this country's security system to strains never experienced before.

Non-traditional threats also continue to grow. While drug con-
sumption in the country is variously reported as either dropping
slightly or at least not growing at the pace of recent decades, the trade
in the drugs is as violent as ever and its international dimensions are

expanding. The growth of international crime, and its penetration into Canada, is also a problem of vast consequences according to the Royal Canadian Mounted Police and provincial and municipal forces across the country. There is nothing to suggest such problems will not have a security element of considerable consequence.

The Canadian Forces are not *above* any of these issues. They are deeply affected by the continuing debate on national unity, they who have the responsibility of serving the whole country in times of danger. Under current circumstances, the loss of faith in national direction affects them as much as anyone. At the same time, their morale has been heavily hit by events across a wide spectrum of national life. The most direct effects have obviously appeared in the form of their own internal scandals, causing a loss of public confidence.[21]

The decline in morale has been compounded by the shattering effect of continued and massive cuts in the defence budget which must have an effect on morale, as they express a lack of public belief in the value of what the services do. The closure of many military bases, educational institutions, and other installations has also meant—since the reserve force is only a shadow of its former presence across the land—the disappearance of the Forces from huge areas of the country where before they were part of the local scene and generally much appreciated.

Another aspect of this situation is reflected in the kinds of personnel and unit cuts within the armed services themselves. Particularly hard hit have been military education and bands. The three military colleges, in Quebec, Ontario, and British Columbia, gave an exceptional exposure of the military to the university scene across the country and ensured the production of a large number of Anglophone as well as Francophone bilingual officers. They provided the military with unique assets such as an automatic entrée into the sometimes hostile environment of university education in this country. This, in turn, helped to create a critical mass of people specializing in security issues nationally, a group who ensured an informed discussion of defence matters something which had not always taken place in the past.

While the Royal Military College in Kingston can take up some of the slack in this area, it is really asking too much of the institution to do it all. The disbandment of the National Defence College was also a blow to military education and to the *ouverture* of the military to the civilian community. With its demise, not only are Canadian senior officers having to go abroad more often for advanced education but they are also very rarely exposed to the various mixes of thinking civilian-military, national-foreign, defence ministry-foreign ministry, and federal-provincial—which the College provided. The loss of these and other military education centres left in doubt the seriousness of the Armed Forces' future attitude to education.

Although bands offer an opportunity for poking fun at the military, the fact is that their presence has been seen by the public as a good the armed services have for long provided. Their availability for public events across the country was well appreciated by organizers and public alike and there has been ample evidence that they heightened the esteem in which the forces were held. And while this is serious enough for the regular force, it has been grave indeed for the reserve units, which have seen such musical assets savaged in recent cuts.[22]

Thus we have national forces less and less visible across the country and particularly with respect to areas of key interest such as education and exposure at major events. This has no doubt fostered the doubts about their role in the post-Cold War era.

The decline in support for peacekeeping now combines with these internal factors. More and more in parliamentary committees and debates, in the national press, and in the public at large, the question is asked whether Canada should be spending its money and risking its soldiers' lives in trying to help those who so often do not seem to wish for help. In an era in which peacekeeping is often seen as the main current reason for having forces, this matters.[23]

It is especially of concern when one considers that, historically, Canadians have rarely shown a sense of need for preparation for war or crisis before it was upon them. And while this behaviour is something of a tradition in this country, at the moment defence preparedness is in a shambles, as repeated conferences on the subject have shown. And defence industries, especially at a time of massive budget cuts and the relaxing of "buy Canadian" policies, are at a crossroads, not to say a potentially final moment of crisis. This must be set against a defence context where there is no longer a Royal Navy behind whose hulls Canada could find the time to arm and prepare for conflict.[24]

This of course is not merely a question of preparation for foreign involvement. In the light of all the domestic concerns mentioned above Canada must be ready for emergencies at home if only to ensure its ability to hold the ring in the event of disorder accompanying unforeseen developments. Armed forces are, after all, in the final analysis about worst case planning, however much that kind of thinking has been pooh-poohed of late. And if they are not going to do that sort of preparation, then it can well be asked why we have them at all.

THE ABSOLUTE REQUIREMENT TO DECIDE ON PRIORITIES

It is surely fair to say that the world and country we know are no longer what they were in the Cold War and that the forces which we maintain in the new era must now be configured in response to this new context. It must, however, also be said that much of the previous world has remained. Countries do still opt to use violence or the threat of violence to force others to fulfil their will. Nations still keep national interests as the guiding light of their foreign policies. We have not reached the "millennium" in that sense. The world is still not a very pretty place when it comes to the ways states interact.

At the moment there is a highly laudable attempt to do as much as possible in all areas which the government and DND have determined to be worthwhile. This means multipurpose forces which, however problematical on a number of scores, are the only solution practicable in an era of uncertainty and reduced budgets. Canada must be able to contribute to multinational forces a level of military commitment commensurate with our objectives as a state. That means *reduced* but balanced forces.

The kind of argument being made here has, after all, been made before. We have too many commitments and we must cut some of them in order to save vital elements of CF capabilities. But muddling through is the Canadian tradition where defence, as so much else, is concerned. Why cannot this continue? It is the contention of this paper that muddling through with all the current roles means we are losing out not only in key areas but are unable to respond to changes being forced upon us because of our being wed to former taskings.

At the time of writing, Canada's land forces are still active in southern Europe although under UN auspices. The Navy has supported in the recent past this activity in operations like the Adriatic patrol (backing up the arms embargo on the Balkans) and still continues to function as part of most NATO maritime arrangements. The Air Force has deployed for a variety of missions in the Southeast of the continent. Minor efforts are also still being maintained through headquarters, surveillance and other arrangements under the NATO umbrella.

As mentioned above, the Canadian Forces, and particularly the Air Force, remain closely tied to their U.S. counterparts in cooperation in defence of North America. This represents the single main commitment of the Air Force today.

Outside these traditional areas, as has also been mentioned, Canada is more active than ever in the Asia-Pacific and Latin American regions. Finally, as is well known, even outside of Europe Canada is still heavily engaged in the peacekeeping area and is counted upon to support a number of probable future missions as well.

On the equipment side, all this means that the Navy, fresh from its long-awaited shot in the arm represented by the new ship deliveries, is doing its best to sustain a serious anti-submarine capability, in support of which it retains an aging submarine squadron of three *Oberon* class boats. In the important area of mine warfare capabilities have recently been improved. In addition, as part of its three-ocean responsibilities, the Navy is also active in sovereignty-related taskings, cooperates actively in search and rescue missions, supports the RCMP in drug interdiction operations, and "shows the flag" internationally.

The Air Force, once the darling of the services in one of the few countries where it was larger and richer than the other branches, is now operating interceptor, reconnaissance, ground support, transport, and training aircraft in support of most of the above-mentioned activities, and it is doing so with aging aircraft. The magnificent *Hercules* air transports are very old indeed, as are most of our helicopters. Even the proud F-18 fighter is no longer a recent acquisition.

For the Army, the picture is no better. The M-113 armoured personnel carrier began to come into service over three decades ago. Despite new purchases, most light armour and wheeled and lightly armoured transport vehicles are out of date, undergunned and inadequately armoured for possible tasks ahead.

It is not, however, merely age which is the problem with the equipment now in service. That would be manageable by means of budgets. The difficulty with all of these issues is that of deciding future direction. What roles should be assigned to these forces? If this question can be answered, it is possible to move on with relative certainty to planning what weapons and equipment should be provided in order to retain effective forces for future national security purposes.

It is inconceivable that the country should go through any but the most obvious purchases of machines and weapons without clearly deciding on what it is actually going to do with them. The parliamentary report and indeed the White Paper sketched the need for choices. But few have really been forthcoming. We still wish to do something of everything. How does the argument go?

As we have said Canadian defence planning is based, as is most such planning, on worst case forecasts. In an era of absolutely extraordinary uncertainty about the future, the view is that our forces must, logically, be flexible and available to be tasked in highly differing circumstances. This is not a flight of fancy but represents sound thinking. Indeed, other middle powers like Australia, Argentina, and Spain are reaching similar decisions about the future of their armed services. Since one does not know what to expect, then only preparing for the unexpected makes any sense. And in such conditions only forces which have the widest possible utility can hope to answer future calls. In no way is this a specious argument but one which is the result of vast military experience worldwide.

It is, however, important to note that the implications of such a decision, when reached in the current Canadian context, may be far-reaching and may dovetail poorly with government priorities elsewhere. It can already be seen that cuts so far made have struck not only at some of the most necessary long-term capabilities of the forces but also at some of their most vital underpinnings.

Peacetime forces serving in unique circumstances such as those described above must first of all have the best network of intelligence possible in order to have their ears to the ground when and where it is most important. In a world where alliance connections become day by day less concrete and where traditional sources of intelligence sharing are not without their problems, this requirement has never been greater. This is all the more true in the light of the especially demanding circumstances in which Canadian foreign policy decisions must now be made.

In these circumstances cuts in our military attaché services abroad are particularly painful. And the inability to find funds to reassign intelligence priorities away from long-term cold war tasks to newer ones in Asia-Pacific, Latin America and the Caribbean, and the Middle East is also unpleasant and damaging in both the short and the long term. There are not nearly enough resources for expanded language training in the Forces. For example, at this key moment, when our connections with the world are broadening mightily and our need for officers skilled in languages other than our own and those of communist or formerly communist nations, there is little reflection of these new requirements within the military training system. And there is little doubt that the reason for this is largely one of funds.

The increasingly obvious weight of the United States in Canadian defence procurement, officer and even senior NCO training, out-of-country service attachments, training and doctrine and the like tends to "continentalize" our armed forces. And with retrenchment our forces are obliged to focus their efforts on cooperation with the United States in continental taskings rather than activities farther afield.

There is of course nothing inherently wrong with a high level of military cooperation with this powerful and generally benign super-power. It can be argued that the connection gives us access to intelligence, technology, new ideas and many other advantages.[25] But it is difficult to deny that what might be called the "cultural" element of national defence can easily be disturbed by too close an embrace of the colossus. This element, transmitted by floods of U.S. films, official publications and training aids, may be hard to define, but it has an impact on young officers and other ranks, not to mention the vital senior NCO cadre, that presents a major problem for the defence of Canada.

An example of note is worth consideration. As has been seen in interviews with a number of officers and observers, the Airborne Regiment was perhaps the first unit in the history of the Canadian Armed Forces to visibly adopt a U.S. model for its own institutional development. The unit, despite excellence in many fields, was soon a well-known destination for personnel who had difficulty fitting into their own regiments because of what might be called excess zeal, or a certain tendency towards "Ramboism." This phenomenon was not in any way generalized but it was there. The cultural dimension it represented was to have the most deleterious impact on the Regiment and on the Forces as a whole. Financial considerations, which were essentially the root of the trouble, must not be allowed to make Canadian training and basic terms of reference too U.S.-oriented. At the same time we must be careful to understand that this is not a U.S. problem. It is a Canadian problem if we accept models from outside which are not in keeping with our traditions and what the Canadian public are prepared to accept.

The Commonwealth and La Francophonie still offer help for us here, especially the former. Canadians serve well and happily with units from most of our traditional partners in the Commonwealth. They are part of our history and our view of ourselves and nowhere is this more obvious or legitimate than in the armed services. Unfortunately it does cost more to exchange officers, send people for training, coordinate military doctrine, and so forth with these smaller and more distant forces than it does to make arrangements with the Americans just to our south.

When money was more abundant it was possible to do more with the Commonwealth (and with the French and Belgians) and thus reduce the relative weight of U.S. influence. But it can already be seen that this practice is giving way under financial pressures. By the calculations, admittedly very vague, of this author, some twenty years ago almost half as many Canadians were on attachments or courses with other foreign and Commonwealth armed forces as were with those of the U.S. At the moment, the figure is closer to eight-to-one "in favour" of the United States. Again, in many senses this is not a problem. But in terms of keeping an armed force which is distinctly Canadian—surely essential if we are serious about sovereignty roles—it is a matter of high importance which should not be disregarded simply because there is not enough money to do everything we would like to do.

Another area for concern is the reserves. More will be said about them later on, but it is important to note that they are at the present time being starved of funds and made the laughing stock of the Forces. This is short-sighted and wrong. If they have been allowed to atrophy, the major fault must be looked for elsewhere than in their own ranks. They did not organize themselves. A country with as small a regular force as ours, and as uncertain a future, cannot expect to do well without a strong reserve element.

It would seem from what has gone before that it is precisely the effort to maintain multipurpose forces that is forcing DND to consider difficult decisions. What is required is another hard look at the way to ensure the most support for our policy goals in circumstances where much less money is available.

Unfortunately, some activities will have to be further curtailed or reorganized. No one in the defence field can find the idea of reorganizing a pleasant one. Three decades of reorganizations have left the Forces confused and shaken. But the harsh reality is that these are tough times for all and DND's effective capabilities will be reduced to virtually nil if tasks and resources are not brought into line. The

Forces have been hearing this for decades but the bite represented by recent cuts is creating a new and evident sense of urgency within the halls of National Defence Headquarters. DND has correctly decided that teeth elements must be retained at all costs. But which ones are essential and which are only, to use the army expression, "nice to have"?

It is impossible to reach a conclusion which allows all areas of current expertise to remain. It is necessary, in the absence of a credible Russian threat against North American air space, to reduce the priority given to air defence. This will probably mean, in the long run, accepting fewer and less sophisticated interceptor forces. On the other hand, air transport and other logistic capabilities have never been in greater demand and this requirement is unlikely to change very much in the near future. It is also true that some fighter ground attack capability must be maintained if we are to be credible within NATO and the United Nations.

The Navy will need to keep a steady eye on its anti-submarine role but may be able to consider ending its own submarine effort. The value of our submarine force is not in question here. It has served well and represents a training, sovereignty, defence and strike capability of some importance. On the other hand, it is difficult to imagine a moment when our own few boats could make much of a difference, given the vast capabilities of the Atlantic Alliance in this area. Such a decision should not be taken lightly. The loss of this operational strength would only be justified if costs were truly prohibitive but this may actually be the case today.

It is hard to imagine where else the Navy can give up capabilities without the surrender having very serious implications. A surface fleet with the current number of ships could not be cut further without emasculating almost totally our ability to operate in the areas of greatest priority to us. The flexibility we obtain by having a surface fleet is enormous. In the near future, however, it will surely be necessary to shift even more to the use of multipurpose ships. The days of specialized antisubmarine forces of great cost and sophistication may well be gone for good.

The Army, for long virtually alone in the peacekeeping business, now jostles daily with its naval and air force counterparts in such operations. Nonetheless the bulk of the work still falls on its shoulders. It is also true that most internal security and related operations depend mostly on Army resources. It will almost certainly be necessary for the Royal Canadian Armoured Corps to abandon its longstanding tradition of maintaining sophisticated and heavily armoured tanks as the touchstone of its arsenal. If heavy armour is to be abandoned surely the tank which is its physical expressions goes too. This will be a painful choice in a century when the tank has tended to be king and it too must only be contemplated if other options mean losing even wider-ranging capabilities.

It is the infantryman who remains the source of maximum flexibility for the Army. And infantrymen are proving a costly resource indeed. Manpower costs are ferocious and may force truly revolutionary analyses of what must now be done with the reserve force. Whatever the findings of the recent study on the reserve force, it remains true that the reservist represents the cheapest source of reasonably prepared manpower in case of national emergency. But it must be underscored that a reserve is just that: a "reserve." "Total force" and other ideas which try to make it something it is not—almost immediately deployable and essentially a part of the *forces in being*—fail to convey what reserves are all about. They constitute the base of expansion when things go really badly. That does not mean one cannot have categories of reserves which are available more rapidly but hopefully not, as is currently the case, at the expense of the mobilization base's ability to respond.

CONCLUSIONS

This is truly an *era* of austerity and its end does not appear to be near. Foreign and defence policy decision makers are well aware of this and are struggling to find the best design for policies fitted to the new circumstances. None of this is easy. Armed forces are always conservative organizations and policies which appear for a long time to suit a country well are not jettisoned when the first bright new idea comes along. It behooves our authorities to consider carefully decisions on which the lives of many Canadians may depend and which may involve vital national interests.

Canada has, in James Eayrs' words, "grown up allied."[26] We have never been alone or, if we have, we did not realize it. The French Empire, the British Empire and Commonwealth, the United Nations in its first years, and then NATO, ensured that "multilateralism" in some form or another became an abiding constant of our policy. We are still anxious to make the United Nations work and never more so than in this new era in which we are uncertain about the comfort we will find in what is offered as a "new world order." We wish to answer peacefully the challenges of our own national future. We wish to contribute to international peace. But we clearly wish to do all these things within financial constraints which we can hardly alleviate.

Under such circumstances, we may be obliged to have Forces which are *maigres*, but we must see to it that they are *thin* because they are fit and not because they are atrophied. That is the challenge of defence policy today. Only hard decisions will ensure that we have forces which respond to a new situation, with new partners and challenges, perhaps not the ones we would have preferred but the real ones we have to deal with today. We cannot be all things to all people. We cannot feast any longer in any pasture. We can, it is to be hoped, choose policies which will allow us to remain grazing in those fields which have the most to offer us, even though it will be certainly painful to reduce our interest in others which have for so long been so lush.

NOTES

1   See the interesting discussion of some of these issues in James Finan and S.B. Flemming, "Public Attitudes toward Defence and Security in Canada," in David Dewitt and David Leyton-Brown eds., *Canada's International Security Policy* (Toronto: Prentice-Hall, 1995), 291-311.

2   Report of the Special Joint Committee of the Senate and House of Commons Reviewing Canadian Foreign Policy, *Canada's Foreign Policy: Principles and Priorities for the Future* (Ottawa: Publications Service, Parliamentary Publications Directorate, 1994), 11. Hereafter cited as Special Joint Committee, *Foreign Policy.*

3   Report of the Special Joint Committee of the Senate and House of Commons in Canada's Defence Policy, *Security in a Changing World* (Ottawa: Publications Service, Parliamentary Publications Directorate, 1994), 20. Hereafter cited as Special Joint Committee, Security.

4   Special Joint Committee, *Security*, 2.

5   Canada, the Department of National Defence, *1994 Defence White Paper* (Ottawa: Minister of Supply and Services December 1994), 9.

6   John Tredennick, "The Defence Budget," in Dewitt and Leyton-Brown, *Canada's International Security Policy* 413-54, especially 413-14.

7   For a U.S. diplomat's view of this aspect, see "Enhancing Stability: Peacemaking and Peacekeeping," in James R. Graham, ed., *Non-Combat Roles for the U.S. Military in the Post-Cold War Era* (Washington, D.C.: National Defense University, 1993), 29-63.

8   Charles Trueheart, "Canada Reassesses Peacekeeping Role," *Washington Post*, 27 April, 1993, A10.

9   John Holmes, "Canadian Security: a Historical Perspective," in Claude Bergeron et al, eds., *Les Choix géopolitiques du Canada: l'enjeu de la neutralité* (Montréal: Méridien, 1988), 107-18, especially 117.

10 This point is discussed in greater detail in H.P. Klepak, "Education and Training for Peacekeeping Forces," in Ernest Gilman and Detlef Herold, eds., *Peacekeeping Challenges to Euro-Atlantic Security* (Rome: NATO Defence College, 1994), 111-25, especially 113-14.

11 Some of these matters are discussed in H.P. Klepak, "Les Forces armées et l'armement au Canada," in Stanley Kirschbaum, ed., *La Sécurité collective au XXIe Siècle* (Québec: Presses de l'Université Laval, 1994), 197-214.

12 See the highly stimulating work by J.L. Granatstein, *How Britain's Weakness Forced Canada into the Arms of the United States* (Toronto: University of Toronto Press, 1989).

13 Indeed, foreign and defence policy statements have for successive years given steadily less play to Europe and steadily more to Asia-Pacific. A comparison of the 1971, 1987, and 1994 Defence White Papers is illustrative of this trend.

14 This point is repeatedly brought forward in James Rochlin, *Discovering the Americas: the Evolution of Canadian Foreign Policy Towards Latin America* (Vancouver: University of British Columbia Press, 1994). See also H.P. Klepak, *What's in it for Us?* Ottawa, Canadian Foundation for the Americas (FOCAL) Paper, 1995.

15 Jean Daudelin and Edgar Dosman, "The New Era in Canadian-Latin American Relations," in J. Daudelin and E. Dosman, eds., *Beyond Mexico* (Ottawa: Carleton University Press, 1995), 1-11, especially 6.

16 H.P. Klepak, "Canada and Security Issues in Latin America," in Daudelin and Dosman, eds., *Beyond Mexico*, 209-236.

17 For the exceptional extent of that cooperation, seen in historical perspective, see J.L. Granatstein, *Ties that Bind: Canadian-American Relations in Wartime from the Great War to the Cold War* (Toronto: Hakkert, 1977).

18 Joel Sokolsky, "The Bilateral Defence Relationship with the United States," in Dewitt and Leyton-Brown, *Canda's International Security Policy*, 171-98, especially 187-93.

19 For longer discussions of both these issues, see this author's "The Impact of the International Narcotics Trade on Canada's Foreign and Security Policy," *International Journal* XLIX, (Winter 1993-4), 66-92; and "Canada's Pull-Out May Mean More than Losing a Brigade," *Jane's Defence Weekly*, 11 April 1992, 614.

20 See the real contribution to this discussion made by David V.J. Bell, "Global Communications, Culture and Values: Implications for Global Security," in Dewitt and Leyton-Brown, *Canada's International Security Policy*, 159-84. And for a fascinating view of the situation as seen by a Third World author see Luis Maira, "América Latina en el sistema internacional de los años noventa," in Francisco Leal Buitrago and Juan Gabriel Tokatlian, eds., *Orden mundial y seguridad: nuevos*

desafíos para Colombia y América Latina (Bogotá: Tercer Mundo, 1994), 25-47, especially 30-32.

21   See Pierre Martin and Michel Fortmann, "Canadian Public Opinion and Peacekeeping in a Turbulent World," *International Journal L*, no. 2, (spring 1995), 370-400 for much useful data on this and other trends, as well as the bibliography included with it.

22   See the series of papers by Anthony Kellett on this and related subjects, published by the Operational Research and Analysis Establishment of the Department of National Defence in the early 1980s.

23   See the last section of Martin and Fortmann, "Canadian Public Opinion."

24   The literature is rich in discussions of this tradition. See the opening chapters of J.L. Granatstein, *The Generals: the Canadian Army's Senior Commanders in the Second World War* (Toronto: Stoddart, 1993), 3-52; the background sections of John English, *The Canadian Army and the Normandy Campaign: the Failure of High Command* (New York: Praeger, 1991); and Dan Middlemiss, "Canada and Defence Industrial Preparedness," in Ronald Graham Haycock and Barry D. Hunt, *Canada's Defence: Perspectives on Policy in the Twentieth Century* (Toronto: Copp, Clark, Pitman, 1993), 242-257.

25   See the interesting discussions of this throughout Joseph Jockel and Joel Sokolsky, *Canada and Collective Security: Odd Man Out*, Washington Papers, no. 121, (New York: Praeger, 1986).

26   James Eayrs, *In Defence of Canada: Growing Up Allied* (Toronto: University of Toronto Press, 1980).

New Challenges
in an Era of Globalization

IV

Canada and the Halifax Summit

The Halifax Summit held last June was the third G-7 Economic Summit hosted by Canada and the twenty-first in a series of leaders' meetings that began on a small scale at Rambouillet, France in 1975. The Halifax Summit may well represent a turning point in the history of these large international events. In substantive terms and in a manner virtually unprecedented in Summit history, leaders in Halifax laid out an ambitious and comprehensive agenda to reform the architecture of the international financial institutions (IFIs). Although the agenda for reform focused on the World Bank (WB) and the International Monetary Fund (IMF), on the last day of the Summit leaders expressed a determination to include the United Nations and its many related agencies in this effort.[1]

To evaluate the results of the Halifax Summit, the event and its substantive preparations must be perceived within the context of the evolution of the G-7 as a consultative group, the emphasis leaders place on any one individual issue, their dynamic as a group as well as the global economic and political events of the day. Contrary to the belief of some, the G-7 does not seek to dictate mandates to international organizations, regional banks or national governments. Its main purpose, as has become clear through the history of this loosely defined and flexible institution, is to identify issues that require the attention of the world and to suggest collective action for their solution. Rather than try to seek solutions independently of other groups, the G-7 nations attempt to provide an impetus to the activities of organizations of which they are often themselves members. Summit follow-up activities for the review of international institutions demonstrate the necessity of the G-7 acting in concert with other countries to achieve progress with the resolution of issues raised.

FROM NAPLES TO HALIFAX

Canada assumed the G-7 chair in January of 1995; Italy had hosted the 1994 Summit in Naples. There are several different tracks of activities required to prepare a Summit, all of which coalesce shortly before the Summit to ensure the effective hosting of a substantively successful meeting. These different activities are carried out in both political and bureaucratic spheres.

In many respects, Naples proved to be innovative in providing greater time for leaders together with an unprescribed agenda. In particular, the tone of the Naples meeting was set at a leaders-only dinner on the first evening that featured two developments: a lengthy discussion on global economic and financial institutions, and agreement among leaders to have more informal exchanges of this kind. Prime Minister Chrétien accepted this challenge and promised at Naples that Halifax would be different. He also indicated that he attached considerable importance to having a thorough discussion on international financial and economic institutions at the Canadian Summit. He remained very active on this file over the following year, exploring options with other leaders and international experts and providing clear guidance to me as to how he wished to see the agenda for Halifax develop.

At the working officials' level, there is an internal Summit machinery which operates throughout the year, involving sherpas—the leaders' personal representatives—sous-sherpas and political directors from the G-7 nations. On the financial side, the Finance sous-sherpas or Finance Deputies meet almost every month, and often on the margins of IMF and OECD meetings to coordinate macroeconomic issues. This group and the quarterly meeting of Finance Ministers that they support represent the most institutionalized aspect of G-7 consultation, a direct outcome of the 1986 Tokyo Summit. The leaders' personal representatives or sherpas (a borrowed Nepalese word meaning "mountain guide") have overall responsibility for the Summit agenda and hold several meetings throughout the year, prior to the Summit, to discuss relevant issues and to build a G-7 consensus in advance of the event. They keep their leaders apprised of developments, take instructions from them to impart to their colleagues and maintain a steady flow of communication amongst themselves. This flow became very significant as the substantive elements for the Halifax agenda grew. The sherpas address both the traditional G-7 agenda, such as macroeconomic issues, growth and employment, and also other issues which have in recent years been included on the agenda, such as sustainable development, international debt, nuclear safety, terrorism and international crime. The detail is provided by teams led by a finance and a foreign affairs soussherpa from each G-7 country (and the EU). Senior foreign affairs officials known as Political Directors round out the teams, and on their network prepare foreign policy issues that are more political/security in nature (Bosnia, for example) for eventual discussion by foreign ministers and leaders at the Summit.

At Naples, the G-7 agreed that Russia would participate fully in this latter group, and the term "Political 8" or "P-8" was coined. It was also agreed in the preparations for Halifax that Russia would participate on a partial basis in the G-7 preparatory meetings with respect to issues that touch it directly: nuclear safety, money-laundering and crime. Other classic G-7 issues, involving monetary and fiscal policies, approaches to the international financial institutions and trade issues, while of undoubted interest to Russia, remained out of reach, a consensual decision based on Russia's transitional economy. The Halifax Summit accomplished much in the way of setting out a mechanism for meaningful Russian involvement at these top-level meetings.

The leaders had given a clear signal at Naples that they wished to have a more focused and substantive agenda for the next Summit and that this wish should be mirrored in a more streamlined preparatory process. My role as host sherpa and Chair of the preparatory process was, therefore, clear: while working towards an agenda that would meet leaders' requirements, I could not let the process of consultation overwhelm the preparations. Finally, the Halifax results should present a calibrated follow-up agenda, so that momentum, particularly on the international institutional reform agenda, could be sustained in the post-Summit period. If this could be accomplished, the Halifax Communiqué would be seen as a blueprint for action in the interval before the next Summit and as the best possible working tool which the next country assuming the chair—France—could use to ensure that the preparations for the Lyon Summit would proceed smoothly. This in fact proved to be the case.

With regard to the preparation of Canadian objectives and agenda items, the first step was a thorough and sharp analysis of the Naples Communiqué and the items which were specifically noted as requiring follow-up discussion in Halifax. To ensure that all these issues were addressed, we as Chair had to follow up with our G-7 colleagues and seek their views on where we were headed, what work was required, and what our subsequent objectives would be for the Halifax Summit. We, of course, presented an unabashedly Canadian view as to how all this could be accomplished. Several issues had been identified in the Naples Communiqué as requiring attention in Halifax, including nuclear safety (Chernobyl closure), international debt, trade and environment issues.

Seeking other country views on the emerging agenda for Halifax involved travel by the Prime Minister to Asia, Latin America, the Caribbean and Europe; by Foreign Minister Ouellet, including his hosting of a meeting of the Association of Southeast Asian Nations (ASEAN) Foreign Ministers and key work by Finance Minister Martin at multilateral economic and financial meetings. All of these efforts featured discussion on matters of substance. While we could not say that Canada was acting in the interests of many smaller states at the Halifax table, it is most certain that the full discussions that took place prior to the Summit represented an unusually wide and substantive consultation that shaped our views as chair and cemented our relations with many countries—particularly when we reported back after the Summit. It should also be noted that the Summit is but one node—albeit an important one—in a comprehensive network of international meetings and events in which Canada is a strong participant. Consultation across international bodies, therefore, assumes key importance. In my capacity as sherpa, I also undertook to visit all G-7 capitals and the United Nations before Canada assumed the chair. This underscored our transparent consultation strategy on the one hand, and on the other established clear lines of communication with my sherpa colleagues, often informal, but essential as we embarked on the preparatory process.

SETTING THE HALIFAX AGENDA

Speculation on the part of pundits and others as to what actually transpires at an in-camera international meeting often revolves around one or two issues that could "derail" the Summit. The Halifax Summit was not exempt from such speculation. It is, of course, up to the Chair to ensure that the Summit agenda, while remaining flexible in response to quickly changing circumstances, is maintained intact and that bilateral disputes do not affect the overall thrust and results of the Summit. Prior to Halifax there was much speculation that the Japan-U.S. auto dispute would influence both the Summit agenda and the atmosphere among leaders. The Canada-European Union (EU) fish dispute was fortunately successfully resolved before the Summit, and was not a factor in it. As the Summit began, there was also a concern that developments in Bosnia could become the dominant issue; this did not happen because as leaders had a full discussion on former Yugoslavia the first evening, released a statement and then focused on the other elements of the Summit agenda. In the end, the agenda was maintained by the dynamic amongst the leaders, the deft chairmanship of our Prime Minister in running the meeting, and its very nature as the product of a more streamlined and focused preparatory process.

The emphasis of the preparatory process was on the institutional review proposed in the Naples Summit Communiqué. The question of how comprehensive this review should be soon became the main focus of both internal Canadian policy deliberation and, subsequently, sherpa discussion at the preparatory meetings. Should the review be narrow and cover only the IMF and the World Bank? Should it be broadened to include not only these institutions but also the economic and social machinery of the UN? Or should it be all-inclusive?

Prime Minister Chrétien had addressed the theme in some detail at Naples and, as a former Finance Minister, was very familiar with the international financial institution issues. His support of the proposed review was based on several factors: a realization that there had been profound changes in the way the global economy functioned, and that with the emergence of new and huge capital markets there were vulnerabilities that did not exist before. In the immediate period after Naples, there were varying degrees of interest in reviewing financial institutional adequacy. However, the Prime Minister remained committed to the institutional review despite the sometimes more sceptical views of other nations. The Mexican peso crisis early in the year served to illustrate several weak points in the international economic and financial system and as a result, the G-7 as a whole became more supportive of the institutional review. Following reflection attention concentrated on strengthening the IMF and the World Bank in the face of emergencies such as the Mexican peso crisis, by means of an "early warning" mechanism and a response capability. While there was a lively interest on the part of several leaders in currency speculation issues, fuelled by the Mexican crisis, the Barings Bank fiasco and the suggestions from numerous non-governmental groups for a comprehensive review of the Bretton Woods institutions, it became clear that the only way to deal with this issue was to address the fundamental problems in each of the economies. Some leaders were open to discussing novel ways of dealing with currency market volatility; however, solutions that were both realistic and operational were not evident.

The agenda for review of the IFIs was all-encompassing: the Prime Minister had devoted much of his time to preparing for a higher, more informed discussion at Halifax on this issue, through meetings with the heads of the IMF and the World Bank and by hosting a meeting of international experts in March. There was never any question that the Halifax Summit would result in a new Louvre or Plaza accord or attempts at formal economic coordination of the variety that had emerged from past Summits. Rather, Halifax was meant to kick-start a process for review following a good discussion amongst leaders. This it did and Canada can claim much credit. The Summit Communiqué urges progress in four key areas: strengthening of the IMF's surveillance activities and early warning capacity; ensuring that it has sufficient financial resources to respond effectively in crisis situations, including an expansion of its General Arrangements to Borrow (GAB); encouraging the World Bank and other multilateral development banks to direct a greater share of their resources to poor countries committed to poverty reduction; and achieving greater cost efficiency and less waste—in short, subjecting the IFIs to the same pressures that are currently faced by most shareholder governments.

There were two prongs to the institutional review proposal: the first and foremost involving the international financial institutions (IMF and World Bank) and the second the UN and its related agencies. The second track of the discussion proved much more unwieldy. In trying to balance the desire for reform while avoiding being seen as a "directoire," sherpas agreed on the objectives and the basic outlines of the sort of proposals for UN reform that should be made in Halifax. This discussion focused primarily on the sustainable development and poverty reduction mandates of UN agencies and the multilateral development banks. At the Summit itself, leaders dealt with the degree of detail and the specificity of the Communiqué. The Communiqué, in fact, sets out an action plan. During the preparatory discussions, Canada, with the support of a few other G-7 members, had advocated an ambitious approach to UN reform, with an extensive post-Halifax follow-up process which would seek to create consensus on reform proposals in wider constituencies and build on the 50th anniversary of the UN in the autumn.

Other issues discussed at Halifax included growth and employment, the former a *de rigeur* subject for discussion in G-7 circles and the latter reflecting domestic policy currents in all G-7 countries, the Detroit Jobs Conference of March 1994 and the subsequent Organization for Economic Cooperation and Development (OECD) study that had guided leaders' discussions at Naples. Leaders agreed to hold another G-7 employment conference in France before the Lyon Summit. The Sustainable Development section of the Communiqué reflects key Canadian concerns on reducing poverty, safeguarding the environment and preventing or responding to crises through greater coordination of efforts by international bodies. Consensus on selling IMF gold reserves to alleviate the burden of developing country debt (a UK proposal that Canada supported) proved to be elusive, but was captured in encouragement to the IFIs to adopt measures to advance the objective. Leaders discussed environment issues in the context of Rio Earth Summit commitments and a clearer delineation of the responsibilities of the United Nations Environment Program and the Commission for Sustainable Development. Natural disasters and crises, such as those that enveloped Rwanda, Burundi and Somalia, led to a call by leaders for better coordination of responses and early warning through the responsible UN bodies and an improved transition from the emergency to the rehabilitation phase of a crisis. One Canadian initiative that was endorsed by leaders was the request to the multilateral institutions to consider trends in military and other unproductive spending when extending assistance to developing countries. Canada can also claim credit for the far-reaching language on international trade included in the Communiqué: the Canadian stamp is apparent in references to consolidating the new World Trade Organization (WTO) and creating the basis for an ambitious first WTO Ministerial meeting in Singapore in 1996, the role of regulatory reform in contributing to trade liberalization and the need to pursue work on trade and environment, competition policy and standards.

Another significant role for Canada at Halifax was our chairmanship of the Nuclear Safety Working Group which had been established at the Munich Summit of 1992. Improving safety at the Chernobyl facility was the primary task of the Group. Throughout 1995, Canada endeavoured to mobilize international support for the safe closure of Chernobyl and provide encouragement for devising a long-term non-nuclear energy strategy for Ukraine. Leaders complemented the work done on nuclear safety at Halifax by agreeing to President Yeltsin's invitation to attend a Nuclear Safety and Security Summit in Moscow in 1996.

In the end, this issue represented a substantive role for Russia at Halifax and due recognition that Russia was a global citizen on a new, cooperative course. The Chairman's Statement, issued on the last day of the Summit, underscores Russia's contribution to the P-8 and President Yeltsin's involvement in discussions on the UN, Asia, Africa and the Americas. The G-7 has been closely involved in coordinating multilateral efforts in support of Russia's historic transition. Russian participation at G-7 Summits has expanded. There was an add-on meeting at Munich in 1992 and Tokyo in 1993 (where a $42 billion assistance package for Russia was endorsed). The Russians participated in the final day at Naples in 1994. At Halifax, the Russian President participated in a working dinner, substantive morning discussions and a final working luncheon. His senior officials were involved in all preparatory meetings dealing with political issues and his Economy Minister participated in a portion of the sherpa meetings.

AFTER HALIFAX

Certainly the most important outcome of the Halifax Summit is the implementation of Halifax initiatives which became known as the "Halifax Agenda." Halifax stands apart from previous Summits, not only because of G-7 and P-8 agreement in new areas but also for well-organized follow-up procedures to which Prime Minister Chrétien is personally committed. He recognized that to enhance its credibility the G-7 needed more than statements of intent. It was essential to ensure that activities related to the Summit, and its achievements, would not end with the closing ceremonies. The onus was on Canada, as Chair, to ensure, in collatoration with its Summit partners, that the Halifax resolutions were implemented. Prime Minister Chrétien and Ministers were firmly committed to this; sherpas and sous-sherpas turned their attention to Halifax follow-up.

Consulting other countries is essential to engendering international support for the Halifax reforms. Institutional reform, particularly UN reform, requires the building of wider coalitions. Just as Canada made a point to consult widely before Halifax, it made a deliberate effort to inform the international community of the Halifax agreements. Prime Minister Chrétien discussed Halifax issues at other Summits (Commonwealth, Francophonie and Asia-Pacific Economic Cooperation (APEC)) and bilateral meetings. Finance Minister Martin sent letters to each of his counterparts in the 178 member countries of the IMF, and our high commissions and embassies were instructed to inform their host countries of the Halifax outcomes and seek their support. By autumn, virtually every country and key international organization had been debriefed on the Summit outcomes.

The second step was to coordinate and oversee the implementation of G-7/P-8 Summit initiatives. Canada presented the G-7 recommendations relating to the instability of financial markets, sustainable development, poverty reduction, the environment and improving institutional efficiency to the Bretton Woods institutions. The World Bank and the IMF have been actively pursuing reform on all fronts in keeping with the Halifax approach, devoting the bulk of the agenda of the WB/IMF annual meetings in Washington in October to these issues. Similar efforts are being undertaken by Canada in relation to members of the Regional Development Banks, the Development Committee Task Force on the Multilateral Development Banks and the G-10 (the coordinating group for the GAB).

Canada has also encouraged the OECD Development Assistance Committee to continue its work in the area of development. Its activities relating to capacity-building, institutional strengthening, private sector development programming and good governance, including the unproductive role of military expenditures, are especially in line with the Halifax message.

Promoting Halifax initiatives on UN reform has proven to be a very challenging task because of the complexity of these issues and the number of actors involved. The P-8 agreed to coordinate their efforts to build wider constituencies for UN renewal and promote Halifax initiatives in their domain.

The Summit on Nuclear Safety and Security, scheduled for next spring in Moscow, will focus on civilian reactor safety and radioactive waste management, security of nuclear materials—including illicit trafficking—the safe disposition of fissile material, and nuclear accounting and control. The Nuclear Safety Working Group plus Russia and the P-8 Non-Proliferation Working Group, led by their Canadian Chairs, have begun the initial preparations.

The Chairman's Statement addressed the growing problem of transnational organized crime by calling for a working group to look at improving P-8 cooperation in crime-fighting before the next Summit. During the summer, Canadian officials toured UN capitals for input to the agenda and process for the meeting of the ad hoc Senior Experts Group on organized crime. The group met in Ottawa in October and again in November to come up with concrete recommendations for strengthening P-8 cooperation and coordination.

A P-8 working group on terrorism also met this fall in Ottawa to prepare the groundwork for a ministerial level meeting on December 12, 1995. The Ottawa Ministerial on Terrorism resulted in an extremely detailed program of action on terrorism by the Economic Summit partners and Russia. The Ottawa Declaration is both a summary of what has been accomplished over the last 17 years as well as a road map for the years ahead. In the Declaration Ministers stated their determination "to continue to provide leadership to the international community, using bilateral and multilateral measures and agreements to counter terrorism."

*   *   *

We attempted to breathe new life into the Summit process. During the Canadian chairmanship, the Prime Minister himself set the tone:

business-like, informal and congenial. In revitalizing the Summit process, Halifax accomplished many things. It allowed for greater spontaneity in leaders' discussions and a more flexible role for Prime Minister Chrétien as Chair; it provided a constructive role for Russia while maintaining the traditional G-7 financial and economic focus of the discussions. A streamlined preparatory process with fewer and more modest meetings led to a business-like event that showcased Halifax/Dartmouth and produced a remarkable level of civic involvement. The far-reaching agenda and the emphasis on substantive follow-up may set the standard for future Summits. This Summit may have, to a significant degree, restored faith in a process that had become the subject of much public and media cynicism. With the passage of time, it may well represent a watershed in the history of these large international events.

NOTES

1   For additional discussion of the Halifax Summit, see also Chapter 14 by Roy Culpeper.

V

Is There Life After Deathstars? Communications Technology and Cultural Relations

KEITH ACHESON AND CHRISTOPHER J. MAULE

In 1993, the Canadian Broadcasting Corporation (CBC) formed a partnership with Power Broadcasting Inc. to supply American-owned DirecTv with satellite signals for delivery to viewers in the United States. Televised news and entertainment from Canada is now available on a continuing basis to American audiences. This outward thrust provides a contrast with the previous half century, in which Canada spent much effort in devising regulations and policies to offset the effects of American media overflow into Canada. A recent concern with regard to inward flows has been the alleged harmful effects on Canadian culture resulting from the new generation of satellite broadcasting services. The "deathstars" have a footprint covering all of North America, and thanks to digital compression can deliver as much or more programming than a state-of-the-art cable system.

The questions we pose concern the likely impact on Canadian cultural industries and policies of developments in communications technology, such as satellites. Do they represent a problem or an opportunity for Canada? Is the protection of our cultural industries from foreign competition either desirable or possible? Does our policy of exempting the cultural industries in trade agreements promote their long-term interests and those of Canadian culture?

Our answers suggest that export opportunities exist and are being recognized by private sector companies as well as the CBC, and that protection is neither desirable nor possible. In fact, we argue that some previous policies have retarded the development of Canada's cultural industries by encouraging them to be inward-looking, and have led Canada to argue for a cultural exemption in international trade agreements that is counter to the industries' best interests.

The trade disputes over culture that have arisen since the passage of the Canada-United States Free Trade Agreement (FTA) and the North American Free Trade Agreement (NAFTA) have not been subject to any formal dispute resolution mechanism, and have involved an informal political bargaining process between Canada and the United States. In contrast to the position taken in negotiating the FTA and the NAFTA, Canada might have fared better by grandfathering existing policies and foregoing an exemption.

Cultural trade issues comprise one set of irritants in Canada-U.S. relations as Jockel notes.[1] At the end of 1995 an issue which had roots in the 1960s came to the fore again with the passage by the Canadian government of a prohibitive excise tax on advertising in foreign-owned periodicals. While legislation had previously affected *Time*, it now targeted *Sports Illustrated*.[2]

In this chapter we address first the nature of cultural concerns, second, examples of emerging communications technology and associated commercial opportunities, and finally the preliminary lessons that can be drawn from recent cultural trade disputes between Canada and the United States. While these few examples do not provide definitive answers, they indicate the forces at work and the direction of change for firms and governments.

WHY THE CONCERN OVER CULTURE?

Canadian concerns have roots in the country's origins as an entity separate from the United States. Numerous royal commissions and official reports at the federal and provincial levels have examined the circumstances of the cultural industries—book, periodical and news-paper publishing, films, music, radio and television broadcasting and the live performing arts.[3] The analysis has usually pointed to the small size of the Canadian market relative to the United States and its fragmentation between French and English speakers. It has also emphasized capturing more of the smaller English- or French-Canadian markets rather than encouraging participation in the much larger English- or French-language international markets.

Those arguing the need for continuing protection point to the inability of Canadian producers to compete in the domestic market against product imported from south of the border, especially in light of the claim that it is dumped or sold unfairly in the Canadian mar-ket.[4] Criticisms are also levelled at distribution systems serving Canada, which are alleged to favour foreign over Canadian material. For example, it is claimed that there is no shelf space for Canadian publications on magazine stands, while Heritage Canada continues to talk about a film distribution policy that will encourage the exhibition of Canadian films in Canada.

Without attempting to dissect these arguments, which we have done elsewhere[5], it is sufficient here to point out that satellites, as one example of evolving technological change, merely increase the ease with which overflow can occur, further reducing the cost and time of delivery while increasing the capacity for transmission and the range of available choice. No wonder some refer to satellites as deathstars because of their ability to rain down signals on large areas of the world. However, satellites should also be seen for the benefits they offer. Consumers have greater choice, while producers with the capacity to access satellites can use them to distribute programs. Producers in a country such as Canada can become outward-looking and use satellites to service a larger market, thereby overcoming the perceived limitations of market size.[6]

A typical expression of Canadian concerns is the following royal commission statement about periodical publications. Magazines are:

the thread which binds together the fibres of our nation. They can protect a nation's values and encourage their practice. They can make democratic government possible and better government probable. They can soften sec-tional asperities and bring honourable compromises. They can inform and educate in the arts, the sciences and commerce. They can help market a nation's products and promote its material wealth. In these functions it may be claimed— claimed without much challenge—that the communications of a nation are as vital to its life as its defences, and should receive at least as much protection.[7]

Comparable statements can be found in numerous speeches and reports dealing with other cultural industries. They are often accompanied by illustrative statistics, showing, for example, that only 4 percent of films exhibited and 17 percent of books and publications sold are Canadian.[8] The social onus placed on periodical publishing by the royal commission is similar to the responsibility assigned to those administering the multiple objectives of the Broadcasting Act, an impossible task with frequently conflicting objectives, but one which is repeated in recently amended versions of the Act.[9]

Canada is not alone in expressing its unease over what some refer to as American cultural imperialism. In Asia, the governments of China, Singapore and Malaysia have attempted either to regulate or to ban the use of satellite dishes for fear that control will be lost over what the population can listen to and watch.[10] Islamic countries in the Middle East have similar concerns and in Europe, France has fought for the passage of policies in the European Union that will limit the broadcasting of foreign programs, whether by satellite or other means, and has lobbied for the exclusion of audiovisual services from trade liberalization measures in the latest General Agreement on Tariffs and Trade (GATT) negotiations.

Cultural concerns are not new and have been recognized, and perhaps sometimes even understood, by American policy makers. In connection with British concerns about the restricted distribution of American films, two U.S. State Department officials had the following exchange as early as 1928:

I honestly do think that the cultural argument is one which can honestly be advanced in good faith and which must be legitimately met. England, for example, I believe was stampeded into their film legislation almost entirely through their patriotic societies who believed that English customs and traditions were in danger.[11]

Almost seventy years later, a related sentiment was expressed by James Blanchard, U.S. Ambassador to Canada, in a CBC radio interview (January 26th, 1995) in which he told Peter Gzowski, "...I would not fault a single Canadian for wanting to protect and preserve, and frankly, promote and spread that culture."

The "imperialism" label refers not just to the imposition of political ideologies and cultural values but also to the economic benefits resulting from the spread of print and audiovisual material. This was recognized at an early date to be an important reason for the U.S. lobbying foreign governments to keep open markets for American films. An editorial in the State Department's Weekly Commerce Reports for January 22nd, 1923, entitled "Trade Follows the Film," notes the benefits to American business from the messages conveyed in movies. At other times, trade officials were critical of American films that portrayed the seamy side of American life.

What has become a hallmark of these discussions at home and abroad is the clash of the opposing views of those who support, respectively, the cultural and the industrial dimensions of these activities. Those favouring the former argue that the cultural industries are different, if not unique, because of the impact of the messages they carry. The latter contend that they are just like any other industry, at least when it comes to their treatment in international trade regimes. The proponents of the cultural view support subsidies and protectionist measures, in contrast to those proposing that market forces should determine the outcome. Arguments for protection on behalf of the Canadian cultural lobby always appear to be self-serving, even on those occasions when the motive is culture. Like lamb and wool, the two can never be separately produced.

In recent years, the debate became a major focus of the negotiations over international trade in the FTA, the NAFTA and the GATT. In each case Canada claimed it should have its cultural industries exempted from the liberalizing provisions of the agreement. In the case of the FTA, Article 2005(1) provided Canada with the exemption that gave comfort to the cultural nationalists, but it was paired with Article 2005,(2) which stated grounds for retaliatory action and supported the American industrial viewpoint.[12] Nobody knew exactly how these provisions might be interpreted in practice, but each side claimed a measure of victory while waiting to have its views tested when an occasion arose. It has since become clear that neither side wants to test the wording.

These provisions were carried over to the NAFTA for Canada's dealings with the United States and Mexico, while the latter two countries claimed no such exemption in dealings with each other.[13] At the time the Canadian government could claim that the cultural industries were not on the negotiating table, which was true in a limited sense only. Exclusion was a bargaining chip which may have resulted in Canada making concessions in some other area. It also meant that when cultural trade disputes did arise they would be dealt with at the political level rather than through the use of an established dispute resolution mechanism. The informal process would pit Canada against the U.S. and the only precedents would be the way similar disputes had been handled in the past when no such agreements prevailed.

In the GATT negotiations, the cultural industries were considered part of the service sector and made subject to the General Agreement on Trade in Services (GATS). The GATS is a new framework agreement which contains a number of general commitments, but which permits each country to decide whether to make each industry within the service sector subject to the trade liberalizing provisions of the agreement, especially in the case of market access and national treatment. Not surprisingly, Canada has chosen, where possible, to exclude its cultural industries in line with its position on the FTA and the NAFTA.

The GATS for trade in services has been described as being at the same stage that the GATT was at for trade in goods when it was first implemented. This means that it will evolve over time as a result of pressures to reduce the restrictions that countries maintain for their cultural and other service sectors. Countries may buy time to make the adjustments but these are likely to come. Even the European Union, a strong opponent of liberalizing trade in the audiovisual sector, has recognized that while concessions may have been obtained in the Uruguay Round, there will be a second round and the contest is not over.[14]

In Europe, some members of the industry now recognize that the policy approach taken in the past may have harmed the prospects for future development and the opportunity to supply domestic and foreign markets. The facts are that the decline of European film audiences from 1200 million fifteen years ago to 550 million now has been almost entirely at the expense of European films while audiences for American films in Europe have remained unchanged.

A report, sponsored by the European Commission and written by members of the industry in Europe, concludes that:,

... too often national systems of aid have perverted their objectives and wasted their resources. Instead of promoting the image of their countries and their regions, public funds have instead shut up their production in a cultural logic that has accentuated its autarchical aspect, depriving them of any possibilities of contributing to their underlying objectives.[15]

German director Wim Wenders refers to an industry with subsidy lethargy "... whose symptoms are frequently artistic self-indulgence, indifference towards the audience or disregard of economic laws."[16]

WHAT DOES THE NEW TECHNOLOGY DO?

In one sense nothing has changed. New ways have been found to record, store and transmit information. The same content, text, data, voice and video messages, can now reach consumers through different channels. In some instances the information is available directly to consumers on a user-pay basis, or on the "net," bypassing the traditional distributors such as broadcasters, movie theatres and music stores. The Internet grew exponentially from 562 computers connected in 1983 to 2.2 million in 1994. At any time between 1983 and 1994, it is estimated that about half the growth took place in the previous twelve months.[17] Interactivity is increasingly possible so that consumers can participate in the process and pay for particular items directly. In this highly decentralized and unstructured system, the ability of governments to regulate content is reduced. For a country like Canada, the arsenal of cultural policies that has been used to protect its industries has been weakened .

Satellites are one example of a technology that merely augments the existing carriage mechanisms, whether it is for a telephone conversation, fax or e-mail message, news, information or entertainment, in an audio or video format. The ability to convert all these forms of content into digital signals means that satellites provide superhighways on which all types of traffic can be carried. However, unlike a highway where a car, truck or motorcycle look different, all digital signals look the same while in transit and become different at a terminal when reconverted into a text, audio or video form. Moreover, a text, for example, can be broken down into parts which are delivered along different routes and reassembled at the endpoint. This makes it difficult for governments to monitor and control the domestic and crossborder flow of different types of information while in transit, a prerequisite for policies concerned with cultural overflow.

Competitors for satellite highways are those developments in cable and telephone delivery mechanisms which now permit a much larger volume of information to be delivered. In the past, governments have been able to regulate cable and telephone companies but this is becoming increasingly difficult as interconnectivity does not respect national borders where jurisdiction resides. A cable system may be terrestrially based and regulated but its "headend" may be provided with a signal delivered by cable, microwave or tape that comes from another national jurisdiction. The Canadian Radio-Television and Telecommunications Commission (CRTC) has claimed powers to regulate satellite delivery, but within a year of the launch of DirecTv in the U.S. it was estimated that there were up to 75,000 grey market dish receivers for the service in Canada.

Possibly the most critical agent of change has been the remote control or "zapper" which places power in the hands of consumers. In the past, viewers and listeners of television and radio were at the mercy of broadcasters regulated by governments. The news had to be watched at 6pm and 10pm because that was when the broadcaster decided news would be scheduled. Consumers could adjust their lives around these programming decisions, something they did not have to do when selecting a book, newspaper or magazine to read. Apart from increasing consumer choice, the remote control can be tied to technology that allows consumers to pay directly for what they watch, instead of programming being advertising-supported or government-funded. Content can be ordered on demand or almost on demand. This development has altered the conditions for advertisers, who now find their audiences not only fragmented but also able to bypass traditional means of receiving commercial messages.

While broader information highways with enhanced interactivity are being provided, another set of developments allows consumers use of alternative systems. Purchase of a book, periodical, newspaper, record or tape is a direct decision by a consumer. Now the same consumer can rent or buy a videotape for use with a VCR and purchase or rent audio and video compact disks for use on home computers.

These developments are merging in the Internet where communications over existing telecommunications systems allow persons to interact directly not only for voice messages, but for the receipt of data and information as well as for audio and video material previously delivered by broadcasters and cablecasters. Systems already available and undergoing refinement enable consumers to pay for whatever information they choose to receive. Use of the Internet for shopping, subscription to magazines and advertising is growing, causing changes to consumer buying habits and the way goods and services are organized for production and distribution.

Canada's Broadcasting Act and regulatory procedures for cablecasting were developed for conditions that pertained to an earlier era. In its decisions the CRTC has attempted to grapple with the onslaught of technology but is always playing catch-up and is reluctant to relinquish its traditional regulatory approach.[18] Publication of the Task Force Report on the Information Highway is an attempt to respond to change, but meanwhile private and commercial interests are making changes that will be hard to undo.[19] The development and use of the Internet is one example of practice getting ahead of policy.

Similarly, the Canadian position on the cultural industries in the trade agreements was predicated on the view that Canada could still effectively implement its licensing, content and subsidy policies and make a difference. The position taken here is, first, that the technological conditions which underlay these policies have changed and, second, that the cultural industries are more likely to flourish in circumstances of reduced protectionism. The former proposition is a statement of fact. The latter will be challenged by cultural nationalists on combined grounds of self-interest and the claim that Canadian culture will be adversely affected.

While technological developments create problems for traditional policy approaches, they create opportunities for Canadian producers and productions to reach larger markets. The CBC/Power Broadcasting Inc. arrangement with DirecTv is one example. Elsewhere Canadian producers engage in co-productions as a means of obtaining financing and gaining access to foreign markets and foreign sources of funds. Canadian firms like Alliance, Cinar, Nelvana and Paragon are selling their productions in foreign markets, while Vancouver and Toronto are being promoted as places where foreigners can produce. For 1994, Atlantis is reported to have earned 85 percent of its licensing fees for television programming from foreign sources.[20]

As the industry develops a critical mass in certain locations, it provides opportunities for local producers to expand their operations. None of these firms is near the size of a Time-Warner, Disney or News Corp. but they have become established in recent years as the opportunities for program sales increase and the number of channels expands. Recognition of Canadian expertise is evidenced by the Walt Disney Company's announcement that it will open animation studios in Toronto and Vancouver.[21]

Some argue that past Canadian policies nurtured an infant industry now able to compete in international markets. Our view is that these policies were often overly protective and discouraged the development of recognized Canadian expertise that could have accessed foreign markets at an early date. Canada was heavily cabled before the United States, but developed no specialized channels for the North American market. Specialty channels like HBO (Home Box Office), ESPN (a sports channel), CNN (Cable News Network) and A&E (Arts and Entertainment) have been the most profitable segments of North American broadcasting in the past decade. Despite Canada's cable base and acknowledged expertise in news and other areas of broadcasting, it missed participating in these profitable developments. Instead, the CRTC busied itself with designing policies on controlling the inflow of American signals into Canada, a relatively futile exercise as is demonstrated by Canadian broadcasters who made promises of performance when receiving their licences from the CRTC, but then failed to live up to them. Satellite technology was another area in which Canada was at one time in the vanguard, but it was never developed to promote the delivery of Canadian programming throughout North America until American-owned DirecTv became operational.

The inward-looking character of Canadian producers and regulators was, in our view, not in the country's best interests and was contrary to the example of other firms. Northern Telecom broke away from being a captive supplier to Bell Canada and has become a major supplier of equipment in the U.S. and other foreign markets. Like Alcan, Bombardier and Seagrams, Northern Telecom looked abroad for growth. Use of communications technology to look outward represents an opportunity for Canadian creative talent and the way to support a thriving cultural sector. At the same time it requires that cultural policy instruments must be adapted to these changes and not provide impediments to growth.

DOES THE CULTURAL EXEMPTION WORK FOR CANADA?

The exemption negotiated for the cultural industries in the FTA and carried over into the NAFTA was supported by all political parties in Canada and strongly opposed by industry interests in the U.S., led by the Motion Picture Association of America. The two sides were familiar with each others' arguments, having been engaged over many years in disputes regarding Canadian cultural policies.[22] The compromise was wording which satisfied both sides but whose meaning would remain unclear until actual cases arose and were resolved.[23] Three disputes have now arisen; the removal by the CRTC of Country Music Television (CMT) from the list of authorized services allowed by Canadian cable operators and its replacement by Canadian-owned New Country Network (NCN) service; the introduction of an 80 percent excise tax on advertising in split-run editions of magazines and aimed at *Sports Illustrated*; and the CRTC's decision regarding the licensing of direct-to-home television services and affecting the Power DirecTv partnership.

Elsewhere we have set out the details of these cases.[24] Here we will comment on the impact of the trade agreements in terms of how the disputes have been managed to the end of 1995, and the impact of technology in present and future cases. None of the cases that have arisen led either party to invoke the exemption/retaliation clauses of the NAFTA[25] because neither side wanted to test the meaning of the clause. If the CMT dispute, for example, had led to a NAFTA Chapter 20 dispute resolution process and one side had lost, it would have meant the other would have had a freer hand to pursue its line of interest. The U.S. sees itself fighting the cultural battle on a number of fronts, especially in Europe, and is loath to allow precedents to be established in other parts of the world which would weaken its position.

A second reason for avoiding the NAFTA is that the U.S. dislikes submitting disputes to a procedure that it does not completely control and one that establishes precedents, especially if it can achieve its objectives in some other way. Without testing the exemption clause, the United States was able to take these disputes to the political arena where there were fewer constraints and, where by virtue of being the larger player, it could exert more influence. It was like two schoolchildren settling their dispute in the schoolyard without the teachers watching, as opposed to an organized bout in a ring with a referee and timekeepers. In both instances the larger person has the advantage, but the advantage is reduced in the ring where there is a referee and foul play is eliminated, at least when it is witnessed.

The tactics used by each side were varied and ingenious and differed, depending on the particular circumstances of cable and satellite television and periodical publication. The CMT case illustrates some of the techniques used. Canada began by using its regulatory authority to replace an authorized foreign country music cable service, which had operated for ten years, with a competing licensed Canadian-owned service. CMT challenged the regulatory decision in the Federal Court on procedural grounds, lost, and was refused permission to appeal to the Supreme Court of Canada. CMT then turned to the U.S. and laid a 301 complaint under United States Trade Law, which triggers a process whereby the U.S. government has to inquire into the legitimacy of the complaint and call for responses by interested parties.[26]

Meanwhile diplomatic exchanges were taking place in the two capitals with one side pointing to the cultural exemption clause and the other, boosted by sometimes exaggerated submissions from the owners of CMT, arguing that the exemption did not apply, retaliation was justified and anyway there were applicable provisions of the NAFTA that were not covered by the FTA.

A great deal of positioning by both sides as well as veiled and not so veiled use of threats by parties in the U.S. ensued, until, lo and behold, on the day the United States Trade Representative (USTR) was to report, in June 1995, the two parties announced they had reached a partnership arrangement that would give CMT 20 percent and its Canadian partner 80 percent ownership of an enterprise known as CMT Canada. At the same time CMT would end its boycott of Canadian country music performers from its services outside of Canada, a boycott that began after its Canadian service was terminated. One other player was involved, the Federal Communications Commission, which was asked by the USTR if there were any applications involving Canadian companies in the U.S. that could be used for retaliatory purposes. Public diplomacy occurred with the aforementioned appearance by Ambassador Blanchard on the Gzowski program, in which he recognized Canada's cultural concerns but noted that Westinghouse, a part owner of CMT, was a major employer in Canada and would be offended by what it considered to be expropriation of its assets.

It has been suggested, but we have no way to confirm this, that both governments were anxious for a private settlement, so as to avoid escalating the dispute, and pressured the companies to reach some agreement. In this way the exemption/retaliation clause would not be tested. At any rate the dispute was handled outside the NAFTA but was probably conditioned by the agreement. Aside from being the bigger player, the U.S. had a fairly powerful array of weapons to use, especially the 301 process which can be activated by private interests and leads the American diplomatic representatives to say they have no options but to follow the procedure dictated by domestic legislation. The Canadian government used a similar argument in stating that the CRTC was an independent body and that the government could not influence CRTC decisions providing they implemented Canadian policy and were procedurally correct. One linkage between this and the *Sports Illustrated* dispute was that Time-Warner filed a response to the USTR in connection with the CMT case in which it articulated its concerns about the proposed excise tax on split-run editions (now Canadian law) and suggested that the two represented a new Canadian offensive against foreign cultural interests.[27]

Canadian ownership policies are highlighted by this case. At the time the partnership was announced in June 1995 a licensed cable operator could not be more than 20 percent foreign-owned. That requirement has now been relaxed so that a holding company with up to 30 percent foreign ownership can hold the other 80 percent. However, even at 20 percent, actual Canadian commercial control was questionable when a large operator like CMT is the foreign partner. This had certainly been the case in the periodical industry when Reader's Digest formed a trust in Canada which was 75 percent Canadian-owned but depended on the American firm for its commercial activities. Seagram's, with its acquisition of MCA/Universal creates further problems for ownership policies, depending on whether it is deemed to be Canadian or American.[28] If the former, it will have difficulties in owning broadcasting licences in the United States; if the latter, then its indirect takeover of cultural firms in Canada will have to be reviewed by Investment Canada.

A second dimension of the trade disputes is the impact of technology. In one sense it was quite limited. NCN would deliver its cable service in the same way as CMT. DirecTv would deliver satellite radio and television services to Canadian audiences, some of which were already receiving satellite services from Cancom. *Sports Illustrated* was shipping its magazine into Canada via satellite as opposed to the use of film and printed copies. Technology has been important in increasing the capacity of delivery systems to audiences and to intermediaries which supply audiences and new possibilities are available, but it is largely the same content.

In the future, however, it can be expected that entrepreneurs will develop new ways of delivering content which are competitive with existing systems. Thus newspapers and periodicals are and will be increasingly made available on the Internet with advertisers seeking ways to reach customers. As ways are found to measure viewership, advertisers will be attracted to these systems at the expense of existing media, with consequences for their economic viability. The Internet increases competition by enabling users to access and pay for material from anywhere in the world. Government control of domestic content, and of violence and pornography, will be reduced unless fairly invasive measures are employed. As well, copyright becomes a problem, with new forms of delivery requiring domestic and international copyright regimes to develop revised concepts to handle the situation.

Another source of competition will come from compact discs with a large capacity for digitized information which can be used in conjunction with home computers. Again the consumer will be put in direct contact with the producer, thus bypassing all those traditional filters that governments have used to impose their cultural policies.

CONCLUSION

Canada's concern over cultural sovereignty remains a political issue, but one that is now conditioned by developments in technology. As flagged in the Task Force Report on the Information Highway,[29] there is a convergence of technologies related to telecommunications and broadcasting which is affecting the way services are delivered and regulated. At present, Canada has separate regimes, the Telecommunications Act to regulate telecommunications and the Broadcasting Act to regulate broadcasting. If administration of the Highway is undertaken as a broadcasting activity, Canada will attempt to extend the reach of its cultural policies, thereby generating further trade and investment conflicts with the United States.

Our argument is that the same technology provides opportunities for Canadian creative talent to service foreign markets. In film and television production, Canadian firms are already outward-looking.

Others should be encouraged to follow their example and forego protectionist and inward-looking policies as represented by Canada's cultural exemption in trade agreements.

NOTES

1   See Chapter 6 of this volume.

2   The earlier treatment of *Time* and *Reader's Digest* is discussed in I.A.Litvak and C.J.Maule, "Bill C-58 and the regulation of periodicals in Canada," *International Journal*, 1980, 70-90. The legislation affecting *Sports Illustrated* was introduced as Bill 103 and received third reading in Parliament in December 1995.

3   See, for example, the Royal Commission on National Development in the Arts, Letters, and Sciences (Massey), (Ottawa: Queen's Printer, 1951); the Special Senate Committee on Mass Media (Davey), (Ottawa: Queen's Printer, 1970); *Report of the Federal Cultural Policy Review Committee* (Applebaum-Hébert), (Ottawa: Supply and Services, 1982). Each of these reports was to lead to further reports on each sector. A more recent comprehensive discussion of broadcasting is contained in the *Report of the Task Force on Broadcasting Policy* (Caplan-Sauvageau), (Ottawa: Supply and Services, 1986).

4   The earliest use we have found so far of the dumping argument is in the *Times* (London), June 18th, 1919 in connection with film distribution. An article entitled "British Film Cooperation Essential" quotes the proprietor of Harma's British Photoplays as saying that because of the pricing of American films abroad, England is "suffering from the evils of dumping in its most virulent form."

5   See, for example, Keith Acheson and Christopher Maule, "Canadian Content Rules for Television," *Journal of Cultural Economics*, 16, no. 1 (1992), 13-24; and "Risk and the Transfer Cost of a Tax Shelter," *Canadian Tax Journal*, 42, no. 4 (1994), 1082-99.

6   The forecast of a 500-channel universe is attributed to John Malone, President of Tele-Communications Inc., who in a media interview, answered "Hell, yes!" when asked if his company would supply more than the current 52. "We're going to have 10 times that!" According to John C.B.LeGates, Director of the Program on Information Resources Policy, Harvard University, the number is probably closer to 150 channels—see *Hope, Hype and the Highway*, published by Deloitte Touche Tohmatsu International in connection with a conference at Le Château Montebello, Quebec, June 15-17, 1994, at page 20.

7   *Report of the Royal Commission on Publications*, (Ottawa: Queen's Printer, May 1961), 3.

8   John Ralston Saul, *Position Paper on Culture and Foreign Policy*, prepared for the Special Joint Committee of the House of Commons and the Senate reviewing Canadian Foreign Policy, August 30, 1994, 10.

9   Broadcasting Act, S.C. 1991, c. 11. Amongst other things, the Act requires the broadcasting system to be effectively owned and controlled by Canadians, to safeguard, enrich and strengthen the

cultural, political, social and economic fabric of Canada, to present varied and comprehensive programming, to provide a balanced service of information, enlightenment and entertainment for people of different ages, interests and tastes, and to adapt to scientific and technical advances.

10   Paul Lee and Georgette Wang, "Satellite TV in Asia; Forming a new ecology," *Telecommunications Policy*, 19, no. 2, (1994), 135-49.

11   From letter of North to Canty, officials in the Bureau of Foreign and Domestic Commerce, Foreign Service of the United States Government, dated October 18th, 1928 and filed in National Archives, Washington, D.C. File RG 151, General Records, 1914-1958, 281 Motion Pictures.

12   Article 2005(1) provides a general exemption for culture while formulating certain specific trade and market access commitments; Article 2005(2) permits either country to "take measures of equivalent effect in response to actions that would have been inconsistent with this agreement but for paragraph 1."

13   The cultural exemption in the FTA is carried over into the NAFTA by virtue of article 2106 and annex 2106 for the cultural industries specified in article 2107.

14   *Report of the Think-Tank on the Audiovisual Policy in the European Union*, Brussels, European Communities, (1994), 21.

15   Report of Think-Tank, 55.

16   Ibid., 34.

17   Douglas E.Comer, *The Internet Book*, (Prentice Hall: New Jersey, 1995), 70.

18   Robert Fulford, "The CRTC Comedy Hour," *Next City*, Fall 1995, 26-31.

19   *Connection Community Content. The Challenge of the Information Highway: Final Report of the Information Highway Advisory Council*, (Ottawa: Supply and Services, 1995).

20   *Queen's Alumni Review*, Nov./Dec. 1995, 11.

21   *The Globe and Mail*, December 1, 1995, B1.

22   Disputes of long standing include Canadian content rules for broadcasting and restrictions on split-run editions of foreign magazines sold in Canada.

23   See endnote 12.

24   Keith Acheson and Christopher Maule, *International Agreements and the Cultural Industries*, Carleton University, Carleton Industrial Organization Research Unit, Working Paper 95-03, Dec. 1995.

25   See endnote 13.

26   Section 301 of the United States Trade Act of 1974 as amended by the Omnibus Trade Act of 1988 (Title 111, Trade Act of 1974, 19 U.S.C 2411 (Supp. 1993)) allows the government or firms or citizens to file a petition with the USTR alleging illegal or unfair actions by governments.

27   As of January 1996 the CMT dispute continues, as the American owners contend that NCN has not lived up to its partnership agreement. *The Globe and Mail*, January 6, 1996, B1.

28   The nationality of Seagrams is under review according to Heritage Minister Dupuy. See *Financial Post*, May 10, 1995, 9.

29   See endnote 19.

VI

Canada and the United States: Still Calm in the "Remarkable Relationship"

JOSEPH T. JOCKEL

President Clinton, avoiding yet at the same time outdoing the old cliché about the "special relationship" between Canada and the United States, told the Canadian Parliament in February 1995 that "ours is the world's most remarkable relationship."[1] The President made it clear that he was referring to the level of integration and cooperation between the two countries.

Equally remarkable, though, is the persistent calm that has taken hold of the bilateral, government-to-government relationship. It is still another cliché of Canada-U.S. relations, relied upon a bit too often by scholars and speechwriters alike, that within such a close partnership conflicts are inevitable. And indeed, in 1995 a host of bilateral differences needed to be addressed by the two governments, especially in the thorny area of subsidies, antidumping, and countervailing duties. Nonetheless, throughout 1995 the list of bilateral economic, military, environmental and even cultural "irritants" between Washington and Ottawa remained, for the most part, far from intractable, when compared to earlier periods of tension, such as the first part of the 1980s.[2] It may well be that the relationship has entered into a period of enduring calm.

Several of the special mechanisms put into place to manage the relationship during that tense period in the 1980s have been abandoned, to be replaced in part by others, especially those mandated by the Canada-United States Free Trade Agreement (FTA) and the subsequent North American Free Trade Agreement (NAFTA). Most visible, and also symbolic, has been Prime Minister Chrétien's continued emphasis on a lower-key prime ministerial-presidential relationship in public. Not only had this relationship been of little practical importance, but it became clearer and clearer that the two heads of government got along just fine without having to engage in an active social life together.

Looming over the calm prevailing between Ottawa and Washington throughout 1995 were events in Quebec, culminating in the October 30 referendum and Quebec's rejection, by the very slimmest of margins, of sovereignty. U.S. officials, up to and including Secretary of State Warren Christopher and President Clinton, sought to stay within the bounds of the longstanding U.S. hands-off policy towards Canada's constitutional and political future, while also trying gingerly to signal their hope that Canada would remain united, especially as the polls during the referendum showed growing support for the "yes".

CHRÉTIEN AND THE AMERICANS: PUTTING NAFTA BEHIND US

It is hard to escape the conclusion that the tranquil tenor of the bilateral relationship is due in large part to Jean Chrétien—not so much for what he has done, but what he and his government have not done. During the 1993 general election campaign anyone taking Liberal speeches or the Liberal Party's vaunted "Red Book" policy statement seriously would have expected the new Chrétien government to pursue policies that would immediately have led to a cooling of Canadian-American ties. A revival of Canadian nationalism, reminiscent of some of the Trudeau years, appeared to be at hand. The "Red Book" called for "new directions in Canada-U.S. relations", especially "rejecting a camp-follower approach in favour of pursuing a partnership with the U.S."[3] NAFTA in particular, for which Canadian implementing legislation had been adopted but not proclaimed under the outgoing Progressive Conservatives, would have to be renegotiated, or Canada would stay out of the deal. Lloyd Axworthy, then the party's Foreign Affairs critic, wrote that in world affairs the Liberals would "develop an alternative to the continentalist views" of the Mulroney government.[4]

Yet within weeks of winning the November 1993 election the Liberals signed on to NAFTA, with only a few fig leaves attached to allow them to claim that the deal had been renegotiated. This step was particularly welcome to the Clinton administration, which, at the time, faced the difficult task of obtaining Congressional approval for the deal in the face of opposition from a significant number from the president's own party.

It also represented nothing less than a crucial development in recent Canada-U.S. relations, second in significance only to the 1988 Canadian general election that had allowed the Mulroney Conservatives to proceed with ratification of the FTA. The new Liberal government's acceptance of NAFTA has, in effect, extinguished effective opposition in Canada to free trade with the U.S., despite its persistent unpopularity among Canadians. This was all the more true because the federal New Democratic Party, which had opposed the FTA and NAFTA even more vehemently than the Liberals, was all but annihilated in the 1993 election.

To put it somewhat differently: while it might have been expected that the Liberals under Chrétien would nostalgically opt for a new variant of the 1972 Trudeau "third option" policy of establishing counterweights to integration with the U.S., they have in substance confirmed the country's commitment to the "second option" of closer continental economic integration. In fairness, though, it should also be pointed out that the original goal of the "third option" was to "reduce the present Canadian vulnerability" to the U.S. and that the protections afforded by the FTA and NAFTA do just that in several aspects of the trading relationship.[5] Moreover, the Chrétien government has been active in pursuing trading relations overseas.

The Liberals' reluctance to challenge the new framework of Canada-U.S. economic relations was confirmed in 1995 by the fate of the most politically important NAFTA concession on which the Chrétien government had insisted in 1993: the creation of two working groups by the U.S., Mexico and Canada, one on dumping and antidumping (AD) duties and the other on subsidies and counter-vailing duties (CVD), with mandates to report by December 1995. This demand arose from the persistent Canadian perception that the U.S. has been overly aggressive in its use of antidumping and coun-tervailing duties against imports from Canada, and from the "holes" in both the FTA and NAFTA where the desired provisions dealing with such disputes should have been.[6]

Ottawa has long favoured wide-ranging reform of U.S. legislation in the areas of AD and CVD and harmonization of competition laws. Previous bilateral working groups on antidumping and countervail-ing duties established under the FTA had made little progress; U.S. officials, in agreeing to the creation of the new groups in 1993, had few expectations of progress in the face of firm Congressional oppo-sition to change. The NAFTA groups began meeting in February 1994 and, as fully expected in Washington, made little headway. The Chrétien government quietly agreed to the extension of the deadline beyond 1995. While a report may be issued in 1996, it will be very surprising if resolution of these issues is found any time soon.

Meanwhile, during 1995 there were a number of subsidy and countervailing issues on the bilateral agenda. These included:

Softwood Lumber
In December 1994 Canada and the U.S. agreed to establish a bilateral consultative process, involving experts and business interests from both sides, to address the longstanding softwood lumber dispute, in which U.S. interests have continued to charge that Canadian provin-cial practices constitute lumber export subsidies. By the end of 1995, with proposals being advanced by Canadian provinces, the U.S. agreed to extend consultations into 1996.[7]

Sugar
Canada pressed the U.S. in 1995 for changes in its sugar import quo-tas affecting Canadian sugar. Meanwhile, the Canadian International Trade Tribunal (CITT) determined that sugar from the U.S. and other countries was being "dumped" in Canada. In 1996 the CITT will deter-mine whether to proceed with consideration of antidumping duties.

Grains
In September 1994 the two countries agreed in a memorandum of understanding to establish a Joint Commission on Grains to examine

all aspects of their marketing and support systems for grains and the impact of these systems on cross-border trade and competition. A dispute arose over surges of Canadian grains (especially durum wheat, other wheat, and barley). Here again, a final report is due in 1996. At the end of 1995 a deal appeared to be in the making.

Other such issues on the bilateral agenda in 1995 included claims that live swine, magnesium, and colour picture tubes from Canada were subsidized, while Revenue Canada initiated an antidumping investigation of imports of bacteriological culture growth media from the U.S. and Britain. Reviews were underway with regard to duties already imposed by the U.S. on Canadian steel. Finally, in 1995 the U.S. and Canada were completing the selection of panelists for a NAFTA dispute settlement panel concerning the application of new World Trade Organization (WTO) tariff equivalents for Canada's supply-managed agricultural products (poultry, dairy, eggs and barley).

It is tempting to speculate as to why the Liberals turned away from their announced approach to the U.S. Perhaps with the Canadian economy still weak and with another crucial battle in Quebec looming, the government decided it did not have the resources to take on Washington. Or, it may have seen an irreversible logic in North American economic integration. In a larger sense, though, Mr. Chrétien's U.S. policy may reflect the cautious approach taken by his government overall to both domestic and foreign issues.

One portion of the bilateral agenda, culture, did seem for a while to be rapidly heating up in 1995. Some expected that, with the Canadian government accepting economic integration under NAFTA, it might choose to take a very firm stand here. The area was ripe for discord, with Canadian "cultural" issues usually appearing to be "economic" or, at the most, "entertainment" matters to the U.S.[8]

Three issues emerged. In the first, the Canadian Radio-Television and Telecommunications Commission (CRTC) sought to remove the U.S.-owned Country Music Television channel from Canadian cable services and to replace it with a Canadian equivalent. The U.S. prepared a list of retaliatory measures. But a settlement was negotiated in June by the commercial parties, under pressure from the two governments, whereby the U.S. and Canadian services established a joint Canadian venture.

Second, the Canadian cabinet issued a directive which, contrary to the preferences of the CRTC, permitted a U.S. concern, DirecTV, to be involved in direct satellite broadcasting in Canada, in partnership with a subsidiary of the Power Corporation. From the U.S. perspective, a level playing field had been established for Canadian and foreign providers.

The third issue, the *Sports Illustrated* case, was not resolved. Bill C-103 received royal assent in December 1995. It will prevent *Sports Illustrated* (and, potentially, other U.S. publications) from publishing modern forms of "split-run editions." Strikingly, a Senate Committee, upon considering the legislation, recommended that Bill C-103 be amended to "grandfather" *Sports Illustrated*, which already had established its electronic split-run edition in Canada. The full Senate turned the recommendation down. The U.S. government views the impact of the new act as confiscatory in its impact on *Sports Illustrated*, much as it viewed the intended impact of the CRTC's actions on Country Music Television. In response to the bill's enactment United States Trade Representative Mickey Kantor directed his officials at the end of 1995 to examine retaliatory options.

MANAGING THE RELATIONSHIP

At the Prime Minister's behest, the two heads of government have pursued a much more formal public relationship than Prime Minister Mulroney had with Presidents Reagan and Bush. But this has had very little practical importance in the day-to-day management of Canada-U.S. relations, partially as a result of the underlying absence of deepseated differences between the two governments, partially because behind the scenes the two men have worked effectively together, especially on the telephone.

In the longer run it may be more significant, especially if the Canada-U.S. relationship ever turns sour again, that the formal commitment of the two countries' foreign ministers to meet four times a year (the mainstay of bilateral management in the 1980s) has been allowed to fall into abeyance, although the two ministers met several times during 1995. In Washington, the position of Deputy Assistant Secretary of State for Canada, which had been intended, when it was created during the Reagan administration, to play a key role in supporting the four meetings a year, has been discontinued. On the other hand, Ambassador James Blanchard, a former Democratic governor of Michigan, has been important, not only in representing the U.S. in Canada, but also in the formulation of policy toward Canada in Washington.

At the same time, many of the trade disputes that used to be handled politically and on an ad hoc basis between the heads of government or the foreign and trade ministers are now addressed through the dispute settlement mechanisms provided by the FTA, and now by NAFTA, most importantly through the procedures whereby the application of national legislation on subsidies, antidumping and countervailing duties can be reviewed by a binational panel. These provisions are certainly not perfect. After all, each country can still legislate in this area. But they are far from toothless and serve, in large measure, to depoliticize disputes. In addition, as briefly discussed above, the two governments have also established new semiformal mechanisms to address the disputes on softwood lumber and grains.

Still, a perennial problem of Canada-U.S. relations, that of the role of the Congress, has intensified with the Democratic loss of control of both houses. As will be discussed below, Republican initiatives have at times threatened to disrupt the otherwise highly cooperative Canada-U.S. environmental relationship. Moreover, the proposed "Cuban Liberty and Solidarity Act," also known as the Helms-Burton bill, championed chiefly by Senator Jesse Helms (R-North Carolina), has threatened to reignite old Canadian grievances about the extraterritorial application of U.S. foreign policy and law. Versions of the bill passed both houses of Congress in 1995, and went to a Conference Committee for reconciliation. The Senate version proposed restrictions on entry into the U.S. of any foreign national who has confiscated property in Cuba owned by a U.S. national (or who has "trafficked" in such property) and would establish new requirements for certification of origin of sugar, syrups and molasses imported into the U.S. The Clinton administration, which shares Canadian concerns, has threatened a veto. Canadian officials also began monitoring the progress of a bill, introduced by Senator Alfonse D'Amato (R-New York) and approved by the Senate Banking Committee in December 1995, that would impose sanctions on persons, including foreign persons, investing in Iran's oil and gas sector.

In 1995 the Clinton administration and Congressional leaders struggled in vain to find a formula that would provide Congressionally authorized "fast-track" negotiating authority facilitating the extension of NAFTA to Chile. Within the complicated maze of issues affecting resolution were the role of environmental and labour side agreements within any negotiation with Chile, proposals for free trade with the West Bank and Gaza, and Congressional anxieties over both the NAFTA dispute settlement provisions (which have handed Canada several significant victories) and the impact of the new WTO panels. It may be that administration officials and members of Congress supportive of NAFTA extension have privately welcomed statements by Canadian officials to the effect that Canada might have to reach an agreement on its own with Chile, as a modest additional spur to Congressional action. In public, however, official free traders in Washington have to lament that Canada, which headed off a Mexico-U.S. arrangement in favour of the trilateral NAFTA, might pursue its own arrangement with Chile.[8]

MILITARY RELATIONS AND ENVIRONMENTAL QUALITY: WHERE HAVE ALL THE DISPUTES GONE?

In two other areas of the bilateral agenda, military and environmental relations, significant disputes have all but disappeared (with the exception of the West Coast fishery issues). There is every reason to believe that in the military case this shift will be very longstanding, inasmuch as the very underpinnings of the Canada-U.S. defence relationship, and the irritants that relationship has often produced, have also disappeared, along with the Cold War.[9]

Since the Ogdensburg Accord of 1940, during the Second World War and the Cold War, Canada and the U.S. have been drawn together for two defence tasks: the protection of North America and the prevention of a potentially hostile power from achieving hegemony in Europe. The first led to friction from time to time, as Americans grew frustrated at what was sometimes seen as the insufficient level of Canadian financial commitment, and Canadians worried about the loss of their territorial sovereignty to the U.S. military and about a close link to the U.S. nuclear deterrent. These Canadian concerns flared up as recently as the early 1980s, especially as a result of the U.S. Strategic Defense Initiative ("Star Wars") and the 1985 Canada-U.S. Air Defence Modernization Agreement, which provided for the revamping of radars across the continent, including the replacement of the old Distant Early Warning (DEW) Line in northern Canada with a "North Warning System" (NWS) and the construction of forward operating locations (FOLs) for fighter interceptors, also in northern Canada. Jean Chrétien was especially caustic, at the time, in his denunciation in the House of Commons of the 1985 deal and its impact on Canadian sovereignty.

The disappearance of the Soviet threat has brought all this to a halt. As a January 1995 statement by Ottawa emphasized, "direct threats to Canada's territory are diminished" and future challenges to Canadian security are likely, to an increasing extent to be of a non-military nature, that is, economic, environmental and demographic.[10] For its part, the Clinton administration's 1994 defence strategy statement scarcely mentioned North American defence.[11]

North American air defence, long a mainstay of Canada-U.S. cooperation, has been put on the backburner. For this task the North American Aerospace Defence Command (NORAD) no longer has "war plans" but "concept plans." Forces have been put in what NORAD calls a "regeneration" category, with the expectation that there would be as much as a two-year strategic warning of any resurgent air threat.[12] Washington has cut back on plans contained in the 1985 agreement. The NWS now will operate with much reduced capacity. Of the four modern air defence radar installations envisaged in 1985 for the U.S. two were cancelled, one was deactivated and the last put on part-time alert status. U.S. funding for the FOLs in northern Canada was completely cut off by Congress. So in recent months it has, ironically, been Canadians who have been irritated by a (relatively) low level of U.S. spending for continental defence.

To be sure, the U.S. may some day deploy a limited ballistic missile (BMD) system in North America or limited theatre missile defences (TMD) for protection abroad, especially if U.S. forces are deployed overseas. It is, though, far from clear how much emphasis the U.S. will eventually put upon North American BMD. The Clinton administration is continuing the emphasis on TMD. Although the new Republican-controlled Congress tried to speed up the fielding of a BMD system to defend the United States,[13] the current legislation still only requires that a BMD system be "developed by 2003, with Congress having to vote again before it can be deployed."[14]

The Chrétien government, in consonance with its cooperative approach to the U.S., and having regard to the end of the Cold War, went further in its *1994 Defence White Paper* than any Progressive Conservative government would have dared to go by signalling its willingness to explore participation in a U.S. missile defence system. The government said that one of its new goals in NORAD was to "cooperate ... in the examination of ballistic missile defence operations focused on research and building on Canada's existing capabilities in communications and surveillance."[15] In an era of tight government budgets, U.S. officials will continue to wonder how much money Canada will have for this purpose. What is more important, though, is that Canada is not essential, for neither Canadian territory nor Canadian personnel are needed for the operation of a BMD system.

NORAD renewal, scheduled for 1996, has also become a non-issue for Ottawa. Changes will no doubt be made in the wording of the agreement reflecting the altered global security environment. Reference will also be made to future potential cooperation in BMD, reflecting Ottawa's new attitude. However, NORAD will still be a pale reflection of its Cold War self. In short, Canada has ceased to be the strategic glacis of the U.S.

Canada's 16 surface warships, (including 12 new patrol frigates) as well as its plans to augment its naval presence in the Pacific and the more recent changes to the underwater surveillance system, will make the Canadian maritime contribution to continental defence actually better than it is at present.[16] The Canadian and U.S. navies can be expected to maintain close contact and cooperation. However, with the dramatic decline in post-Soviet naval power, purely national sovereignty protection duties, as opposed to bilateral roles, are much more likely to be the main focus of the Canadian Navy in the waters surrounding North America, as is evident from its actions against Spanish fishing vessels in the spring of 1995.

For the first time in this century, no potentially hostile power threatens hegemony in Europe. As a result, Canada has removed all its military units deployed in Western Europe, while the U.S. presence has been dramatically reduced. In the future, to the extent there will be Canada-U.S. military cooperation, it will be focused "out of area," that is outside the NATO area of Western Europe and North America.

It is still far too early to say how extensive such "out of area" cooperation between the U.S. and Canada will be. The current debates in the two countries over military posture are strikingly different. In the U.S., there is widespread willingness (especially in the Republican Congress) to *pay* for extensive armed forces, but great reluctance to actually *use* them. The success or failure of the U.S. involvement in the Bosnian peace enforcement operation, which began in December 1995, will no doubt be decisive in shaping the still badly divided U.S. attitudes towards the deployment of forces in areas and conflicts not central to U.S. security interests. Republicans will remain largely sceptical. But as is indicated by the guarded support for the Bosnian deployment of Senator Robert Dole, the likely presidential candidate of his party in 1996, Republican opposition to such involvement is not completely solid.

Canadians and their governments, on the other hand, have recently been unwilling to sustain significant levels of military spending, but much more willing to use them, at least for peacekeeping operations. The U.S. asked for and received assurances, during the call of former Foreign Affairs Minister André Ouellet on Secretary of State Christopher in October 1995, that Canada would participate in the Bosnian peace enforcement operation. But clearly Ottawa was ambivalent. Ouellet and the Prime Minister soon seemed to be backing away from a pledge to send combat forces, saying that Canada would participate "only if absolutely necessary."[17]

Ottawa's eventual decision to send a force of 1,000 troops reflected this ambivalence. Given the nature of the mission and the dangers, the force is more heavily armed than previous Canadian units in the former Yugoslavia and will have the authority to defend itself under the more robust rules of engagement under which NATO is operating. But over half the force, 500-600, is assigned to support British soldiers by providing a headquarters unit, including communications staff, west of Sarajevo and only 300 to 400 are expected to be combat troops. Ottawa also made it clear that the deployment would be for only one year. In justifying the small size of the force, the Minister of National Defence, David Collenette, cited Canada's three-year long participation in U.N. peacekeeping in Yugoslavia. "This is what Canadians would expect us to do."[18]

There is little doubt that, in making this commitment, Ottawa was trying to mend fences with NATO. As Mr. Collenette noted, Canada had a "moral obligation" to support the alliance[19] at this "historic time for NATO."[20] In the final analysis, though, the decision can probably be explained simply by the continuing Canadian desire not to be entirely left out of a major American-led Western undertaking.

Washington was glad for what it could get from Canada. To be sure, the Clinton administration might have liked to have had a larger, more combat-capable Canadian contribution as it rounded up the NATO posse for Bosnia. However, the U.S. is not going to put any heavy pressure on Canada to do more. Militarily and operationally it makes little difference. Given Canada's continuing budgetary crises and recent policy decisions, there is little the U.S. could do. More significantly, such entreaties would not be worth the effort. It was far more important for the Clinton administration to garner West

European contributions and the participation of some of the Partnership for Peace countries, especially Russia. Should the U.S.-brokered settlement on Bosnia flounder on the killing fields of Yugoslavia or in Congress, then little importance will be attached to Ottawa's ambivalence or the size of the Canadian commitment.

Canada is showing a new interest in the countries of the Far East and those of Latin America. Ottawa clearly believes that as Canada seeks out new trading opportunities, there should be some commensurate augmentation in military links with regions and countries outside the traditional North Atlantic triangle. The *1994 Defence White Paper* also reflects this attitude. It documents the way in which Canadian interest in the security of the Asia Pacific region has become much more active, through the encouragement of regional security dialogues such as the Asia Regional Forum, the Council for Security Cooperation in Asia Pacific, and the Canadian Consortium on Asia Pacific Security. Canada will expand the current program of bilateral military contacts with a variety of Asian nations, including Japan, South Korea, and members of the Association of South East Asian Nations.[21]

Increased Canadian military ties in Latin America, the Pacific and elsewhere might involve some cooperation with the United States. But this new interest cannot be equated with a Canadian commitment to the security of these regions, a commitment necessitating greatly expanded military operations. So, bluntly put, for the U.S. Canada's quite limited military commitment to regional security and any future war-fighting coalitions is of secondary importance, even less important than in the Cold War when much more political symbolism was attached to Canadian diplomatic support. The U.S. military knows full well that the Canadian forces lack the capabilities to make a significant military contribution out of area. Moreover, for the U.S., promoting regional security will depend upon cooperation with regional powers and, at times, powerful external actors such France and Britain, and even Russia. If Washington cannot get these other nations to follow its lead, then it will either act alone, if its vital interests are deemed to be at stake, or it will not act at all.

The election of a Republican president would, in all probability, enhance this trend. Continued Republican scepticism about the UN has already placed limits on the Clinton administration's support of that body. The administration has consequently backed away from its early enthusiasm for U.S. participation in classic international peace-keeping operations and the U.S. is still behind in its payments to the

UN. At a time when support for the UN is a mainstay of Canadian foreign policy, a change in U.S. administrations could lead to a significant divergence between the approaches of the two countries to international organization.

Nonetheless, the U.S. does have an interest in Canada's maintenance and use of its limited peacekeeping capabilities, especially as many Americans remain squeamish about their own country's involvement in peacekeeping. The Clinton administration was especially pleased with the presence in Haiti of 470 Canadian peacekeeping military personnel and 125 Canadian police officers.

Well before the Clinton administration and the Chrétien government took office, acid rain, the most significant environmental dispute between the two countries, was taken off the table thanks to the 1990 re-authorization of the U.S. Clean Air Act and the Bush-Mulroney Canada-United States Air Quality Agreement of 1991.[22] Acid rain was an unusual bilateral environmental dispute inasmuch as most causes of the degradation were concentrated in one large region (the industrial heartland of the U.S. Midwest), while the effects were largely felt elsewhere, in the eastern U.S. and Canada. With one large region pitted against others, finding a solution was especially difficult, and was, of course, made more so by the scepticism of the Reagan administration.

With this issue resolved (for now) Canada-U.S. environmental relations have returned to their normal pattern, involving, first, more localized disputes which arise periodically and which can be referred to the Canada-U.S. International Joint Commission for study and recommendation and second, but more importantly, Great Lakes water quality issues. (In recent years, though, no new environmental disputes have been referred to the Commission.) The Great Lakes ecosystem is obviously a large region. But with the causes of Great Lakes pollution arising, and their effects being felt, in the same transboundary area, finding the regional will to support abatement and cleanup is far easier there than was the case with acid rain.

Moreover, the Clinton administration's commitment to the environment has undoubtedly extended to Great Lakes water quality. The U.S. Environmental Protection Agency's (EPA) 1995 draft "guidance" document for the Lakes is especially stringent as it pertains to discharge permits. In fact, the U.S. grew concerned in 1995 that budget cuts to Environment Canada would delay Canada's ability to keep pace in meeting deadlines on the Great Lakes.

Especially looming as a threat to bilateral environmental progress is the Republican Congress, whose leadership sought several times in 1995 to weaken domestic air and water quality legislation, with potentially significant implications for the ability of the U.S. to live up to its obligations to Canada under the acid rain agreement and the several bilateral Great Lakes Water Quality Accords. The Republicans launched another assault on environmental programs through the budgetary process, attempting to reduce EPA funding significantly.

At the end of 1995 the outcome was far from clear, and only partially because of the ongoing budget deadlock between Congress and the administration. Joining Democrats, roughly 50 "green" Republicans in the House of Representatives, bolstered by support in the Senate, successfully thwarted their leadership's attempts to gut environmental legislation. Speaker Newt Gingrich was obliged to admit in 1995 that the Republicans in Congress had mishandled the environment.[23]

The Republicans in Congress have also sought to enact legislation permitting oil and gas exploration in the Arctic National Wildlife Refuge (ANWR) in Alaska, on the Yukon border. The Canadian federal and Yukon territorial governments have opposed this step, which is supported by the Democratic governor of Alaska. President Clinton has promised to veto any legislation opening up ANWR, if it emerges from the Congress.

Finally, reference may be made to an environmental issue not involving pollution: the two countries reached an impasse on the application of the 1985 U.S.-Canada Pacific Salmon Treaty. At issue are starkly differing views on the allocation of stocks.

WASHINGTON AND QUEBEC: STRETCHING THE "MANTRA"

Quebec was a substantial preoccupation in 1995 of U.S. officials responsible for relations with Canada, up to and including the President. How could it be otherwise, with the President, during his February visit to Ottawa, briefly meeting Bloc Québécois leader Lucien Bouchard and speaking to a Canadian Parliament that had 54 Bloc MPs, and with the Quebec sovereignty referendum being held at the end of October?

Official U.S. policy concerning the possibility of an independent Quebec has for the most part remained constant since the 1970s.[24] While it remained fundamentally unchanged in 1995, it was slightly, yet significantly, "stretched."

The policy consists in essence of a firm determination to stay out of the debate in Quebec and the rest of Canada over the country's future. In form, it consists of two elements: first, carefully phrased, formulaic public statements, and second, a universal refusal on the part of U.S. officialdom to enter into discussion of how the U.S. would react if Quebec moved toward independence or actually became sovereign.

Among private analysts and the business community in the U.S. there is striking unanimity of opinion about the interests of the U.S.: they lie with a united Canada. Still, most would also agree that if Quebec ever does move irrevocably towards independence, it would then be in the interest of the U.S. to pursue second-best options and to establish as close a relationship as possible with the new state. Indeed, it would also be in the interest of the U.S. that a sovereign Quebec and Canada should reach a close relationship with each other.

Public statements by U.S. officials have always included a recognition of the value of Canada (usually "a united Canada") to the United States, swiftly followed by the observation that Canada's future constitutional and political arrangements can only be determined in Canada itself. The shortest version of such statements is what is called at the State Department the "mantra", which any U.S. official dealing with Canada is prepared to chant at the drop of a hat. The 1995 form of the mantra has run, "The United States enjoys excellent relations with a strong and united Canada. Canada's political future is naturally for Canadians to decide."[25]

In Canada, much is sometimes made of relatively minor changes which occasionally have been made in the first part of the mantra. Sometimes the U.S. officially has "preferred" a united Canada. And emphasis was laid on the fact that during his address to the Canadian Parliament President Clinton said, to the applause of most members, that "Canada has stood for all of us as a model of how people of different cultures can live and work together in peace, prosperity, and respect." He went on to quote with great approval remarks once made in the same place by President Harry S. Truman about "Canada's notable achievement of national unity."[26]

Nonetheless, just like officials chanting the mantra, the President was careful to point out, in this case to the great applause of Bloc MPs, that "your political future is, of course, entirely for you to decide."[27] Even more significantly, again in the firm tradition of U.S.

policy, he managed to avoid any other comment on future U.S.-Canada-Quebec relations, even in the wake of his visit with Mr. Bouchard.

So while the President's speech no doubt reflected a real desire on his part and on the part of his senior officials to go as far as possible in praising Canadian unity, the real significance of all these formulaic statements is not to be found in any changes of nuance or emphasis within them. Rather, they were all Washington was prepared to say about Canada's constitutional and political future and about the future of U.S. policy towards Canada and Quebec.

In other words, these statements were intended to bring U.S. public utterances to an end. A host of questions that were on the minds of Quebecers as they pondered their future remained unanswered, among them, whether the U.S. would want to admit Quebec to NAFTA, and whether the U.S. would recognize a unilateral declaration of independence issued by Quebec.

Nonetheless, statements made by separatist leaders since the 1994 Quebec election have precipitated a significant "stretching" of the U.S. mantra. Such public statements, especially by P.Q. spokespersons, have sought to create the impression that Quebec would, by legal mechanisms, "automatically" be admitted to NAFTA and other Canadian agreements with the U.S. Sovereignty would, in that regard, be made much less painful, economically speaking. Much was made, in particular, by the P.Q. government of an advisory legal memorandum it commissioned in early 1995 from the New York law firm of Rogers and Wells. The impression was created that the memorandum supported the notion of "automaticity," although a careful reading of it reveals that this is not at all the case.[28] The original draft Sovereignty Bill, tabled in the National Assembly by the P.Q. government in late 1994, also asserted that "in accordance with the rules of international law, Québec shall assume the obligations and enjoy the rights set forth in the relevant treaties and international conventions and agreements to which Canada or Québec is a party on the date on which Québec becomes a sovereign country, in particular [NAFTA]."[29]

Such an interpretation is not at all shared in Washington. Serving U.S. officials, constrained by the bounds of the mantra, could not openly respond. Nonetheless, they hit upon the formulation relied upon both by Ambassador James Blanchard and by Secretary Christopher, among others, and appended, as it were, to the mantra, to the effect that the U.S. had given "no assurances" about the nature of Quebec-U.S. relations, in the event that Quebec actually did become independent.

Charles E. Roh, Jr., as a former Assistant U.S. Trade Representative for Canada and Mexico, was no longer bound by official constraints. So he could set out the U.S. understanding in an important study released in Washington in October 1995:

1. An independent Quebec would not have any automatic rights or obligations under existing trade agreements, including the NAFTA, the WTO Agreement, and the Auto Pact. Instead, Quebec would have to negotiate terms of accession to those agreements.

2. The U.S. President has no authority under U.S. law to give an independent Quebec the preferential trade benefits Quebec now enjoys as part of Canada, unless and until Quebec has acceded to the NAFTA and Congress has approved and implemented that accession. The termination of those preferences, even for a short time, would be most costly and disruptive for Quebec, but would also hurt U.S. interests.

3. Despite historic friendships, negotiations for an independent Quebec's accession to the WTO, the NAFTA, and the Auto Pact would likely prove difficult. Many of Canada's obligations would produce a different substantive result if transposed without change to an independent Quebec, and thus require substantive negotiations. U.S. negotiators, pressed by Congress and the private sector, are likely to seek improvements in sensitive areas: sectors such as agriculture, textiles, cultural industries, and reviews of unfair trade rulings.[30]

Those same U.S. officials undoubtedly sighed guardedly with relief when the referendum results came in. Not only had the "remarkable" relationship not been ruptured, but Washington would not be faced immediately with such issues regarding Quebec and NAFTA and the even thornier problem which could have arisen if Quebec ever were to knock on U.S. doors with a unilateral declaration of independence in hand. Still, Washington officialdom knows, like Quebecers and other Canadians, that in the wake of the close referendum the question of Canada's future is far from settled and that in the future Quebecers may well be called upon by their provincial government to leave Canada.

For now, Washington will keep quiet. Should Quebec eventually move towards sovereignty, U.S. policy would, of course, have to be entirely reformulated. There can be little comfort for Washington in Robert A. Young's observation, in his recent study, *The Secession of Quebec and the Future of Canada*, that "Foreign powers will play an important role in the secession.... The most important actor will, of course, be the United States."[31]

CONCLUSION: THE YEAR AHEAD

During 1996, Quebec will recede, if only briefly, from its prominent place in Canada-U.S. relations as its new premier, Lucien Bouchard, settles into office and hones his strategy to achieve sovereignty. While Canada is drawn inward once again into another round of national unity agonizing, the moments between now and the next Quebec referendum (or election) on independence will be ripe for U.S. officials, should they chose to do so, to rewrite the "mantra." It bears watching to see if "no assurances" for Quebec will be fully incorporated into any future versions of it.

It takes no real foresight to predict that there inevitably will be new trade "irritants" on the Canada-U.S. agenda and that those unresolved in 1995 will require further attention. At the end of 1995 it was easy to doubt whether the report of the NAFTA working groups on antidumping and countervailing duties would lead to progress. Yet there were reasons for optimism about the positive impact of two other bilateral reports in 1996, on grains and softwood lumber. The defence agenda will, in all probability, be quiet, and the NORAD agreement will be renewed with little fuss.

The U.S., for its part, will be drawn into presidential and Congressional elections. At the end of 1995 it also appeared that the overall stalemate between the Republican Congress and Democratic White House, which affected Canada-U.S. relations in several areas, especially the environment, would carry over into the November 1996 elections. In the lead-up to the campaign and during the campaign itself there may well also be "tough talk on trade" that could make resolving trade irritants somewhat more difficult. But Canada will rarely be the direct butt of such talk.

The best bet is still that the "remarkable relationship" will remain calm in 1996. Both countries are locked into the free trade framework. Moreover, while Lloyd Axworthy became Minister of Foreign

Affairs in a January 1996 cabinet shuffle, any temptations he may still have to put a greater distance between Canada and the U.S. will probably be held in check by the Prime Minister's cautious approach, which has so strikingly set the tone for Canada-U.S. relations since 1993. Besides, Chrétien, his cabinet and Canadians in general will no doubt be heavily pre-occupied in 1996, not with the U.S., but with domestic affairs.

NOTES

1   The White House, Office of the Press Secretary, "Remarks by the President to the Canadian Parliament," February 23, 1995.

2   For a discussion of the cycles of tension in Canada-U.S. relations, see Joseph T. Jockel, "The Canada-United States relationship after the third round: the emergence of semi-institutionalized management," *International Journal*, XL, no. 4 (Autumn, 1985), 689-715.

3   Liberal Party of Canada, *Creating Opportunity: The Liberal Plan for Canada*, (Ottawa: September 1993), Chapter 8.

4   Lloyd Axworthy, "Canadian Foreign Policy: A Liberal Party Perspective," *Canadian Foreign Policy*, 1, no.1 (Winter 1992/93), 7. Axworthy became Minister of Foreign Affairs in January 1996.

5   In 1972 Mitchell Sharp, then Secretary of State for External Affairs identified three options:
    — Canada can seek to maintain more or less its present relationship with the United States with a minimum of policy adjustments.
    — Canada can move deliberately toward closer integration with the United States.
    — Canada can pursue a comprehensive long-term strategy to develop and strengthen the Canadian economy and other aspects of its national life and in the process reduce present Canadian vulnerability. Mitchell Sharp, "Canada-U.S. Relations: Options for the Future," *International Perspectives*, Special Issue, Autumn 1972.

6   For a good introduction to NAFTA see Gilbert R. Winham and Heather A. Grant, "NAFTA: An Overview," in Donald Barry, ed., *Toward A North American Community: Canada, the United States, and Mexico*, (Westview Press: Boulder, CO: 1995), 15-33.

7   A tentative agreement to reduce Canadian exports of softwood to the United States and to raise taxes on softwood shipments, either through increased stumpage fees or an export tax was reached in mid-February 1996. Negotiation over the details of implementation continued through March in an effort to meet an April 1, 1996 deadline. See Drew Fagan, "Canada to cut softwood exports," *The Globe and Mail*, February 17, 1996, A1, A2 and Peter Morton, "Canada back to bargaining over softwood exports today," *Financial Post*, March 20, 1996, 3.

8   For similar reasons related to Congressional reluctance and opposi-
     tion, Clinton administration officials welcomed Canadian support for
     and contributions to the assistance package to Mexico in the wake of
     that country's peso crisis.
9   See also the discussion of Canadian defence policy in Chapter 3.
10   Canada, Department of Foreign Affairs and International Trade,
     Canada and the World (Ottawa: Canada Communication Group,
     1995), 24.
11   United States, White House, *A National Strategy of Engagement and
     Enlargement* (Washington, D.C., July 1994).
12   Remarks by Deputy CINCNORAD Major General J.D. O'Blenis to a
     conference sponsored by the Canadian Institute of Strategic Studies
     and Center for Strategic and International Studies on "Rethinking the
     Canada-United States Military Relationship," Ottawa, March 19-20, 1994.
13   Eric Schmitt, "Foreign Policy Plan of G.O.P. Is Set Back Over Missiles,"
     New York Times, February 16, 1995, A9.
14   Helen Dewar, "Senate Backs Missile Plan, Adds Funding for
     Weapons", *The Washington Post,* September 7, 1995, 2.
15   Canada, Department of National Defence, *1994 Defence White Paper*,
     (Ottawa: Minister of Supply and Services Canada, 1994), 26.
16   See Canada, Department of National Defence, Maritime Command,
     *The Naval Vision: Charting The Course for Canada's Maritime Forces
     into the 21st Century* (Halifax: 1994), 17-25.
17   Paul Koring, "Chrétien hedges on Bosnia mission", *The Globe and
     Mail*, October 20, 1995, A5.
18   Cited in Jeff Sallot, "Canada Commits force of 1,000 to Bosnian
     Mission," *The Globe and Mail*, December 7, 1995, A1.
19   Jeff Sallot, "'Moral obligation' seen in Bosnia," *The Globe and Mail*,
     December 6, 1995, A1, A6.
20   Quoted in Sallot, "Canada Commits," A6.
21   *1994 Defence White Paper*, 37.
22   For an excellent overview, see Alan M. Schwartz, "Canada-U.S.
     Environmental Relations: A Look at the 1990s," *American Review of
     Canadian Studies*, 24, no. 4 (Winter 1994), 489-508.
23   See Margaret Kriz, "The Green Card," *National Journal*, no. 37,
     September 16, 1995, 2262-67.
24   The standard history of U.S. policy towards the Quebec independence
     movement remains Jean-François Lisée, *In the Eye of the Eagle*
     (Toronto: Harper Collins 1990).
25   Text courtesy of U.S. State Department.
26   See endnote 1, above.
27   See endnote 1.
28   Rogers and Wells, "Advisory Memorandum Regarding the Effect of
     Independence of Quebec Upon Treaties and Agreements with the
     United States of America," March 7, 1995. Text courtesy of the
     Délégation générale du Québec, New York.
29   Quebec, National Assembly, Draft Bill, "An Act respecting the sover-
     eignty of Québec," First session, 35th Legislature, 1994.

30   Charles E. Roh, Jr. "The Implications for U.S. Trade Policy of an
      Independent Quebec," "Decision Quebec" Series, October 5, 1995.
      (Washington: Center for Strategic and International Studies and
      Ottawa: Centre for Trade Policy and Law).
31   Robert A. Young, *The Secession of Quebec and the Future of Canada*,
      (Montreal: McGill-Queen's University Press, 1995), 203, 204.

The UN System:
50th Anniversary Review

Reflections: Ambassadors' Round Table

VII ROBERT FOWLER

VIII LOUISE FRÉCHETTE

IX GEOFFREY A.H. PEARSON

VII

ROBERT R. FOWLER

The UN at 50 finds itself in "mid-life crisis." It has not fulfilled all of its youthful expectations, it has yet to find its post-Cold War role, and it is hamstrung, politically and financially, by the ambivalence of its principal shareholder, the United States. Nevertheless, at the 50th anniversary Special Commemorative Meeting last October, Prime Minister Chrétien and the leaders of all the UN member states re-affirmed their commitment to an organization which would have to be renewed and invigorated to meet the global challenges of the next half century. How can the UN be in such trouble while at the same time continuing to be considered indispensable? Let me suggest some answers to these questions.

The *raison d'être* of the UN was the collective determination of the nations who were achieving victory in the Second World War to avoid a repetition of such carnage. It was designed, first and foremost, as a collective system in which the major powers assumed the principal responsibility, through the Security Council, for maintaining international peace and security. The Cold War, however, produced a superpower stalemate that paralyzed the UN system of collective security. These inauspicious circumstances did, it is true, give rise to the concept of peacekeeping: the monitoring under UN colours of a cease-fire with impartial, lightly armed troops provided by member states, a formula that helped to prevent resort to arms but fell far short of enabling enforcement of peace as envisaged by the UN Charter.

With the end of the Cold War it was too quickly assumed that the UN could finally discharge its original mandate, a view that was reinforced by the success of the Gulf War. This assumption, and the expectations, however unrealistic, that accompanied it, are now being closely scrutinized. The end of the Cold War meant that traditional rivalries—ethnic, religious, racial, territorial, economic and tribal—could be removed from the freezer to which they had been relatively briefly, but unnaturally, assigned.[1] These rivalries proliferated, unchecked by super-power hegemony, in the immediate post-Cold War period. The international community was simply unprepared to deal with the vicious wars and rebellions spawned along these all too traditional fault-lines.

Faced with war, anarchy and chaos in various parts of the globe, the member states—effectively the members of the board of the UN—failed to give the United Nations the political direction and resources required to allow the Organization to respond effectively. Instead, they attempted to apply Cold War concepts (e.g., "classic" peacekeeping) to situations (e.g., the former Yugoslavia) that required deep and long-term commitment and more robust responses. And they did so without making the consequent changes in UN mandates and resource requirements. My point is not so much that the world remains troubled, but that the members of the international community have tended to prescribe old-think solutions to very current problems such as those of failed states. In doing so they have at best been loath to take the necessary significant risks or to make the large investment required to see the job done right. At worst, member states simply shirked or abdicated responsibility and accountability for finding effective solutions. The result has been frustration over the "UN's failure" in Somalia and what was its supposed inability to stop the fighting in the former Yugoslavia. These situations have caused an unprecedented outpouring of criticism of "the UN's impotence." In fact the recent history of the UN's unfulfilled promise is one that has been characterized by member states simultaneously raising unrealistic expectations of what the UN can achieve, while withholding from it the means and the mandates to accomplish the missions assigned to it.

It was not "the UN" that decided to deploy a huge force to Somalia to bring about, *inter alia*, "... the early implementation of the disarmament of all Somali parties, including movements and factions...."[2] at a total cost of U.S. $1.5 billion. It was not "the UN" that came up with the concept of "safe areas"[3] in Bosnia and then refused to provide either the troops or the mandate to defend them. These were Security Council decisions and it was in the Security Council that the compromises and omissions were brokered and agreed to.

To suggest, then, that somehow the UN has failed or, more particularly, has failed the most important and influential of its members, is simply a travesty of the facts. It was not "the UN" which failed to stop the genocide in Rwanda. The Secretary-General of the UN repeatedly called for troops and a mandate to halt the slaughter. Member states simply failed to respond. The will to do so was not there. Canada's Major-General Dallaire, his tiny staff and his enormously brave, under-strength Ghanaian battalion were not reinforced and thus could not effectively intervene. Whenever I hear the diatribes against the UN which appear to be becoming increasingly popular, I am reminded of Pogo's wise counsel (*hommage* à Oliver Hazard Perry): "We has seen the enemy, and they is us."

The UN is neither a country nor a supranational authority. It is an organization of sovereign states that can only do what its members decide should be done. Its successes are those of its members, as are its failures. The UN is merely what we make of it, no more, no less. Unfortunately, however, member states have found that it is all too easy to make the UN a convenient scapegoat for their own failure of political will, failure to provide adequate resources, or failure to risk casualties.

The reasons for this abdication of political responsibility are various. Members of the European Union, for instance, appear, quite understandably, to be most immediately concerned with finding and maintaining political consensus on the issues of the day, rather than with providing leadership to the broader community of nations. Isolationist and unilateralist tendencies have strengthened in the

United States and, coupled with a growing reluctance to put American lives at risk, have made it difficult for the U.S. Administration to lead by example. Most other countries continue to place rather narrowly defined national interests well ahead of the collective good of the international community.

This vacuum of political will is revealed most starkly in the financial crisis faced by the UN. One of the labels frequently applied to the UN is "bankrupt." The Secretary-General himself has so declared in an article in the *The Washington Post* in August '95, referring to the financial crisis caused by the failure of member states to pay their assessed contributions. The crisis is real, and serious enough to have forced the UN to freeze all payments to troop-contributing nations, as well as recruitment, procurement, overtime, travel and other day-to-day expenditures. In this context, I am pleased to note that not a single peacekeeper has been withdrawn as a consequence, despite the fact that a large number of soldiers from some of the poorest countries in the world continue to perform their peacekeeping assignments without compensation from the UN.

The Secretary-General's remarks do, however, need to be qualified. The UN is not bankrupt in the strict sense that its liabilities exceed its assets, but its assets are mainly in the form of unpaid contributions - uncollected and, in some cases, uncollectible receivables. The UN is meeting its current requirements: in the 18 months to June 30, 1995, it collected about U.S.$1.8 billion in contributions, and expended U.S.$1.5 billion.

The UN cannot go broke because it does not and cannot borrow externally. It cannot spend more than it receives in contributions. So, when contributions do not match appropriations, the UN has no choice but to curtail expenditures. It maintains its liquidity by over-budgeting, under-spending and delaying payment of the amounts it owes to troop contributors like Canada. It also leaves undone some of the new priorities that member states have assigned to it, some of which are significant.

This, clearly, results neither in sound budgetary practice nor in good management, but is the direct result of the refusal of the majority of member states to pay their assessments on time, in full and without conditions. As of November 15, 1995, only 15 out of 185 member states had fully paid up both their regular and their peacekeeping contributions that were due the end of January, 1995. The total of outstanding assessed contributions stood at U.S.$2.7 billion on November 15, 1995. The financial crisis, in my view, raises the question, not only of economic ability to pay, but also of the political support which the Organization should be able to expect from its members.

That this situation has arisen despite the fact that all UN appropriations, as well as the scale of assessments by which they are apportioned, are approved by consensus must give us pause for serious reflection. The vast majority of UN members appear to be quite content to approve programs, appropriations and assessments, apparently without any serious intention of honouring the obligations which they voluntarily incur.

There are two sorts of countries which receive a special break through the nature of the agreed scale of assessment. The first is a large group (87) of the poorer countries who pay less than their percentage share of world income. The second is the United States which, according to the formula to which it had agreed, should be contributing a little more than 30 percent of the UN's regular budget costs but now pays no more than 25 percent. Recently, the U.S. unilaterally restricted its contributions to peacekeeping expenses, which in 1995 are three times higher than regular budget expenses, from 31 percent to 25 percent. This negated not only the validity of the formula, but also the fundamental premise that the permanent members of the Security Council have special rights (they create, and can veto, peacekeeping operations and mandates) and obligations (such as paying an increment above the regular budget assessment which in the case of the U.S. is the difference between 25 percent and 31 percent). In fact, all this is, unfortunately, a little academic in that the United States actually pays far less than 25 percent of either the peacekeeping or the regular expenses of the United Nations. By mid-November 1995, the U.S. had paid only 13.2 percent of the UN's current annual regular budget and 11.9 percent of the equivalent peacekeeping budget.

In the post-Cold War era there is only one surviving super-power—and the world community looks to the United States for leadership. Nowhere is this more evident than in the United Nations. Yet the main source of the UN's financial difficulties is the United States. As of November 15, 1995, the U.S. owed over U.S.$414 million of the U.S.$646 million outstanding on the regular budget, and over U.S.$817 million of the more than U.S.$2 billion outstanding on peacekeeping contributions. Fully 44 percent of all monies owing were, as of November 15, 1995, owed by the United States. In 1995, only 22 countries had paid their regular budget contributions by the January 31 deadline. The United States was not one of them, but Canada was, and so was Micronesia. It is hard to lead when you are so far in arrears.

One of the most worrisome things about the present state of the UN, therefore, is the attitude of its most important member. The United States has called for reform of the UN bureaucracy, and reforms are certainly necessary. At 50 years of age the UN needs renewal and reform. Some of its organs and functions have become obsolete (in some cases through their own success, e.g., the apparatus created to combat apartheid) and the bureaucrats involved in them are now redundant. These functions should be eliminated and the officials reassigned or released. Management reform has indeed begun, but it needs to be applied both forcefully and intelligently.

The U.S. is right in holding that there is a need to eliminate obsolete, redundant and low-value programs and activities. This problem needs to be approached not only within the context of the UN regular budget, but as part of a coordinated and comprehensive action across the UN system.

We Canadians also support review of the UN budget and administrative processes, and agree that the UN's oversight mechanisms need to be made more transparent, accountable and efficient.

The U.S. has also called for a revised, equitable scale of peacekeeping assessments reflecting the realities of each country's financial strength, and Canada very much agrees with this approach. Such a move should, however, focus on the regular scale of assessments, on which the peacekeeping scale is based. The scale should continue to reflect the special responsibility of the permanent members of the Security Council, and provide a measure of relief to developing and least-developed countries.

It is nevertheless disturbing that calls by the United States for reform of the scale of assessments have been accompanied by unilateral measures which run counter to the Charter obligations which bind all member states. As noted above, the U.S. has passed legislation which unilaterally reduces its share of the peacekeeping budget to 25 percent, effective October 1, 1995. Canada has made it clear that it cannot support a unilateral decision by one member state to reduce its assessed contribution. Aside from the legal and financial ramifications for the member state and the United Nations, the concern has been expressed by Canada that such action could lead other members to attempt to abrogate their Charter obligations.

When this article went to press in early 1996, it was not at all clear whether the U.S. Administration would be successful in negotiating a deal with Congress that would allow for the payment of its dues and arrears or, indeed, what kind of a deal it might be. Would such a deal eliminate all U.S. arrears or provide for a payment schedule spread out over several years, which would, of course, have the effect of prolonging the UN's financial crisis in its currently acute form? Would conditions be attached to such a restructuring of the U.S. debt to the United Nations, by, of course, the Americans?

Following the debate about the UN in the U.S. Congress leads to the conclusion that a significant number of U.S. legislators would be happy to see the United States out of the UN. While such a development is by no means likely or in any way desirable, it is mooted in UN corridors and does deserve analysis.

The UN would be poorer, not just for the U.S. financial contribution, but also for the active participation of a strong and generous country which has traditionally stood for the best in human aspirations. Most countries would have to pay a greater share of the UN's expenses (Canada's would rise from its present 3.07 percent to just over 4 percent). The UN's pursuit of international peace and security would be severely constrained, and, in many instances, would likely become nugatory. The UN could certainly pursue its worthwhile activities in the economic and social sectors, but the Security Council's role would probably be supplanted by other mechanisms outside the UN framework. In this scenario the Gulf War, the intervention of the Multinational Force (MNF) in Haiti, and the North Atlantic Treaty Organization's (NATO) role in the former Yugoslavia could all have been undertaken but without the sanction of the UN, and these examples could provide the paradigm for the future; and a more parochial future it would be.

In any event, the use of multilateral coalitions to undertake enforcement action on behalf of the UN is in fact being increasingly advocated, only in part because the UN is so desperately short of financial resources. This issue lies at the heart of the debate over the security vocation of the UN in the post Cold War era to which I referred at the outset.

For example, the Secretary-General following the line he first put forward in his Supplement to an Agenda for Peace, argued in

September 1995 against a military role for the UN in the enforcement of the Bosnian Peace Agreement.[4] He noted that the Organization simply did not have the resources, financial and material, to
conduct an operation of the size and complexity of the NATO
Implementation Force (IFOR). Given the United Nations Protection
Force (UNPROFOR's) cost, at the time, of U.S.$5 million per day, the
Secretary-General knew he would never have access to the resources
required to field a force three times the size of the resources committed in the former Yugoslavia, however ironic it might be that 20,000
UN troops had been sent to Bosnia to keep the peace when there
clearly had been no peace to keep, and yet 60,000 NATO fighting
troops were to replace them when peace seemed to be at hand.

While it can be argued that the use of such coalitions are consistent with the provisions of the Charter, if sanctioned by the Security
Council,[5] their use holds two very real dangers. The first is that we
run the risk of legitimizing "spheres of influence" for the major powers. It is only the major powers that have the necessary political
influence to obtain the sanction of the Security Council for enforcement action and the military muscle, including complex command
and control facilities, for any such operation. Over time this type of
intervention can only lead to a geostrategic situation of counterbal-
ancing influences that would be eerily reminiscent, if not exactly of
the Cold War, then, perhaps, of the period before the First World War
began in the Balkans.

The second suggests that an examination of why such coalitions
were formed to deal with the takeover of Kuwait, an illegal regime
in Haiti and ethnic cleansing in the former Yugoslavia, but were not
launched to limit the ravages of civil war in the Sudan or Liberia (inci-
dentally, more people have been killed in the Liberian civil war than
in Bosnia) or genocide in Rwanda, would, I submit, lead to the conclusion that multilateral coalitions have been highly selective in their
determination of what constituted a "threat to international peace and
security." This cannot be what the framers of Article 1 of the Charter
had in mind. Having signalled through its action in Haiti that respect
for the principles of sovereignty and non-interference in the internal
affairs of states has to be informed by moral and humanitarian
considerations, the Security Council should be at pains to ensure that
this new approach is not applied in a discriminatory manner. To do
otherwise would be to risk validating some of the most cynical
stereotypes of the post-Cold War North-South divide.

I have explored at some length the political and financial crisis at the UN because its impact is so pervasive in this time of the Fiftieth Anniversary, and because it is so critically important, from a Canadian perspective, that it be solved and soon. The effective and impartial maintenance of international stability remains crucial to us. I continue to believe, as Lester Pearson and so many other Canadians have done over the last 50 years, that the UN is the best hope for maintaining order in our ever more complex world. Our livelihood and standard of living depend very directly on a stable, predictable international environment: predictable in the sense that business people want to know that they can conduct their affairs over the long term in a peaceful environment, but also in the sense that the rules and regulations they encounter will be fairly and uniformly applied. Some of the UN's greatest successes have been in setting standards for acceptable international behaviour, whether it is the field of environment, fisheries management, aviation and communications or the maintenance of health standards and respect for human rights; and all of these contribute very directly to Canadian well-being.

Canada has not been a pioneer and leader in UN peacekeeping simply because of our reliance on a stable trading environment. Our concern for international stability has been informed from the outset by a strong moral, humanitarian impulse. The UN provides us with the mechanism and the legitimacy to engage situations such as those in Rwanda or Haiti or the former Yugoslavia; neither Canada, nor any other country, has the resources or the authority to "go it alone."

Some claim that smaller nations need the UN more than larger ones. The UN does, however, serve the interests of the large and powerful very directly. Peacekeepers on the Golan Heights, mine clearers in Cambodia and observers in Tajikistan, Liberia and Georgia all make it less likely that the most powerful will have to intervene. No nation can realistically assume a "let it happen" posture in the face of the calamities which so routinely beset most of the world.

Every nation needs the UN. Every nation benefits from the acceptance by the international community of standards of behaviour. Every nation needs the UN because there are some problems that do not lend themselves to solution by any one country, no matter how powerful. The international trade in narcotics, terrorism, diseases such as AIDS, and environmental degradation are cases in point. Every nation benefits from the UN because it is less expensive and more efficient to tackle such problems collectively than to attempt to do so individually or unilaterally. This applies equally to issues of peace and security and to the sharing of the costs of peacekeeping operations. Stability in Central America, democracy in Haiti, peace in the Middle East, and order in Africa serve the interests of every one of the member states of the United Nations.

The retreat from accountability that I have been describing is also occurring in the development area. It is not only in Canada that budgets allocated to development assistance are declining; Western Europeans, even some of the Nordics, historically among the most generous of donors, are reducing their development budgets, and the world's fastest growing economies in Southeast Asia and Latin America show little sign of taking up the slack, at least in any significant way. Japan is one of the few countries that is bucking the trend and giving generously.

Part of the rationalization for this is, of course, that the "rich" are no longer becoming richer at anything like the rate they experienced only a few years ago. Although the gap between rich and poor continues to grow, Northern nations are less willing to part with their share of a pie that, however large, seems to be shrinking. The retreat from accountability thus seems to be accompanied by a retreat into new forms of "beggar thy neighbour" attitudes, and this state of affairs cannot but diminish all of us.

The development side of the equation is further complicated by the fear on the part of developing countries that the "reform" agenda being pushed by Western countries, principally the United States, is designed primarily to provide the rationale for cutting funds available to the UN's development programs. What we might view as at worst irrelevant and at best duplicative agencies (United Nations Industrial Development Organization, for instance) the developing world views as organs that provide a focus for their efforts at industrialization. One way of mitigating the hostility of four-fifths of the UN membership to reform would be for the developed world to undertake to direct into development programs any monies freed up as a result of the elimination of overlap and duplication. However, the prevailing climate I have described above makes this an extremely unlikely proposition.

In conclusion, I would simply state what has become all too obvious: there is a desperate need to add political muscle to the rhetoric of last October's commemorative session. A solid, predictable base of financial support is obviously *sine qua non*, and political pressure must be focused on those who enjoy the benefits of representation without the responsibilities of taxation (to repeat Prime Minister John Major's evocative phrase). More than that, however, member states, in particular those on the Security Council, must learn to discipline themselves in the face of the "CNN factor." Another resolution is not necessarily the best answer to the latest atrocity on "Headline News." Empty bluffs and further posturing will only diminish the effectiveness of the Security Council.

The Council has two choices. The first is to respond to each crisis, or possible commitment, with a comprehensive, well thought out strategy—involving if necessary the use of Chapter VII authority—designed to accomplish political objectives and to prepare the ground for post-conflict peace-building. Appropriate means must be given to the UN to carry out clear and achievable mandates that enjoy the general support of the international community and of troop-contributing nations. The second choice—if all those elements cannot be brought together—is probably to resist the "CNN factor" and do nothing. If we have learned one lesson from our recent peacekeeping experience, it is precisely that ill-conceived and ill-equipped operations are bound not to solve the problem on the ground while bringing the Organization into disrepute. UN operations must be given appropriate and very carefully considered and practicable mandates and the human and material resources with which to achieve success. Above all, UN missions must have political objectives which have been understood and agreed to within the Security Council and are explainable and explained among the general membership, particularly the troop-contributing community.

There are a number of issues critical to the future viability and effectiveness of the UN that I have not touched upon; the most important of these is indeed Security Council reform. The legitimacy of Council decisions is under attack. Expansion of the Council is one, but not the only, remedy; a greater sense of its responsibility and accountability for global well-being is called for.

The reader might be forgiven for coming to the conclusion that my prognosis of the UN's future is uniformly bleak. It is not. The UN continues to register impressive achievements in the eradication of disease, in the elimination of poverty, and in assisting failed states to put the pieces of their societies back together. It is also beginning to demonstrate that it understands the need to match objectives and resources (its efforts in both Haiti and Angola suggest that this lesson is being learned, albeit slowly and painfully).

The UN is also beginning to take the requirement for reform seriously. The Secretary-General has set up an Efficiency Board with a mandate to identify cost-saving measures and efficiencies that could be implemented within the Secretariat. He has also set up thematic task forces (for poverty, women's issues and environmental sustainability) that will attempt to rationalize the Organisation's efforts in these areas. For their part, member states of every ideological persuasion are beginning to see that their interests are best served by an effective UN that also continues to benefit from the participation of its largest shareholder.

The current challenges to the Organization, as I have described them, are clearly enormous, and the solutions are anything but clear; they are certainly not guaranteed. It is the exercise of political will, or the failure to exercise it, that will determine the outcome.

The UN deserves Canada's continued steadfast support. It is in our own national interest to offer such support, particularly in the current crisis of resources and confidence. One of our most pressing challenges in the next few years will be to convince others that it is also in their best interest to ensure that the UN is able to respond effectively to the tasks we give it.

NOTES

This chapter was written in close collaboration with the staff of the Canadian Mission to the United Nations, most particularly, the Deputy Permanent Representative, Ambassador David Karsgaard, and Counsellor for Financial Affairs, Sam Hanson. All responsibility for content and editorial opinion is, however, entirely my own.

1   The irruption of traditional rivalries and the challenges they pose to the UN has been explored by many observers, including Professor Thomas Flanck, "A Holistic Approach to Building Peace," 25th Vienna Seminar, Peacemaking and Peacekeeping, Royal Institute of International Affairs, 1993; Thomas G. Weiss, "Intervention: Whither the United Nations?," *The Washington Quarterly*, 17, no. 1, (Winter 1994), and Mohamed Sahoun, *Somalia: The Missed Opportunities* (Washington, D.C.: U.S. Institute of Peace, 1994).

2   Security Council Resolution 837 (1993) of 6 June 1993, operative paragraph 3.

3   Security Council Resolutions 824 (1993) of 6 May 1993 and 836 (1993) of 4 June 1993.

4   In his letter to the President of the Security Council, S/1995/804 of 18 September 1995, the Secretary-General said "the aggravation of the Organization's financial crisis makes it even more unrealistic to envisage UNPROFOR being enlarged to perform the task that will be required."

5   Charter of the United Nations, chapters VII and VIII.

VIII

LOUISE FRÉCHETTE

The UN celebrated its 50th anniversary a few months ago amidst widespread criticism of the Organization's effectiveness. The mantras are familiar: "paralyzed in the face of crisis," "incapable of reforming itself," "weighed down by a bloated and ineffective bureaucracy" and "on the verge of bankruptcy." It is hard to relate these sombre headlines to the enthusiastic and confident atmosphere I found in New York in January 1992. The end of the Cold War had led to an unprecedented degree of cooperation in the Security Council. The last veto had been cast more than 18 months earlier, on May 31, 1990. Building on this new found comity, the UN had undertaken several successful, high-profile missions notably in Namibia and Central America.

Nothing exemplified the newly found cohesion better than the UN-mandated campaign to reverse Iraq's invasion of Kuwait. The international community had come together to restore Kuwait's sovereignty, protect Iraq's Kurdish population and dismantle its program for the development of weapons of mass destruction.

The election of a new Secretary-General, Mr. Boutros Boutros-Ghali, who took over from Mr. Perez de Cuellar on January 1, 1992, signalled the beginning of a new era in the Secretariat as well. The main topic of conversation among members of the Secretariat and the local missions in those early days of January was the imminent nomination of the Secretary-General's new management team.

Mr. Boutros-Ghali's election had been greeted with mixed feelings. His vast experience of world affairs and his exceptional intelligence were widely recognized, but doubts lingered about his capacity to steer the Organization through what promised to be a most challenging time. Would he be able to breathe new life into the Secretariat and force greater cohesion within the sprawling UN system? Was he too much of a diplomat to confront powerful member states and impose respect for the office he now held? Would he have the stamina to keep up with the brutal pace imposed on a Secretary-General?

Mr. Boutros-Ghali quickly proved these fears to be misplaced. He is leading the United Nations with a firm hand and has shown a surprising—and welcome—propensity to speak his mind. He has an enormous capacity for work—and little time for the niceties of diplomatic life. He is a hands-on Secretary-General, deeply involved in the management of the numerous political crises that invariably land in the UN's lap. Like all his predecessors he has had to walk the fine line between serving the interests of the member states and protecting the integrity of the Organization. He has done so with great skill.

The job of Secretary-General of the United Nations has to be one of the most thankless on earth. Power rests almost entirely with the member states. They are quick to take credit for the UN's successes, but are only too prone to blame the Organization for failures of which they are often the cause. Mr. Boutros-Ghali is remarkably philosophical on this subject. As he has said himself, if it is helpful to the world to use the UN as a scapegoat, he is ready to oblige.

At the end of January 1992 the Security Council met at the Heads of State level—a first in the history of the Organization. The declaration adopted on that occasion, though cast in broad terms, had far-reaching implications for the UN. It reflected a vision of international security that went beyond the concerns of states to include those of individuals and their rights to economic, social and political security. Expressing their willingness to act together in defence of collective security, the members of the Security Council mandated the Secretary-General to prepare an "analysis and recommendations on ways of strengthening and making more efficient, within the framework and provisions of the Charter, the capacity of the United Nations for preventive diplomacy, for peacemaking and for peacekeeping."

Mr. Boutros-Ghali's answer to this call was *Agenda for Peace*, a seminal document issued in June 1992. In preparing his report, the Secretary-General consulted broadly with member states, regional agencies, non-governmental organizations and others to solicit ideas and proposals. Canada, jointly with Australia, New Zealand and the Nordic countries, presented a submission that reflected the views of a group of countries long involved in peacekeeping.

Agenda for Peace offered a forward-looking vision of the UN's role. As the Secretary-General wrote:

In these past months, a conviction has grown, among nations large and small, that an opportunity has been regained to achieve the great objectives of the Charter—a United Nations capable of maintaining peace and security, of securing justice and in the words of the Charter, "social progress and better standards of life in larger freedom". This opportunity must not be squandered. The Organization must never again be crippled as it was in the era that has now passed.

To achieve this goal, the Secretary-General put forward a number of proposals and introduced several new concepts, including the preventive deployment of peacekeeping forces, a stand-by arrangement system and measures to respond more swiftly. The report went beyond the mandate given by the Security Council to address postconflict peace-building, reminding member states that conflicts too often find their origin in poverty and inequality. It also promoted cooperation with regional organizations.

Member states gave broad support to *Agenda for Peace*, the focal point of most speeches to the 1992 General Assembly. It proved difficult, however, to translate this support into meaningful resolutions in the General Assembly. Most of the practical suggestions contained in the report were eventually incorporated in resolutions emanating from the Special Committee on Peacekeeping. Canada, as Chair of the Committee's Working Group, led the drafting and negotiating process. Attempts to reflect the more politically significant elements of *Agenda for Peace* were, however, less successful. A number of the more conservative member states, determined to preserve intact the concepts of sovereignty and non-intervention in internal affairs of states, insisted on repeating in the resolutions the exact wording of the Charter, thus making the drafting exercise basically meaningless. This experience convinced those who had been thinking of proposing a full-scale reform of the Charter to postpone this endeavour until more propitious times.

Although little progress was made in codifying the new concepts of security defined in *Agenda for Peace*, some of the more ambitious forms of peacekeeping were already being tested on the ground. In November 1991 the UN sent an advance mission to Cambodia which would pave the way for the UN Transitional Authority in Cambodia (UNTAC), established in March 1992.

UNTAC was the largest and most ambitious mission ever undertaken by the UN. It was a complex operation involving nearly 20,000 military and civilian personnel and performing a wide range of functions, including supervising a cease-fire, demobilizing and disarming the warring factions, repatriating refugees, organizing elections and disabling landmines, as well as developing related education programs. Furthermore, the UN was given the daunting task of supervising five key ministries and implementing a vast program of reconstruction and rehabilitation.

To say that UNTAC was greeted with a certain amount of skepticism is an understatement. I heard predictions of disaster from every quarter. How could the UN, so notorious for its inefficiency and sluggishness, meet this impossible challenge? The mission got off to a shaky start and in the early days its performance owed more to the ingenuity and dedication of its military and civilian members than to precise planning and organization.

By the time it ended in 1993, UNTAC could be described as a genuine success. Refugees had been returned to their homes, an election had been held, a legitimate government had been installed and the country enjoyed relative peace for the first time in decades.

Though successful, this mission was to highlight many of the difficulties that the UN would later encounter in similar large-scale operations. For one, the mission's mandate was extensive and the resources required never fully materialized, particularly the military personnel needed for the demobilization of the warring factions.

Second, the mission consisted of a large civilian component which placed additional demands on the military forces who had to ensure their safety. Problems of coordination and command and control arose. These obstacles—the lack of resources, the need to coordinate the various actors on the ground and the ill-defined lines of authority—would be among the many issues that would resurface in later operations, particularly in Somalia and the Balkans.

For all its innovative aspects, UNTAC essentially fitted the mould of classic peacekeeping missions. A peace agreement was in existence and the various factions had agreed to its deployment. The mission to Somalia followed a different logic.

When the Security Council decided in April 1992 to create the United Nations Operation in Somalia (UNOSOM) it was responding first and foremost to a humanitarian concern. With the country in near-anarchy, many of its people were threatened with starvation. The mandate given to UNOSOM was to monitor the ceasefire concluded in March 1992 by the warring factions and provide security for the delivery of humanitarian aid. But the conditions were not ripe for such an operation. The ceasefire was short-lived and without an effective national authority the country fell deeper into chaos. UN peacekeepers, caught between the factions, threatened by all sides and too few in number to impose respect for their authority, were eventually reduced to protecting themselves as well as they could in this hostile environment.

As the situation deteriorated and UNOSOM confirmed its inability to respond, appeals to "do something" intensified. In December 1992, at the initiative of the United States, UNOSOM I was replaced by a U.S.-led, multinational coalition of member states. The Unified Task Force (UNITAF) was authorized explicitly under Chapter VII of the Charter to create, by force if necessary, a secure environment for the delivery of humanitarian aid, and to disarm factions before handing the operation back to the UN.

This was a landmark decision. For the first time, the international community seemed to recognize that humanitarian concerns and therefore the rights of people (as opposed to the rights of countries) were a legitimate basis for action by the Security Council. The Security Council decision also consecrated the use of force as a legitimate response to an exceptionally severe humanitarian crisis. While some developing countries expressed concern over the precedent this created, UNITAF was widely welcomed, including in Africa, and a large number of countries quickly signed up for the mission.

UNITAF was only a partial success. With security provided by the troops, food aid reached the population in sufficient quantities to avert famine. But the factions were not disarmed and when UNITAF was replaced by UNOSOM II in May 1993 there had been little progress in stabilizing the political situation. Once again, the UN was plagued by resources insufficient to earn the respect of the factions. The death of 17 American Rangers was a turning point for the mission. Public support in the United States evaporated and the emboldened Somali factions intensified their attacks on the peace-keeping forces. The last year of the mission was a bitter, humiliating experience for the UN. When UNOSOM II was finally withdrawn, after several successive reductions in the size of the contingents, there were few voices to argue for the continuation of a UN presence. UNOSOM had become an orphan, without support or promoters.

This was never the case for the UN mission in the former Yugoslavia. The conflict touched a broad cross-section of UN member states: European countries worried about an extension of the conflict to other parts of Europe, Muslim countries anxious to support the government in Bosnia-Herzegovina, the United States pressured by its public opinion to do something short of committing its own troops, and the many countries like Canada which felt the senseless killing and ethnic cleansing could not be left unchallenged. In my three years at the UN, no other issue generated as much passion and as much soul-searching. I can recall endless discussions with colleagues, some of them at social occasions, about the best course of action. For many, the war in Bosnia was a clear case of foreign aggression against a sovereign member state entitled to protection under Chapter VII of the Charter. For others, it was a civil war which called for an essentially humanitarian and human rights response, directed equally at all parties to the conflict.

The United Nations Protection Force (UNPROFOR) had begun as a traditional peacekeeping operation in Croatia. With the deployment in Bosnia-Herzegovina, the mission acquired a new character. Operating in an extremely volatile environment, peacekeepers faced constant challenge in fulfilling their mission of protecting the lifelines first to Sarajevo—its airport and land routes—and, later, to all of Bosnian territory. In New York, sympathy rested overwhelmingly with the Muslims and every new barbaric act by the Bosnian Serbs, such as the bombing of the Sarajevo market and the attacks on

Srebrenica and other enclaves, increased the pressures for more robust action on the part of the UN forces.

The incremental expansion of the mission's mandate, "mission-creep" as it became known, created two kinds of problems for the peacekeepers. First, while additional responsibilities were added to the mission, the necessary resources failed to materialize. Indeed, there were instances when the Security Council knew full well that UNPROFOR would not have the means to enforce the mandate it was being given. I recall vividly the Security Council's meeting which declared Srebrenica a "safe area." By referring to Chapter VII of the Charter, the resolution implied a readiness to use force if necessary to protect the safe area. Yet it was known that all UNPROFOR could do was to dispatch a small contingent of about 150 Canadian peace-keepers to Srebrenica. I pleaded with the President of the Security Council to define the mandate in terms that would reflect the reality more accurately, but to no avail. The UN paid dearly for its pretence. When Srebrenica fell, the UN was rightly blamed for letting down those it had seemingly promised to protect.

Second, UNPROFOR was asked to perform tasks that often seemed contradictory. As the mission undertook new mandates requiring the use of force, it did not abandon its other traditional peacekeeping functions. As a result, several tasks depending on impartiality and consent for their execution were being jeopardized by parallel but more robust operations. The co-existence of Chapters VI and VII mandates had not been tried before. Each time a new step was taken—no-fly zone, close air support to protect the peacekeep-ers, full-fledged air strikes—there was a risk that the mission would be pushed over the edge, placing the troops in grave danger.

One particularly innovative aspect of the mission in the former Yugoslavia was the unprecedented partnership which was forged between the UN and NATO in 1993. This partnership did not develop without significant difficulties. Disputes arose over issues of command and control as well as the coordination of the efforts of the respective organizations. The battle of the "two keys"—the need for both UN and NATO commanders to agree for air strikes to be launched—had to be fought time and time again, with Canada usually in the forefront of those defending the UN's need to retain control.

UNPROFOR was a much maligned and misunderstood mission, particularly during the last 18 months of its existence. In Bosnia-Herzegovina, it was not a traditional peacekeeping mission since there was never any peace to keep. But neither was it an enforcement mission since it never had the means to impose its will on the warring factions. It was thus open to attack from all sides, from those who thought too much was being asked of lightly armed soldiers, and from those who saw the necessary caution exercised by the field commanders as cowardice. Yet for all its internal contradictions UNPROFOR played, in my view, an extremely useful role. It helped save countless lives by bringing food and medicine to besieged populations and prevented the widening of the conflict to the rest of the Europe. In many respects, the mission in Bosnia-Herzegovina was an enormous gamble. There was no previous experience with this kind of operation and each escalation in the use of force was a step into the unknown. It is tempting to conclude that a more robust approach to the mission from the very beginning would have accelerated the end of the conflict. Perhaps. But one thing is clear: the Dayton accords were just the final step in the long process of UN attempts to contain the conflict and bring it to an end. The UN is regrettably receiving very little credit for the fragile peace now extant throughout Bosnia-Herzegovina, but it had a major hand in making it happen.

When the crisis in Rwanda erupted, disillusionment with the UN's ability to quell civil conflicts had set in very deeply. Stopping the massacre would have required the instant deployment of significant numbers of well-armed troops. No one volunteered. As Rwandans were dying by the thousands, and millions were seeking refuge in neighbouring countries, the question debated in New York was whether to withdraw completely the UN mission already on the ground, since it was too small and too poorly armed to take on the killers.

The UN and its member states did redeem themselves somewhat by moving with considerable efficiency to provide relief to the refugees. The coordination of humanitarian assistance had been a sore point at the time of the Kurdish crisis. The creation in the fall of 1991 of the post of Coordinator of Humanitarian Assistance was designed to force better cooperation among the various UN agencies and between them and the NGO and bilateral donor community. The concept was first tested in Somalia, with mixed results. Aid agencies quarrelled and, for the most part, went their own way. The relationship with the military was uneasy. Many agencies worried about losing their neutral status by too close association with armed forces.

The performance was much better in the former Yugoslavia, thanks in large part to the very efficient leadership of the UNHCR. In Rwanda, the Coordinator for Humanitarian Affairs was able to perform its role as intended. Military forces dispatched by a number of member states worked productively with UN agencies and NGOs to mount what was probably the most massive humanitarian relief effort ever undertaken.

If the conflict in the former Yugoslavia was the number one issue for the UN as a whole, Haiti received at least as much attention within the Canadian mission. Canada had made a strong commitment to the cause of democracy in Haiti and had worked hard to help organize the elections which brought President Aristide to power. When a coup forced him into exile, we turned all our efforts towards achieving his return.

Not long after my arrival in New York, I was asked by Ottawa to assess the likelihood of the Security Council imposing mandatory sanctions on the Haitian regime. I did not entirely rule this out but thought things would have to get much worse before the Council would agree to take action. Many member states would be leery of such an obvious intervention in the internal affairs of a state without the justification of a threat to international peace and security as prescribed in Chapter VII of the Charter.

The decision on July 31, 1994 to authorize the use of force was the culmination of a gradual engagement of the United Nations in the issue. In the first instance, the initiative rested with the Organization of American States (OAS), while action at the UN took place principally in the General Assembly and the Commission of Human Rights. When it became evident that the efforts of the OAS would not succeed, the UN moved to centre stage.

The nomination of Mr. Dante Caputo as Special Representative of the Secretary-General provided the necessary focal point in the UN for active management of the issue. The formation of the Group of Friends—composed of Canada, France, Venezuela and the United States, later expanded to include Argentina—ensured very close coordination between the UN and those countries most committed to a resolution of the Haitian crisis. The strategy to move the issue to the Security Council was greatly facilitated by the fact that three of the members of the Group sat on the Council. Furthermore, the Latin American members of the Group could act as a conduit to their regional group, the support of which was essential for success in the

Council. For Canada, membership in the Group gave us as much of a voice as if we had been members of the Council. We participated in the drafting of every resolution and, since the Group worked by consensus, our consent was required for proposals to move forward.

After months of fruitless negotiations with the Haitian junta, the Council agreed, in June 1993, to impose mandatory sanctions to force the junta's hand. The gambit seemed to work. The Governors Island Agreement providing for the deployment of a UN mission and the return of President Aristide was signed a few weeks later. Our hopes were dashed, however, when a crowd of thugs prevented the landing of the mission. This was followed by another year of negotiations and further pressure through tightened sanctions. When the authorization to use force was finally voted by the Council, it was perceived by most as the logical final step in a process that had explored every conceivable avenue of negotiations.

Such a decision, which stretched the notion of what constitutes a threat to international peace and security, would have been unthinkable a few years earlier. Now it was greeted with satisfaction by most member states. Of course, the American backing of the operation was not an insignificant factor in the Council's deliberations, but those who thought the action improper were clearly a minority. Need I add that for Canada, which had been the first to advocate Security Council involvement, this decision was a source of great satisfaction.

Throughout the three years I spent at the UN, the Security Council kept a frantic pace, meeting practically every day. New issues kept appearing on its agenda: El Salvador, Angola, Mozambique, Western Sahara, Nagorno-Karabakh, as well as old ones like Cyprus, Iraq and the Middle East. The increasing influence of the Security Council rekindled the perennial issue of reform. At the 1994 session of the General Assembly, a working group was created to pursue the matter and report to the next assembly.

The difficulty encountered in drafting the mandate of the group gave a foretaste of the task ahead. Some countries like the permanent members of the Council and those aspiring to that status wished to focus the work exclusively on the expansion of the membership and avoid meddling by the general membership in the functioning of the Council. Others, including Canada, attached as much importance to the work methods of the Council as to the question of membership. Enlargement would add only a few seats to the Council, including perhaps some permanent ones. While this would make the Council somewhat more representative of contemporary world realities, it would provide little comfort to those who felt that this body was not sufficiently responsive to the concerns of the membership at large.

Because of the increased workload, the Council increasingly carried out most of its work in informal sessions, behind closed doors. What the Council gained in efficiency, it lost in transparency. Non-members, particularly troop contributors, were largely excluded from a decision-making process to which they had much to contribute and which directly affected their interests. Canada took the lead in demanding that the Security Council consult with the troop contributors before making decisions. We were largely successful in improving the situation in this regard. Meetings of troop contributors, chaired by the Secretariat but with Security Council members in attendance, became a regular practice. We also believed that mechanisms, such as groups of friends, should be expanded as a means to involve more closely those countries which had a particular stake in an issue. Our goal was to consolidate and formalize this practice through the Security Council reform process.

The working group toiled in earnest throughout 1994. At the end of a year of remarkably thoughtful debates, reform seemed as distant as ever. Views were deeply divided. How many seats should there be on the Council? Should there be new permanent members? If so, how many and which ones? Should they have a right of veto? Since agreement seemed almost impossible on the selection of permanent members from developing regions, the notion of shared or rotating seats among groups of middle powers was advanced by a number of countries. There were almost as many permutations as there were members of the UN.

By the time I left New York, I had become highly skeptical that reform would occur in the short term. I do not consider this a calamity, however, so long as the Council makes determined efforts to reach out to the general membership and operates in a more transparent way.

Peacekeeping may have been the dominant issue during my tenure in New York, but the UN also showed considerable dynamism in the economic and social areas as well. A number of major conferences were held and others were in preparation when I left. Often criticized as useless extravaganzas, these conferences, when well prepared, in fact serve the vital purpose of defining new priorities for the entire UN system, a task which regular meetings of other bodies simply cannot perform.

The United Nations Conference on Environment and Development (UNCED), held in Rio de Janeiro in June 1992, produced a major action plan on world-wide sustainable development, *Agenda 21*, which offers a blueprint on how to make development socially, economically and environmentally sustainable. It also concluded binding agreements on the complex issues of climate change and biodiversity. Furthermore, preliminary steps were taken to launch new negotiations on such issues as forestry protection and high sea fisheries. This latter decision was a major victory for Canada, given the European Union's strong opposition. Late last year, negotiations were concluded on a legally binding agreement which should help resolve the problems of over-fishing outside our 200-mile zone.

The 1993 Vienna World Conference on Human Rights was another significant achievement. All 171 states represented in Vienna endorsed the human rights principles defined in the Universal Declaration on Human Rights and reaffirmed the duty of all states, regardless of their political, economic or social systems, to protect those rights. The Conference also affirmed the crucial linkages between human rights and the other central purposes of the UN by embracing an integrated approach to the objectives of peace, democracy and human rights and the requirements of development. In 1994, the General Assembly authorized the appointment of a High Commissioner for Human Rights to coordinate and strengthen the work of the Commission on Human Rights and other related UN agencies, a step which had been strenuously resisted by a small but very determined group of developing countries.

The World Conference on Population and Development was held in 1994 in Cairo. One of the most important achievements of the conference was the new approach to population issues, which recognized that social and economic development, rather than demographic targets, was central to achieving a balance between the number of people on Earth and their demands on the world's ecosystems. Unprecedented consensus was also reached on the issue of international migration where the need for cooperation between receiving and originating countries was stressed.

The UN World Conference on Women and the World Summit for Social Development, held in 1995 in Beijing and Copenhagen respectively, articulated a broad vision of development and human security and set the parameters of UN action continuing into the next century. For most developing countries, however, the vision which emerged from these conferences is incomplete since it leaves undefined the role of the UN in economic affairs. Developing countries would like the Economic and Social Council and the General Assembly to have a greater say in the policies of the agencies involved in economic affairs. Developed countries also agree that the economic side of the UN is in great need of reform, but their priority is on the rationalization of the system and the elimination of duplication among the various intergovernmental bodies and agencies. Following the publication of the Secretary-General's report entitled *An Agenda For Development* on May 6, 1994, a working group of the General Assembly was struck to consider these issues. Negotiations will likely be very difficult, and great care will have to be taken to avoid recreating the great North-South divide, which was not in evidence when I was in New York.

There were many other memorable events during the three years I had the privilege to serve as Canada's Permanent Representative. The Tribunal for War Crimes in the former Yugoslavia was created and its jurisdiction was later extended to cover similar acts committed in Rwanda. It may well be the embryo of a future International Criminal Court. A Convention on the Safety of UN and Associated Personnel was negotiated in record time, thus filling a dangerous void in international law. The impasse over the Law of the Sea Convention was finally broken. It entered into force on November 16, 1994, after a hiatus of 22 years. For a while, UN finances were in reasonably good shape, with many countries beginning to pay down the arrears in their contributions. The number of members, which stood at 159 when I arrived, had reached 184 by the time I left, and for several blissful months there were seven, yes seven, women Permanent Representatives, the largest representation ever.

When I was recalled to Ottawa in November 1994, I knew that I had lived through a particularly positive and productive period in UN history. I also sensed that the wind had changed. The problems encountered in Somalia, Rwanda and Bosnia, the deepening financial crisis, and the aggressive criticism of the UN in the American Congress heralded a period of relative retrenchment, exemplified today by the dwindling number of UN peacekeepers deployed around the world.

The calls for reform are fully justified. Marginal activities must be shed and efforts focused on the real priorities. Inter-agency rivalries and duplication must cease and a leaner, more coherent system emerge. Administrative practices must be improved and management modernized. But the UN is not nearly as inefficient as it is portrayed to be and it delivers a great deal for the relative size of its budget. Furthermore, it is unrealistic to expect a "big bang" of reform. One hundred and eighty-four countries, each with its own priorities and political constraints, must be accommodated. Consensus takes time and change is more easily achieved in an incremental way.

I do not believe the prophets of doom who have already condemned the UN to oblivion. The institution is resilient and will traverse this new crisis as it has others. It can count on the loyalty and dedication of many outstanding staff members, whose contribution to the common welfare of the world is too rarely recognized. But it will require the firm support of its member states which, in this era of interdependence and globalization, need the UN more than ever.

IX

GEOFFREY A.H. PEARSON

IN THE BEGINNING: FAITH

Prime Minister Mackenzie King spoke to the San Francisco Conference in April 1945, in idealistic, if not to say utopian, terms about a "time without parallel in the history of human affairs," a time "to lay the foundations of a new world order," a time "to bring into being a world community." Canada's only purpose, he said, was to help in creating an organization "which over the years and decades to come will be strong enough and flexible enough to stand any strains to which it may be subjected." "It is for each nation to remember," he concluded, "that over all nations is humanity."[1]

No doubt it is a North American temptation to use this kind of language on solemn international occasions (one is reminded of President Wilson at Versailles), but there is also something uniquely

Canadian about Mr. King's address. What other national leader would have denied that "considerations of national pride or prestige" would impinge on his government's policies towards the new organization? Most of the fifty governments represented at San Francisco brought a good deal of national baggage to the Conference. Canada brought much less, for it had barely emerged from a semi-colonial status, and looked to the UN as a kind of guardian of the newly independent strength it had forged during the war. With Australia, New Zealand and South Africa, Canada could pretend to act as a bold and innocent youth in this company of grizzled veterans of the state system.

Mr. King also revealed, however, that Canada *did* have national concerns (which other delegations might have thought had something to do with pride and prestige) about the place in the new security structure of what he called "the smaller powers" (the concept of "middle power" was to emerge from the deliberations of the Conference). These too, he said, ought to have their fair share of the task of "preserving the peace."[2] Indeed, Canada had already urged on the authors of the draft Charter (the U.S., UK, China and the USSR) the view that Canada and other similar powers should be given a greater role in the work of the Security Council, both by explicit acknowledgement of their credentials as potential members of the Council, and by consultation with them before any decision was taken to call upon their forces for cooperation "in a particular task of enforcement." The Canadian memorandum had noted the Canadian record in the two Great Wars as a reason for such treatment, pointing out that the elected members of the Council should be capable of "contributing to the discharge of the Council's obligations."[3]

These views were pressed as well by Australia, and they were to result in amendments to the draft Charter that went some way to meet them (Articles 23 and 44). But, in practice, they were to be disregarded. The Cold War frustrated realization of the Charter concept of collective security, and, later, a tide of new members washed away the principle of capacity to contribute, replacing it by "equitable geographic distribution" as a criterion for election.

Canada had less success in attempting to restrict the use of the veto by the Permanent Members to actions involving the use of sanctions, including military force; this move was blocked by the USSR. Mr. Louis St. Laurent, the Secretary of State for External Affairs, was not overly discouraged, however; reporting to Parliament later, he said that Canada had agreed to accept the veto provisions of the

Charter because the great powers had promised that this privilege "would be used with a sense of responsibility and consideration for the interests of smaller states..."[4] But this too was not to be, and by 1947 he was suggesting the need for a new association "of democratic and peace-loving states" willing and able to keep the peace (the North Atlantic Treaty Organization—NATO—was born the following year).[5]

Canada's election to the Security Council in 1947 was followed by two years of active diplomacy over disputes between Jews and Arabs in Palestine and between Hindus and Muslims in Kashmir, as well as the process of bringing Indonesia to independence. This activity partially restored Canadian faith in the UN, and when the UN responded to aggression in Korea in June 1950 by authorizing the use of force under American leadership it was hoped in Ottawa that the crisis would lead to a new effort to form a permanent UN force, possibly made up of volunteers. While this concept too turned out to be premature, Canadian participation in the Korean operation would begin the practice of earmarking Canadian units for UN duty and eventually lead to the Canadian commitment to peacekeeping.

ALONG THE WAY: DOUBT

For the next four decades the UN made little progress in achieving the security purposes of the Charter, i.e., to prevent or repel aggression by one state against another. Instead, it found a role, pioneered by Canada and by Dag Hammarskold, in helping to end conflict and to deter its resumption in those parts of the world, chiefly in the Middle East, where neither the U.S. nor the USSR wished to intervene directly for fear of provoking a nuclear crisis (when they did intervene with force, as in Eastern Europe or in Vietnam, the UN was powerless). However, the entry of one hundred or more new members during the period and the resulting growth of non-alignment as a political testament meant that agreement on common standards of behaviour, and on collective action, would be harder to reach, whether on matters of human rights, the use of violence to end colonial status, or the duties of members in support of peacekeeping. Indeed, the peacekeeping operations of the period, in the Middle East, Cyprus, the Congo and Central America, could only be organized ad hoc, despite the efforts of Canada and like-minded members to work out agreed procedures in advance.

Nevertheless, Canada served in each of the sixteen UN peace-keeping operations authorized from 1956, the year of the establishment of the UN Emergency Force on the Israel-Egypt border, to 1989, when the Cold War came to an end and the Security Council began to function free of the veto. Paul Martin, the Secretary of State for External Affairs from 1963 to 1968, explained this commitment in 1967 as a function of three main factors: geography (a need "to look outwards"), history ("we have few illusions about the past to shape our conception of the national interest"), and resources ("some extra margin of wealth and stability ...").[6] He might have added that peace-keeping also served two other Canadian interests: it was popular, both in English- and in French-speaking Canada, and the operations in the Middle East served as a convenient excuse to justify Canadian rhetoric about impartiality towards the parties to the Arab-Israel dispute, a stance that was to be sorely tested a month after Mr. Martin spoke when Colonel Nasser ordered the UN force out of Egypt, beginning with its Canadian component.

This episode initiated a period of relative Canadian disenchantment with the UN, although the government agreed to participate in three more UN operations around the borders of Israel during the 1970s. By then, there were almost 130 UN members, mostly developing countries. They gave priority to issues of racism in South Africa, Rhodesia and (they claimed) in Israel, and to the demand for "a new international economic order," leading to accusations in the West about the "tyranny of the majority." Canadian officials wondered, in these circumstances, whether it would be wise for Canada to stand again for election to the Security Council; but, in the end, it was decided that membership would help to demonstrate support for the UN at a time when it was subject to increasing criticism, especially in North America. During its fourth term on the Council in 1977-78 Canada therefore worked to strengthen a UN reputation for practical and agreed action, focusing on the common goal of ending apartheid in South Africa by imposing a mandatory arms embargo and by taking the first step towards the independence of its colony, Namibia (not finally achieved until 1990). By the end of 1978, some 14,000 soldiers were serving under UN command in five peacekeeping operations, with Canada supplying over 10 percent of the total. Much remained to be done to improve the command, control and financing of such operations, but the prospects for Soviet-American cooperation that might make this possible looked somewhat better.

These prospects were destroyed by the Soviet invasion of Afghanistan in 1980, leading both to a dramatic rise in East-West tensions and to a demonstration of the essential irrelevance of the UN in matters affecting the great powers. Changes in Soviet policy after 1985, however, gave birth to new hope, and by the time Canada joined the Security Council again in 1989, having been elected with the support of 127 out of 157 members, the Cold War was coming to an end. A UN good offices mission was already operating in Afghanistan, and by the end of 1989 four new UN operations had been agreed upon in Africa and Central America.

Apparent confirmation of new life for the UN with the end of the Cold War was to be given during 1990—the second year of Canada's term on the Council—when the U.S. was able to rally support for the use of sanctions against Iraq after its invasion of Kuwait. Here was an example of the kind of aggression the founders of 1945 had had in mind when they outlined the steps in Chapter Seven of the Charter for dealing with breaches of the peace. In light of Canada's strong and early support for the concept of collective security it was no surprise that it voted in favour of such action, including, in November 1990, the key Resolution authorizing member states "to use all necessary means" to expel Iraqi forces if Iraq made no response to the order to do so by January 15, 1991. While it is true that this timing was driven by American military planning, and was questioned by many who otherwise accepted the need to apply sanctions in this case, the fact that the Council adopted the Resolution gave it an undeniable basis in law. It demonstrated, as Canada was to put the matter to the Assembly later, "that the UN has the will and the capacity necessary to repel armed aggression."[7] Yet a UN enforcement operation so dominated by one member, and so hastily implemented, appeared to run counter to the spirit, if not the letter, of the Charter, and its conduct raised doubts in Canada that were to reappear in the following years as the Council tried to make enforcement work in quite different circumstances.

Despite brave words ("over all nations is humanity") and stirring sentiments ("we, the peoples ..."), it was never the intention of the founders that the UN should intervene with force to protect minorities, as it would do in 1991 to protect Iraqi Kurds, or to promote democracy, as it was to do later in Haiti, or to police the delivery of humanitarian aid, as in Somalia. However, in the same 1991 address to the Assembly already cited, the Canadian Secretary of State for

External Affairs, Barbara McDougall, signalled a change in thinking: "the concept of sovereignty must respect higher principles, including the need to preserve human life from wanton destruction."[8] She was referring to the breakdown of civil order in Yugoslavia, and it was this breakdown, along with the later carnage in Rwanda, that was to pose the major challenge to the primary purpose of the UN in the next few years.

This challenge has taken two main forms: the need to develop agreed criteria for UN intervention in cases of domestic conflict which may be said to threaten the peace; and the absence of a legitimate capacity for a rapid reaction to threats to the peace, however they may be defined, instead of the resort to ad hoc coalitions of states prepared to act alone, or of failing to act at all or in time. Besides these needs there are more basic questions of the reform of the structure and the management of the UN itself after fifty years of existence.

TOWARDS THE FUTURE: HOPE?

The fact that, from 1990 to 1994, some twenty new UN missions were established, almost all of which involved the monitoring of domestic disputes, ceasefires or human rights, or the provision of relief supplies, is testimony enough to the erosion of the domestic jurisdiction clause of the Charter (by October 1995, eleven of these operations, and five that had been previously authorized, were still in place, comprising some 60,000 soldiers and police, and over 8,000 civilians). But this record also reveals that, where the parties or factions involved are unwilling to make peace, as in Somalia, Rwanda, and ex-Yugoslavia, the UN too is unwilling or unable to enforce it. Moreover, domestic conflicts as intense as, or more enduring than, those attracting UN intervention, e.g. Afghanistan, Sudan, Sri Lanka, have received little or no attention from the Security Council, although other UN agencies may do what they can to provide relief.

Clearly, the UN cannot be equally and simultaneously present in all the world's trouble spots. The doctrine of national sovereignty remains a powerful barrier to intervention, despite the breaches already made in it, even if some states fail to provide a minimum of civic order. There appears to be a need for a triggering mechanism, or international alert, which would point to cases of egregious civilian suffering calling for outside help, either by the UN or by the appropriate regional organization. To overcome the perception of double standards that is widely current, the Secretary-General, perhaps with the assistance of an advisory body of NGOs, could perform this function if he were to report regularly to the Council on such situations, applying criteria that might be approved by the General Assembly.

Whether or not such a procedure is politically feasible, the Council is bound to continue making its decisions on a case-by-case basis, achieving consensus whenever it can. Finding the means to enforce its decisions, however, is a process that can be greatly improved by advance planning. It was for this reason that Canada presented to the 50th Session of the Assembly a report entitled "Towards a Rapid Reaction Capability for the United Nations." Its main proposal is that the UN "assemble, from member states, a multifunctional force of up to 5,000 military and civilian personnel and, with the authorization of the Security Council, quickly deploy it under the control of an operational-level headquarters."[9]

In addition, the report suggests a number of more modest ways to strengthen advance planning, both by the Secretariat and in liaison with contributors of personnel to peacekeeping operations. More radical steps, such as a standing police capability and a military volunteer force, are left for "the long term."

These proposals for improved stand-by and planning arrangements are certainly welcome. But it is fair to ask how much difference they will make as long as they remain subject to agreement by a Security Council that no longer represents fairly a UN membership of 185 states, and the strongest member of which, the U.S., is both the UN's leading debtor and the most reluctant to commit troops under UN command. Unless and until the Council acquires greater political legitimacy and is able to rely on firm financing for its security operations and on forces volunteered for this purpose, peacekeeping and peace enforcement may have to be done by those states which believe their vital interests are most affected in each case, acting with or without the stamp of UN approval. The regional organizations can serve such purposes, although, with the exception of NATO, they usually lack the funds and/or the military strength to engage in large-scale operations.

Improving the UN's performance as a security agency may depend, above all, on reform of the procedures and membership of the Council. The emphasis placed by Canada in 1945 on the capacity of member states to contribute to international peace and security as a major criterion for membership needs to be revived, and buttressed by evidence that they are willing to perform such tasks. The criterion of capacity to pay should also be revived, as in the case of Germany and Japan. A second Canadian objective in 1945 was "no taxation without representation." Contributors to UN operations ought to have a voice in the decisions made, and perhaps even a vote.

Thirdly, the Canadian goal of restricting the use of the veto, while attained in practice, might now be legally entrenched in the Charter. Given such reforms, and assuming they enhance the legitimacy of Council decisions, the machinery envisaged in the Charter for the formal earmarking of forces for implementing Council resolutions might be made to work.

Changes of this kind would require amendment of the Charter, and there is little reason to expect that agreement will soon be reached on them. The question of adding to the permanent membership is especially divisive. Canada has agreed to the objective of Council expansion but has said next to nothing about the means, except to indicate support in principle for the addition of Germany and Japan. A Council of twenty or more members might, it is true, leave Canada in an awkward position, for Canada can hardly aspire to permanent membership itself, and the demand for stronger representation from Asia, Africa and Latin America is difficult to deny. Nevertheless, we are not alone. It would be consonant with our past record to work with other middle powers (Italy, Australia and the Netherlands, for example) to devise a system of rotating seats for members whose capacity to contribute and willingness to serve qualify them for regular attendance at the table. Thought might also be given to ways of increasing the oversight responsibilities of the General Assembly.

The ghosts of the Canadian founders of the UN would approve of such activism. It is hardly to be expected, so far have we moved from the utopian heights of 1945, that a Canadian statesman would repeat publicly that, if the UN moves in the direction of world government, "then the Canadian delegation wholeheartedly supports world government."[10] But perhaps we can still agree with Mr. St. Laurent's view, expressed in 1947, that "we in Canada regard our membership in the UN not as a temporary expedient but as a permanent partnership."[11]

NOTES

1 R.A. MacKay, *Canadian Foreign Policy 1945-1954*, (Ottawa: Carleton University Press, 1971), 13-14.

2 *Canadian Foreign Policy*, 14.

3 *Canadian Foreign Policy*, 7-8.

4 *Canadian Foreign Policy*, 20.

5 *Canadian Foreign Policy*, 97.

6 Department of External Affairs, *Canada's Role in Supporting UN Peacekeepers*, Statements & Speeches No. 67/12. (April 26, 1967).

7 Department of External Affairs, Statement No. 91/49, (September 25, 1991).

8 Department of External Affairs, Statement No. 91/49, (September 25, 1991).

9 Department of Foreign Affairs and International Trade, Statement 95/53, (September 26, 1995).

10 Mackay, *Canadian Foreign Policy*, 99.

11 *Canadian Foreign Policy*, 103.

The UN System

X

The Security Council: Trial and Error in Moving to a Post-Westphalian International System

HARALD VON RIEKHOFF

Under the rules of the Charter, the United Nations Security Council has primary responsibility for the maintenance of international peace and security. It is the principal executive agency of the UN and the only body in the entire UN system that is authorized to make mandatory decisions that are binding on member states (Article 25 of the Charter). As its founders intended it, the Security Council was designed to be lean—originally it had 11 members, a number increased to 15 in 1965—and if not mean, then at least effective. The original efforts to keep the Cold War outside the gates of the UN were short-lived, and by 1947 the Organization, like most other international institutions, had succumbed to the systemic bipolar confrontation. The Charter provision which gave a veto to each of the five permanent members of the Security Council made it relatively easy to render this body *hors de combat*, although in retrospect it would appear that the frequent use of the veto was as much a symbol of paralysis as the true cause of the dysfunctional state of the Council. Given the international context in which it operated, it would have been prevented from operating effectively even if the voting rules had been less restrictive. Between 1946 and 1989, the period generally corresponding to the Cold War era, the Security Council passed a total of 646 resolutions.[1] One can contrast these with the 194 formal vetoes which were cast during roughly the same period, from February 1946 to May 1990.[2] In addition, the mere prospect of a veto had a general chill effect which frequently inhibited the exploration of opportunities for joint action. To be sure, even at the height of the Cold War, the Security Council can be credited with taking several important decisions that affected international security, notably by negotiating ceasefires and dispatching peacekeeping missions in order to protect the Great Powers from being drawn into escalating local wars. Moreover, other UN agents, in particular the Secretary-General and the General Assembly, partly succeeded in stepping into the breach left by an impaired Council.

The demise of the Cold War, whose existence had for so long curtailed the operations of the UN, produced an unexpected consensus among the five permanent members of the Security Council which expanded the frequency, scope and range of the organ's activities to an unprecedented level. Since 1989, the Council has authorized a full-scale collective enforcement action in the Gulf which resembled the Charter ideal of collective security more closely than any previous operation in UN history. As well, during the past six years, the Security Council has initiated a greater number of peacekeeping operations—which have also been more comprehensive in scope—than at anytime in its preceding 45 year history. In a brief summary, Secretary-General Boutros-Ghali's *Agenda for Peace* documents this exponential increase in activities: Security Council resolutions increased five-fold (15 for the year preceding January 31, 1988 as compared with 78 for the year 1994); there was more than a seven-fold increase in the number of UN peacekeepers deployed on active missions (9,570 military personnel in January 1988 as against 73,393 in December 1994); and the UN's total peacekeeping budget rose by a factor of fifteen ($U.S. 230.4 million for 1988 as against $U.S. 3,610 million in 1994).[3]

More important, perhaps, than this quantitative growth in UN security-related operations is the qualitative change which has been manifested in innovative UN practices:

1. the creation of an international war crimes tribunal for the former Yugoslavia and Rwanda;

2. the new focus on *peace-building*, displayed in the UN's major efforts to reconstruct societies which had been ravaged by civil strife, as in El Salvador, Namibia, Cambodia, Somalia and Angola;

3. the restoration of democratic governments as in Haiti; and

4. the increasingly intrusive tendency of the Security Council to mandate limited enforcement actions in response to large-scale humanitarian emergencies, as in Bosnia, Somalia and Rwanda.

Even though Chapter VII of the Charter has been invoked on these occasions, the principal motivation was not as much a traditional concern for international peace and security as compassion for human suffering under conditions of civil war or attempted genocide.

The first reason for this qualitative change, as explained by Secretary-General Boutros Boutros-Ghali, stems from the general shift in the prevailing nature of warfare. In the post-Cold War era, intra-state conflicts have become a far more frequent phenomenon than the classical inter-state conflicts which the United Nations was meant to remedy. Of the more than 100 armed conflicts reported since 1989, all but five were internal conflicts.[4] Consequently, of the eleven UN peacekeeping operations established since the beginning of 1992, all but two relate primarily to intra-state conflict situations.[5] The shift toward domestic conflict situations marks a fundamental problem shift in the security orientation of the UN, bringing with it much uncharted political ground, uncertainty, complexity, and high risk.[6]

The second qualitative change is the growing tendency of the Security Council to authorize the use of UN forces for the protection of humanitarian operations rather than for their original goal, the maintenance of peace. Boutros-Ghali cites the situation in Somalia and Bosnia, where the Security Council authorized the local and limited use of military force under Chapter VII for essentially humanitarian reasons without an accompanying mandate to stop the aggressor or impose a cessation of hostilities.[7] In both instances, however, the UN goal of preserving its neutrality and impartiality towards the warring parties was critically undermined by its humanitarian interventions, however altruistic their aim, thereby exposing the UN to the dilemma of pursuing a mission whose objectives were essentially irreconcilable.

CONSENSUS-BUILDING IN THE SECURITY COUNCIL

Substantive decisions of the Security Council require a majority of nine from the fifteen members, including the affirmative votes of the five permanent members. By convention, abstentions by permanent members are not counted as vetoes. During most of the Cold War period the UN Security Council was divided into three competing blocs. First, the Western bloc, led by the United States, Britain and France and two non-permanent members from the so-called West European and Other Group (WEOG), which includes Canada. Second, the Soviet bloc, led by the USSR and supported by one of its East European satellites as a non-permanent member. Finally, one could identify a bloc of non-aligned countries, consisting of seven non-permanent members from Latin America, Africa and Asia. China, though close to the non-aligned group, tended to play a rather passive and low-key role which negated its high status as the fifth permanent member of the Council.

During the Cold War era, inter-coalition politics of the Security Council were complex and highly unpredictable, as none of the three principal blocs commanded an assured majority; however, each group was capable of blocking a decision: the Western and the Communist groups by virtue of their constitutional veto power, and the non-aligned group by disposing of enough votes to prevent a necessary majority of nine, thus exercising what has been referred to as a collective veto. For the Security Council to take a decision required the active collaboration of two groups, as well as the benevolent neutrality of members of the third group capable of blocking an outcome by an individual or a collective veto. Needless to say, such outcomes required prolonged negotiations and were rare and highly unstable.

The end of the Cold War, which conventionally is often dated with the fall of the Berlin wall in 1989, arrived somewhat earlier in the United Nations. As early as April 1986 the Soviet Union signalled a more cooperative attitude toward the United Nations when it announced its willingness to pay up its peacekeeping arrears. This was followed by a British proposal for cooperation by the permanent members to achieve an end to the Iran-Iraq war. The British initiative led to Security Council Resolution 598 in July 1987, containing a Chapter VII determination which, as Sally Morphet argues, "can in retrospect be seen as the precursor of the greatly enhanced use of

Chapter VII Security Council Resolutions from 1990 onwards."[8] As well, it was evidence of the fundamentally changed nature of post-Cold War decision-making by the Security Council.

At the height of Cold War confrontation, Security Council decisions were made in formal sessions at which the goal of scoring rhetorical and propagandistic debating points frequently outweighed the desire to reach a constructive decision. Despite this overall unsatisfactory context, the situation did offer certain benefits to some member states. The complex politics of Cold War coalition building provided non-permanent members of the Council with considerable scope for manoeuvre and the opportunity to mediate between the principal protagonists. Non-permanent members were thus less in danger of becoming marginalized in the process of Security Council deliberations and decision-making than they are at present, when the agenda is largely controlled by the permanent members acting in concert. Moreover, the formal nature of Council debates provided greater transparency than the informal and closed consultations which have come to be the prevalent norm during the post-Cold War period.

At the present stage, most items which are of concern to the Security Council are initially negotiated in private and informal consultations by two, or three, or all five permanent members, which form a kind of self-appointed steering group. In addition, the President of the Security Council has a legitimate responsibility for initiating consultations and for sounding out the parties to a dispute with a view to determining its seriousness or offering his/her good offices. The President's catalytic function in this consultative and exploratory process is constrained by the brief one-month tenure of the position and may, moreover, be negatively affected by the lack of status or unpopularity of the country which he/she represents.

The undisputed gatekeeper role in initiating Security Council consultations and in guiding their progress is held by the United States. In this task the U.S. is strongly supported by the other two Western permanent members, the UK and France. Theirs is not merely a supporting role as they have often been responsible for important initiatives: for example, British Prime Minister Major's proposal in January 1992 to hold a heads of government summit meeting of the Council in order to prepare the groundwork for its future operations in the new post-Cold War environment. This summit set useful guidelines for future Security Council functions and commissioned what subsequently became the Secretary-General's comprehensive *Agenda for Peace*. Once the Western Three are in agreement, the next natural step is to bring the remaining permanent members, Russia and China, "on board," to enable the permanent five to present a united front to the non-permanent members. The latter are brought into the consultations as the need arises and as individual permanent members want to bolster their own stand. Naturally the consultation loop varies according to the precise issue being considered. During the prolonged and intricate diplomatic negotiations which preceded the Gulf War, China was particularly opposed to the actual use of force and, instead, wanted the UN to achieve a diplomatic settlement. To overcome Chinese inhibitions, the prevailing strategy for consultations was to unite the other four permanent members on an item, then get support from practically all of the non-permanent members, and then to face China with a united front. Non-permanent members have recently complained that they have become marginalized with the current system of informal consultations and that they are all too often confronted with a *fait accompli*. In their opinion, they are asked to endorse the final text of a Council resolution into the drafting of which they may have had little or no input and whose underlying arguments they may not even fully comprehend.[9] Moreover, much of today's voting in the Council takes place without a preceding debate and thus deprives them of the opportunity to seek clarification or express their respective national views.

The central feature of the politics of the Security Council in the post-Cold War era is its predominantly consensual nature, as contrasted with the adversarial spirit that characterized its behaviour during the Cold War phase. One important indicator of this transformation is the dramatic decline in the use of the veto. In the period between 1946 and 1970, the Soviet Union cast 103 vetoes, whereas the United States, profiting from its predominant position which commanded an automatic majority in the UN, cast none. The situation was subsequently reversed when the Soviets frequently found themselves in a majority position. In the period between 1970 and 1989, the U.S. cast 67 vetoes, compared to a mere 11 from the USSR.[10]

In sharp contrast to the prolific occurrence of vetoes in former days, there have only been four instances of Security Council vetoes since 1990. What is notable is not only their infrequent occurrence but also their relatively insignificant and transient impact. In 1993

Russia vetoed a proposal to change the nature of financing for the UN peacekeeping mission in Cyprus from voluntary to compulsory assessment. The revised formula, which sought to bring financing for Cyprus into conformity with standard UN peacekeeping practice, would have added to Russia's financial obligations at a time that it was hard-pressed economically. The veto was therefore based on very practical considerations. But only a month later, Russia reversed its stand and accepted a resolution that corresponded in essence to the one it had recently vetoed.[11] In 1994, Russia used its veto to protect a friendly power, the republic now known as Yugoslavia (Serbia and Montenegro), against a proposed tightening of UN sanctions. In May 1995, the United States vetoed a draft resolution in which the Security Council called on Israel to rescind the expropriation of land in East Jerusalem. In the view of the other Council members, the matter affected international peace and security insofar as the expropriation decree violated the fourth Geneva Convention; moreover, it threatened to jeopardize the fragile peace process between Israel and the Palestinians. U.S. representative Edward Guehm defended his nation's veto by arguing that "debates in the Council on issues which are for the parties to address will only distract them from their efforts and have a negative impact on the process."[12] Regardless of the attempted censure by the Security Council, the Rabin government revoked the controversial decree soon thereafter, because it had generated a domestic political storm in Israel that threatened to break up the governing coalition. Given the minimum actual use to which the veto has shrunk, it is ironic that the right of veto should present such a significant obstacle to the diverse proposals for reform of the Security Council which are currently being circulated and which will be addressed below.

As Morpeth notes in her analysis of the influence of groups of states in the Security Council and General Assembly, by the mid-1980s the distinctive role of the USSR and its East European ally, trying to block a Council decision or working with the non-aligned group to gain a majority, began to disappear. Instead of the three competing blocs in the Security Council two groups were beginning to identify themselves. One consists of the five permanent members of the Security Council, operating very much as a concert in the manner envisaged by the founders of the UN Charter. This group can generally count on close support from the three non-permanent members from East Europe and the WEOG group, the former aligned with Russia and the latter generally cooperating with the three Western permanent members. The other identifiable group in the Security Council consists of the seven non-permanent and non-aligned members. On the whole, the interests of these two groups appear to coincide, insofar as they operate in a highly consensual manner not only within each group but also towards each other. As an indication of the high level of consensus, one can cite the fact that, between August 1990 and July 1994, the Security Council passed 263 unanimous resolutions out of a total of 310. This indicates almost 85 percent unanimity in a body known throughout most of its history for its fragmentation and its cantankerous atmosphere.[13] The permanent members voted together on 63 percent of the resolutions passed by the Security Council between 1980-85; 86 percent of those passed between 1986 and July 1990; and for the period between August 1990 and December 1994 the figure is 92 percent. The corresponding figures for the non-aligned group in the Council were even higher at 95 percent, 100 percent, and 90 percent respectively.[14]

The non-aligned members have generally been supportive of the many Council resolutions which have established peacekeeping missions to end regional conflict in places like Central America, Namibia, Angola, and Cambodia. Both the permanent members and the non-aligned groups have supported Chapter VII mandates which have taken the form of economic sanctions (e.g., against Yugoslavia, Libya, Haiti, and Iraq) and/or limited peace enforcement measures (e.g., Somalia, Bosnia and Rwanda). There was evidence of considerable dissent among non-aligned members on the use of force against Iraq during the Gulf war. More recently, certain divisions have surfaced in connection with the war in the Balkans. Many non-aligned members have retained close ties to Yugoslavia which was a prominent leader of the non-aligned movement during Tito's rule. In contrast, Islamic members within the non-aligned group have naturally been more sympathetic to the fate of the Bosnian Muslims.

Divisions between the permanent members of the Security Council and the non-aligned members have appeared most visibly with regard to two categories of issues: humanitarian intervention and the expansion of Security Council responsibility into non-traditional fields of security. However pressing the argument for international humanitarian interventions might be on compassionate grounds they pose a very real dilemma for developing countries. Third World countries are inclined to be critical of humanitarian intervention as running counter "to the imperatives of state-mak-ing."[15] Developing countries are very sensitive to what they see as collective imperialism operating under the guise of a UN humanitar-ian mandate. Such a mandate might furnish the Great Powers with a pretext to violate the fragile territorial integrity and sovereignty of inherently weak states. This concern surfaced most visibly in con-nection with Security Council Resolution 688 in April 1991, following the Gulf war ceasefire. Cuba, Yemen and Zimbabwe voted against SCR 688 and India abstained. Although the Resolution did not for-mally authorize a Chapter VII operation, it was a highly intrusive measure which demanded that Iraq give unimpeded access to inter-national humanitarian organizations so that they could operate on Iraqi territory in aiding the Kurdish refugee population.

The non-aligned members have also blocked attempts to involve the Security Council in monitoring national elections or verifying per-formance on human rights, unless such action was an integral part of a UN peacekeeping operation. They preferred to entrust electoral and human rights monitoring tasks to the the General Assembly, in which non-aligned members exerted more influence and which lacked the Security Council's authority to undertake more intrusive types of action. Moreover, these members have indicated a preference for a more conventional definition of security instead of a more compre-hensive treatment of the concept. In the terminology of academic discourse, they would be followers of Buzan rather than of Booth or Homer-Dixon.[16] Acting in this manner, the non-aligned members on the Security Council have opposed attempts to entrust the Council with novel, non-conventional security tasks in areas such as the envi-ronment and traffic in narcotic drugs.[17]

REFORMING THE SECURITY COUNCIL—MEMBERSHIP AND VOTING RIGHTS

The Need for Reform
The most logical reason for undertaking a reform of the Security Council is to make it more reflective of the reality of post-Cold War international relations and thereby enhance its legitimacy and credibility.[18] "Despite its recent flurry of activity," notes one critic, "it looks as if the [Security Council] ... is running out of steam and showing clear signs of obsolescence."[19] While there have been obvious successes in responding innovatively to new and essentially

post-Westphalian security and humanitarian challenges, today's Security Council suffers from the birth defect of its unrepresentative and archaic composition, from operational over-commitment and consequent operational fatigue, from financial insolvency and from a lack of criteria to guide Chapter VII-type missions, all of these factors making the Council a target of criticism for its apparently inconsistent, erratic and discriminatory behaviour.

A more active and less moribund Security Council creates greater expectations and thereby, inevitably, will generate criticism from a variety of quarters. During the Cold War, the principal criticism was that the Council was not doing enough and was failing to discharge its Charter responsibilities. The present criticism, at least from Third World states, focuses on three basic issues: one, the Council's membership is unrepresentative and does not reflect contemporary power realities; two, in the protection of human rights and democratic institutions, the Council is exceeding its legitimate authority; and three, its performance is inconsistent and therefore intentionally or unintentionally discriminatory.

The problem of the San Francisco model of the UN is that in essence it reflects the traditional Westphalian order of sovereign states—albeit modified by the introduction of the principle of collective security—in a world that is quickly outgrowing its Westphalian origins. The designation of five Great Powers as permanent members of the Security Council with a privileged veto position was a realist concession to a global Organization that was otherwise governed by liberal-internationalist principles. At San Francisco the rank-and-file members accepted the privileged position of the Great Powers, however reluctantly, as the price paid to secure their active membership in the Organization and to avoid the problem of absentee Great Powers that had plagued its predecessor, the League of Nations. The privileged status also appeared to be justified in view of the enormous sacrifices which the Great Powers had made to win World War II and to take account of the fact that the same Great Powers would provide the lion's share of any future Chapter VII collective enforcement operations. But as Zimbabwe's Foreign Minister, Nathan Shamuyaria, has argued before the Security Council, the time of World War II victors and their special privileges has come to an end. "After the Cold War we believe we are all victors and there should be no losers. Consequently, no one deserves any special privileges."[20]

Even from a realist perspective, these assumptions, which were already tenuous at the time of San Francisco—France and China were then Great Powers by courtesy and diplomatic fiction rather than in fact—have become patently unrealistic in our age. The permanent members of the Council have not been the principal participants in UN peacekeeping operations, and during much of the Cold War they were barred from direct participation in peacekeeping. This experience has somewhat undermined the argument that military power ought to be the predominant criterion for permanent membership in the Council. Moreover, economic power, which has become an increasingly significant component in the international power equation, is grossly under-represented in the Council with Japan and Germany excluded from permanent seats, just as demographic power is belittled by the exclusion of countries like India, Indonesia and Brazil. The Permanent Five, argues Sutterlin, neither represent the most powerful states in today's world nor represent those regions in which conflict is most likely to occur.[21]

From whatever perspective one may choose to approach the problem, it is an undeniable fact that the present composition of the Security Council provides a highly distorted and badly skewed representation of the international community at large. Four of the five permanent seats are occupied by members of the Northern tier of industrialized states, three of them, moreover, being European states. The disparity in representation between Northern and Southern members exists also with respect to non-permanent seats, although it is less blatant than the maldistribution of permanent seats. There are 22 Asian members competing for one non-permanent seat in the Council, compared respectively to 17 members from Africa and Latin America, 12 from West Europe, and 10 from East Europe.[22] This shortcoming in representation is magnified by the fact that the Security Council is the only UN body which can make binding decisions. What further aggravates the maldistribution is the conspicuous mismatch between the geographic location of security problems—most of them originating as civil strife and humanitarian emergencies in the Third World—and the Northern domination in the Council's present composition. In the long term, it is probably an untenable "division of labour," where the problems originate in the South, while the solution, if there is to be one, will be determined by members of the Northern tier in accordance with the existing structure of the Council.

In order to prevent permanent alienation and loss of credibility and trust among developing countries, it is essential that the overall number of Council members from the Southern tier be increased as rapidly as possible. Such an increase was achieved in 1965 when the number of non-permanent seats was increased from the original six to ten. This was one of the rare instances of a successful amendment to the UN Charter—the other two were increases in the membership of the Economic and Social Council (ECOSOC)—and it was motivated by the desire to provide more representation for the many newly independent countries, most of them from the Southern tier, which had recently been admitted to the United Nations. Of all the many proposals for Security Council Charter reform which are now being circulated, the proposal to add another four or five non-permanent seats for developing countries from Asia, Africa and Latin America has the greatest chance of being accepted and quickly implemented.

Such a reform would, in part at least, solve the problem of making the Security Council more representative in nature. This is above all other considerations a matter of political justice and also of prudence, for it would create a more favourable "constituency" for the Security Council in the international community at large. As the Qureshi-Weizsäcker Report argues, "the Security Council must become more representative of diverse perspectives if actions are to command full respect in all parts of the world."[23] But in order to prevent the Council from becoming an anachronistic and essentially symbolic institution, consideration must also be given to the dimension of power, and additional permanent seats should be created in recognition of the fact that power is not merely defined in traditional realist and military terms but also of more diverse characteristics such as global economic influence and regional political leadership.

There has been a plethora of proposals from member states, organizations and individual analysts for the reform of the Security Council. Only a small sample of these will be addressed here in order to demonstrate the diversity of thinking and the accompanying problems raised. The UN itself has helped stimulate this search for reform. In December 1992, the General Assembly passed a resolution asking the Secretary-General to ascertain the views of member states on a possible review of the membership of the Security Council that would take account of the alterations in overall UN membership and other international changes.[24] Approximately one hundred member states have submitted their views on this matter, which indicates that Security Council reform is widely regarded as a priority issue. As well, in December 1993 an "Open-ended Working Group on the Question of Equitable Representation on and Increase in the Membership of the Security Council" was set up by General Assembly consensus.[25] Despite the hope expressed by the Secretary-General that the working group might come up with specific recommendations by the end of the UN's 50th anniversary year, the group is completely immobilized after two years of deliberations. The only agreement that has emerged from the Open-ended Working Group is the expression of a general consensus that the size of the Council should be increased to a total number lying somewhere between 20 and 25 members. But otherwise the group remains deadlocked on the more controversial issues of determining the number of permanent members, designating the candidates for permanent seats and modifying voting rules, especially as these apply to the veto.

A Two-Track Approach to Security Council Reform

The UN Charter shares with the Canadian constitution the dubious distinction of being virtually amendment-proof. UN Charter amendments have to face a dual hurdle: first, ratification by two-thirds of all member states, which in to-day's terms would require over 120 affirmative votes and, second, the concurrent vote of the five permanent members. Any proposal that does not go far enough in rectifying the current imbalance by opening additional seats to developing countries and curtailing the veto privileges of the permanent members would fall short of the required two-thirds majority. In turn, any attempt to diminish the privileges of the incumbent permanent members would fall under the axe of their veto. The magic formula for Charter amendment would have to be one that satisfies the under-represented members without alienating the privileged ones. It is a recipe for class warfare.

Given the difficulty of amendments, it would be wise to pursue a two-track approach. Track One would be the more ambitious route of seeking formal Charter reform. Track Two would be the more pragmatic method of producing de facto changes in the operation of the Security Council that fall short of formal Charter amendments. To cite examples of de facto changes, one could refer to an important interpretative ruling, which the Security Council made in 1946, to count an abstention by a permanent member as a concurring vote rather than a veto. This interpretation greatly diminished the potential scope of the veto. In 1991, again without a formal Charter amendment, the Council decided to treat Russia as the successor to the permanent seat previously occupied by the Soviet Union.[26] In the same second track manner, the permanent members could make a solemn declaration of their intention to restrict the exercise of their veto to a more confined range of issues, such as Chapter VII and peacekeeping decisions. Another voluntary restraint would be acceptance of a so-called dual veto, that is, an agreement not to cast a veto except in conjunction with another permanent member's negative vote. The concept of dual veto has recently been introduced to facilitate decision-making in the Organization for Security and Cooperation in Europe (OSCE). A group of Canadian experts has recommended an even more stringent provision, namely a triple veto.[27] Such voluntary restraints, while not legally binding, might make prospective candidates more inclined to accept the status discrimination implied in occupation of a permanent seat without a veto. It is, indeed, a great irony that most of the obvious aspirants for permanent membership have themselves been critical of the veto role; they are nevertheless reluctant to settle for an inferior status to that enjoyed by the original five permanent members.

Admitting More Permanent Members

Germany and Japan have indicated that, while they have no special interest in the veto, they are naturally reluctant, to cite German Chancellor Kohl, to accept second class membership.[28] To do so would be to run the risk of domestic repercussions, since both Japan and Germany now contribute more to the UN budget than all of the current permanent members except the United States.[29] In an interesting transmigration of the historical concept, one now hears Germans making the argument of "no taxation without representation."[30]

Since 1993, Japan and Germany have openly promoted their claim to a permanent seat in the Security Council; Prime Minister Morihiro, in a very oblique Japanese manner, has told the UN General Assembly that Japan is prepared to do all it could to discharge its responsibilities in a reformed United Nations.[31] Germany has followed suit in a somewhat more direct way. The Permanent Five have been cautiously supportive of these claims. One advantage of the admission of these two countries would be the possibility of easing the UN's current fiscal crisis, as Germany and Japan might be prepared to buy their way into the Great Power club. But the Permanent Five adamantly insist that this reform be accomplished in a controlled surgical manner that does not open the way for an entire restructuring of the Security Council. There is a widely held view among developed states that Germany and Japan are de facto Great Powers and that their formal readmission to the concert of Great Powers is long overdue. After all, it took post-Napoleonic France only two years, following Waterloo, to rejoin the European concert, and Weimar Germany was admitted as a permanent member of the League of Nations Council in 1926, eight years after the November armistice of 1918. There is also considerable support for Japan's candidacy among developing countries—somewhat less for Germany— because Japan is an Asian power and expected to help neutralize U.S. predominance in the Security Council.[32] But most of this support is highly conditional and depends on a more fundamental reform of the Security Council, notably with respect to the role of the veto and the admission of developing countries to permanent seats. It is because of inability to disentangle these factors that consensus has so far evaded the Open-ended Working Group and other interested fora. If a solution is to be found, it will in all probability have to be in the form of a broad package solution. The first and easier step, as indicated above, would be to admit more developing countries to non-permanent seats in order to make the Security Council a more representative body. The second and more difficult step would be to arrange a package deal, serving the principles of equity and efficiency under this arrangement: Germany, Japan and at least one regional power from Africa, Asia and Latin America, respectively, would be admitted to permanent seats, without a veto, in return for a substantial de facto or formal Charter curtailment of the veto rights for the original five permanent members.

Such an arrangement would, in fact, give rise to a three-tiered Security Council:

a.   the original five permanent members with curtailed veto rights;

b.   five new permanent members without veto rights;

c.   approximately 15 non-permanent members.

One way to overcome the systematic discrimination between two categories of permanent members would be to introduce a form of qualified majority voting in which the votes of the Great Powers would be assigned different weights according to some explicit criterion such as population, GNP or contribution to the UN budget. The set of weighted votes could be recalculated periodically and would permit discrimination between permanent members. In order to be assigned a higher weight, members might even be willing to increase their share of the UN budget, a very unlikely contingency under normal circumstances. Weighted voting is the accepted method of decision-making in a number of important organizations, International Monetary Fund (IMF) or the Council of Ministers of the European Union, for handling issues falling under the Single European Act. It reflects a commitment to realism which deviates sharply from the one-nation-one-vote principle that governs decision-making in the UN. There is, of course, a hidden weighted vote inherent in the Security Council veto, for it gives a permanent member a potential weight of 6, i.e., the power to reduce a potential majority vote of 14 to an outcome that is equivalent to a failed minority of 8 or fewer votes.

As if a three-tiered Security Council was not complex enough, a few of the national proposals made in response to United Nations General Assembly Resolution 47/62 have advocated the creation of a new semi-permanent category. The Italians, who are unlikely to attain permanent membership under any arrangement, have been the most vocal supporters of semi-permanent membership. Under their scheme, 20 designated countries, making special financial or other contributions to the UN, should be able to alternate with one another for 10 available seats spread over all five continents.[33] The Netherlands have proposed a somewhat different approach to establishing semi-permanent seats. Under the Netherlands scheme, each region would be allowed one extra seat which could be exempted from Article 23(2) of the Charter which rules out re-election for non-permanent members. By waiving this Charter restriction, members of a regional group would be allowed to decide who should be exempted from this particular restriction. This would create de facto semi-permanent seats at the discretion of regional groups and would strengthen the influence of some particularly qualified actors inside a regional group.[34]

Canadian Perspectives on Security Council Reform
Canada has traditionally stressed the qualitative aspect of Article 23 of the Charter, under which the eligibility of non-permanent members

is to be determined in accordance with their ability to contribute to the maintenance of international peace and security. If strictly applied, this criterion could lead to something approximating semi-permanent membership for countries like Canada which have made a very conspicuous contribution to UN peacekeeping and peace-making.[35] In practice, it has been very much diluted by the competing criterion, according to which non-permanent members are chosen on the basis of equitable regional distribution. During the 50-year UN history, Canada has served on the Security Council for five terms, i.e., for a total of ten years. This certainly falls short of semi-permanent membership, but it is distinctly more frequent than it would have been if the selection had proceeded on a purely random basis.

In her speech to the General Assembly on October 13, 1994, Canada's Permanent Representative to the United Nations, Louise Fréchette, welcomed the concept of semi-permanent seats to be shared for two-year periods by two or more countries. The creation of such a category "would have the double advantage of allowing countries that more fully meet the requirements of Article 23 of the Charter to sit more frequently on the Council, and would lessen the number of candidates for non-permanent status."[36] Canada was also open to other possibilities: creating new permanent seats, without, however, expressing support for any specific candidates,[37] establishing additional non-permanent seats, with or without the possibility of re-election, or reviewing the composition of the existing regional groups.

Ambassador Fréchette stressed four underlying objectives which should guide the expansion of Security Council membership:

1.   Making the Security Council more representative;
2.   Improving its efficiency;
3.   Improving its credibility;
4.   Enhancing its equity.

The first and third objective largely reinforce each other, for an expanded Security Council would be more credible if the new com-position reflected the emergence of important new actors in international relations. There may, however, be a genuine contradiction between making the Security Council more representative while retaining its capacity for quick and effective decision-making. The majority of reform proposals submitted so far envisage an enlargement of the Security Council from its present membership of 15 to a total between 20 and 25. An optimistic interpretation might argue that an enlarged Council could provide more credibility and talent and thus enhance its effectiveness.[38] Most commentators take a contrary view. The mere numerical increase of members will tend to complicate decision-making, particularly if the Council were to adopt a system of three or four-tiered membership. Canadian and foreign diplomats who have served on the Security Council are of the general opinion that flexibility and intimacy, qualities which facilitate efficient decision-making, would deteriorate once the number of Council members exceeded 20.[39] An astute observer of UN affairs, James Sutterlin, has warned that the addition of members from developing regions could complicate decision-making on the most sensitive aspect of conflict prevention, i.e., internal conflict and nation-building.[40]

As a major contributor to UN peacekeeping missions Canada has for some time been vocal in insisting on improved and more structured methods of communication between the Security Council and troop-contributing countries (TCC)—most of them not members of the Council—when renewing mandates or when important events occur in the course of peacekeeping operations. In 1994, the UK, fearing an open rebellion from the ranks of troop-contributing countries and responding to the energetic efforts of non-permanent members like New Zealand, persuaded its colleagues on the Council to accept certain changes. The most important of these has been the new practice, adopted by the Security Council, of consulting more widely with troop-contributing countries. Regular consultative meetings are now scheduled between members of the Council, troop-contributing countries and Secretariat staff to discuss different aspects of peacekeeping operations, including renewal and changes of mandates.

Other innovations intended to make decision-making by the Security Council more transparent and more responsive to the needs of non-members include the following:

- daily or twice-weekly briefings given by the President of the Security Council to non-members of the Council;
- daily publication in the UN Journal of the provisional agenda of formal meetings of the Council, and informal consultation of Council members;

- monthly circulation of the Council's tentative program of work for the forthcoming month;
- improvements aimed at making the activity of the Council's sanctions committees more transparent.

The Open-ended Working Group has commented favourably on these changes and has noted that they have taken place without impairing the effectiveness of the Security Council. The reaction of individual troop-contributing countries has been more mixed. While it is generally conceded that the innovations represent a long over-due move in the right direction, there exist many shortcomings that still need to be resolved. Canada and other TCC members have crit-icized the Security Council for not allowing enough time to prepare for these consultative meetings, for not providing adequate informa-tion and, most of all, for the passive role adopted by permanent members. The latter are determined not to let their authority be diluted by sharing it with a new tier composed of troop-contributing countries, and the Secretary-General, like the catchy advertisement for Calvin Klein jeans, will not let anything, including troop-con-tributing countries, come between him and the Security Council.

CONCLUSION

Following the termination of the Cold War, the UN Security Council has proceeded with remarkable vigour to take on a variety of com-plex missions, many of them quite unprecedented in nature. Its track record has, at best, been a mixed one and has given rise to a slightly more self-critical and introspective mood, as compared with the euphoric spirit that prevailed during the immediate post-Cold war years. Apart from any reform of its composition and voting proce-dures, the evolution of the Security Council will depend largely on the way in which the concept of security will be treated in future. The traditional concept, i.e., the protection of states from foreign aggres-sion, which is embedded in the UN Charter, is gradually giving way to a much more encompassing definition which is concerned with "protection from deadly harm for both states and populations."[41] Given the high level of domestic turmoil that is encountered in almost all parts of the world, the Security Council will increasingly be drawn into problem areas such as humanitarian assistance, ethnic conflict, strengthening of democratic institutions, and reconstructing failed sates, all lying outside its traditional mandate to maintain international peace and security.[42] To be capable of responding effectively, the Security Council will have to develop clear criteria to guide decisions on future interventions, build an international constituency to support its expanded activities, and mobilize the necessary financial and personnel resources to permit such ventures to be sustained. In its recent operations, the Council has encountered severe problems in all three dimensions. The criteria used were often vague, contrived and inconsistent. International support was, at best, divided, and the available resources inadequate.

The Qureshi-Weizsäcker Report fully endorses a comprehensive concept of security and recommends the creation of two additional councils to operate in tandem with the Security Council. Collectively, the three UN councils would be able to address the full scope of security needs, although the report is unclear as to whether the Security Council will have a superordinate status in its relationship with the other two bodies. The proposed Economic Council would become a very much improved version of ECOSOC that would integrate the work of all UN agencies and international institutions concerned with economic issues. Furthermore, it would be responsible for coordinating efforts to rebuild weakened or failed states. The Social Council would supervise UN work on social development, education, health, and women. Moreover, at the request of the Security Council and of political groups in distressed states, the Social Council could be given custodianship over failed states to help restore their social and political integrity and the capacity to exercise their sovereign rights.[43]

The Security Council is not unaccustomed to dealing with civil war issues, as for example in the Congo, Cyprus and Lebanon. The new feature in the post-Cold War era is the almost complete shift of the balance of UN involvement from inter-state to intra-state conflict situations. What is less clear and more controversial than UN involvement in the negotiation and supervision of ceasefires ending civil wars is the Security Council's more intrusive humanitarian intervention (e.g., Somalia, Rwanda, the Kurdish part of Iraq, and Bosnia), the reconstruction of failed states (e.g., Somalia, El Salvador and Cambodia), and the restoration of democratic institutions (e.g., Haiti). During much of the Cold War, UN decisions were generally guided by a strict sovereignist interpretation based on Article 2(7) of the Charter, which prohibited UN intervention in matters which were essentially within the domestic jurisdiction of member states. For some time, it has generally been accepted that, if violations to international humanitarian law are so gross and pervasive as to threaten international peace and security, the Security Council is empowered to take military or non-military action.[44] The January 1992 Security Council heads of government summit recognized that "non-military sources of instability ... have become threats to peace and security."[45] After the end of the Cold War, the sovereignty/non-intervention mind-set is less predominant in the United Nations, and member states are more disposed to accept the view "that matters of domestic jurisdiction must be understood in the light of other principles in the Charter, and in particular the commitment of UN members to promote respect for human rights and fundamental freedoms."[46] Perhaps even more pronounced than the shift in the view of member states is the general trend in international public opinion. In his address at the University of Bordeaux, Secretary-General Pérez de Cuéllar stressed that we "are clearly witnessing what is probably an irresistible shift in public attitudes toward the belief that the defence of the oppressed in the name of morality should prevail over frontiers and legal documents."[47]

But while there may have been a shift in interpretation, we have not yet arrived at an international consensus. Haas recognizes this when he notes that "we are a long way from a consensus on the primacy of a right to intervene on behalf of refugees, starving people and democracy."[48] Forsythe makes the same point when he notes that since 1945 all cases of humanitarian intervention have been "unclear, controversial, and contested by someone."[49] While states have come to accept the principle that human rights are a legitimate subject for diplomacy, as has been stated in the 1993 Vienna Declaration, they are "reluctant to use the international authority inherent in the Charter to have the Security Council systematically override state autonomy concerning human rights."[50]

Given the absence of consensus and the controversial nature of the topic, it is essential that the Security Council draft general principles and flexible guidelines, to be applied when it is considering whether a domestic situation warrants international action by the Council or by regional organizations. To give an example, the Council might define how massive and intolerable human rights violations must be before they can trigger an international intervention authorized by the Council; it could stipulate whether there must be a demonstrable threat to international peace and security before such intervention is justified; it might outline what requests by relevant domestic groups must precede an authorization by the Council to reconstruct failed states or restore democratic institutions. Sutterlin calls for informal and flexible guidelines "for determining when an internal crisis constitutes a threat to international security warranting intervention by the Council." Such guidelines need no formal Charter revision as they could be incorporated in the repertoire of the Council on the basis of an agreed statement by its President.[51] Once the Security Council has agreed to such guidelines and criteria, it is important that they be applied in an impartial and consistent manner. There has been strong criticism, particularly from developing countries, to the effect that the Security Council applies standards that are neither consistent nor impartial. Critics of the Council will argue that Russia has been accorded a sphere of influence that leaves it free to operate in the region of the former USSR without fear of UN censure, intervention or reprisal. The Council is deemed to have shown much greater concern for situations which are of direct interest to permanent members (e.g., Bosnia or Haiti), or in which intensive exposure by Cable News Network (CNN) cameras has raised the level of Western discomfort (e.g., Somalia and Rwanda), while ignoring equally pressing disaster areas like Sudan, Liberia and Sierra Leone, because they do not directly impinge on Great Power interests or awareness.

What is urgently required is the development of new norms and principles which define the role of the United Nations in humanitarian crises, the reconstruction of failed states and the strengthening of democratic institutions. Such a task would best be undertaken in close collaboration between the two principal bodies of the United Nations, the Security Council and the General Assembly. The widely held belief that the Security Council is dominated by the permanent members has led to some unhelpful competition between the General Assembly and the Council. The General Assembly has found ways to evade Article 12(1) of the Charter which tries to prevent the Council and Assembly from dealing with the same issue simultaneously. Since 1990, the Annual Report of the Security Council to the General Assembly, which used to be accepted in a purely perfunctory manner, has been subjected to much greater scrutiny and criticism. Members of the Assembly have called for greater transparency in the operations of the Council, more detailed reports, more accompanying statistics and analysis, and better insight into its actual decision-making. Just as the Security Council tried to forestall a rebellion of troop-contributing countries in 1994, it has issued a similar response in an attempt to pre-empt a further barrage of criticism from the Assembly. It has announced some remedies, notably more detailed reporting and regular consultations between the President of the Council and the President of the General Assembly. In future, statements of the President of the Security Council will be included together with resolutions as a regular part of the Annual Report.[52]

Even if there appears to be some competition and tension between these two bodies, they complement each other extremely well for the purpose of articulating a new set of international rules and norms. By virtue of its universal membership and its function as an open debating forum, the General Assembly is particularly well suited to act as the conscience of the world, and in that capacity it can play a role in formulating such norms. It would then be the responsibility of the Security Council to translate the norms and principles into more precise operating guidelines and, finally, to take the necessary decisions to put them into practice.

NOTES

1   Günter Altenburg, "Deutschland auf dem Prüfstand," *Europa-Archiv*, 24, (1994), 694.

2   Helen Leigh-Phippard, "Remaking the Security Council," *The World Today* (August-September 1994), 168.

3   Boutros Boutros-Ghali, *Agenda for Peace 1995*, 2nd. ed. (New York: United Nations, 1995), 8.

4   Report of the Independent Working Group on the Future of the United Nations, co-chaired by Moeen Qureshi, former Prime Minister of Pakistan, and Baron Richard von Weizsäcker, former President of Germany, *The United Nations in Its Second Half-Century*, (New York: Ford Foundation, 1995), 3 hereafter cited as Qureshi-Weizsäcker Report.

5   Boutros-Ghali, *Agenda for Peace*, 8.

6   James Sutterlin, "United Nations Decision-making: Future Initiatives for the Security Council and the Secretary-General," in Thomas Weiss, ed., *Collective Security in a Changing World*, (Boulder: Lynne Rienner, 1993), 121.

7   Boutros-Ghali, *Agenda for Peace*, 10.

8   Sally Morphet, "The Influence of States and Groups of States on and in the Security Council and General Assembly," *Review of International Studies* 21, (1995), 444.

9   Sydney Bailey, *The UN Security Council and Human Rights*, (New York: St. Martin's Press, 1994), 128.

10   Benjamin Rivlin, "The Changing International Political Climate and the Secretary-General," in Benjamin Rivlin and Leon Gordenker, eds., *The Challenging Role of the UN Secretary-General*, (Westport: Praeger, 1993), 8. Since 1970 China has cast a total of 7 vetoes; France 13; USSR/Russia 10; UK 24; and U.S. 66.

11   Bailey, *The UN Security Council*, 127.

12   *Journal of Palestine Studies* 25, (Autumn 1995), 134-36.

13   Morphet, "The Influence of States," 436.

14   Morphet, "The Influence of States," 457.

15   Mohammed Ayoob, "Squaring the Circle: Collective Security in a System of States," in Weiss, *Collective Security*, 57.

16   Barry Buzan, *People, States and Fear*, 2nd. ed., (Boulder: Lynne Rienner, 1991); Kenneth Booth, "Security and Emancipation," *Review of International Studies* 17, (1991), 313-26; Thomas Homer-Dixon. "Environmental Scarcity and Intergroup Conflict," in Michael Klare and Daniel Thomas, eds., *World Security*, 2nd. ed., (New York: St. Martin's Press, 1994), 290-313.

17   In August 1986, the UK government proposed that the Council deal with the problem of drug trafficking. The non-aligned countries pre-empted this move by calling for a special session of the General Assembly on narcotics and the UK withdrew the proposal.

18   Modesto Seara-Vazquez, "The UN Security Council at Fifty: Midlife Crisis or Terminal Illness?," *Global Governance* 1, (1995), 285-96.

19   Leigh-Phippard, "Remaking the Security Council," 168.

20   Verbatim Record of the 3046th Meeting of the UN Security Council (S/PV.3046), January 31, 1992.

21   Sutterlin, "United Nations Decision-making," 130.

22   Morphet, *"The Influence of States,"* 451-52.

23   Qureshi-Weizsäcker Report, 15.

24   UN General Assembly Resolution 47/62, December 11, 1992.

25   United Nations General Assembly Resolution 48/26.

26   Bailey, *The UN Security Council*, 8.

27   Canadian Committee for the Fiftieth Anniversary of the United Nations, "Canadian Priorities for United Nations Reform," (Ottawa: Canadian Committee for the Fiftieth Anniversary of the United Nations 1994), 8. [Hereafter cited as "Canadian Priorities."]

28   Cited in Wolfgang Wagner, "Der ständige Sitz im Sicherheitsrat," *Europa-Archiv* 19, (1993), 537. It is interesting to note that German Foreign Minister Klaus Kinkel has taken a more flexible position than his Chancellor by indicating a willingness to see new permanent members like Germany and Japan join the Council without a veto.

29   Winrich Kühne, "Erweiterung und Reform des UN-Sicherheitsrats," *Europa-Archiv* 24, (1994), 690.

30   Karl Kaiser, "Die ständige Mitgliedschaft im Sicherheitsrat," *Europa-Archiv* 19 (1993), 547.

31   Fujita Hiroshi, "UN Reform and Japan's Permanent Security Council Seat," *Japan Quarterly* 42, (October-December 1995), 436-42.

32   Miroshi, "*UN Reform*," 439.

33   Italy's response to UN General Assembly Resolution 47/62, December 11, 1992; cited in *Europa-Archiv* 19, (1993), D388.

34   Netherland's reply to UN General Assembly Resolution 47/62, December 11, 1992; cited in *Europa-Archiv* 19, (1993), D396.

35   Harald von Riekhoff, "Canadian Attitudes and Approaches to the United Nations Security Council," *Background Paper* 26, (Ottawa: Canadian Institute of International Peace and Security, 1989), 2.

36   Louise Fréchette, "Statement to the 49th Session of the United Nations General Assembly," (New York: Permanent Mission of Canada to the United Nations, October 13, 1994), 2.

37   Prime Minister Mulroney had indicated Canadian support for permanent seats for Japan and Germany. The Chrétien government has not repeated this promise. There is little to be gained from fighting in the trenches for any new permanent member, particularly because almost any Security Council reform is likely to work to the detriment of Canada's influence.

38   "Canadian Priorities," vii.

39   Confidential interviews.

40   Sutterlin, " United Nations Decision-making," 131.

41   Ibid, 121.

42   Ibid, 137.

43   Qureshi-Weizsäcker Report, 29-40.

44   Bailey, *UN Security Council*, 123.

45   UN Security Council, Document S/23500, January 31, 1992.

46   Bailey, 123.

47   Secretary-General Pérez de Cuéllar's address at the University of Bordeaux, United Nations Department of Public Information (UNDPI), (New York: UN Department of Public Information, Press Release, SG/SM/4560, April 14, 1991).

48   Ernst Haas, "Collective Conflict Management: Evidence for a New World Order?," in Weiss, *Collective Security*, 81.

49   David Forsythe, "The UN Secretary-General and Human Rights," in Rivlin and Leon Gordenker, *The Challenging Role*, 221.

50   Forsythe, "The UN Secretary-General," 221.

51   Sutterlin, "United Nations Decision-making," 124.

52   Morphet, "The Influence of States," 446-49.

XI

Canadian Public and Governmental Perceptions of United Nations Reform

GREGORY WIRICK

"At a time when we are preparing to celebrate the 50th anniversary of the UN, there is no more urgent task than intensifying our efforts for reform in order to give our organization the second wind it needs."

André Ouellet, Minister of Foreign Affairs, before the 49th UN General Assembly, September 29, 1994

"The United Nations system is the only existing global organization.... The challenge is somehow to improve the present structure as a basis for reducing the worst global problems, and for contributing to the solution of as many others as possible."

Canadian Committee for the Fiftieth Anniversary of the United Nations, Canadian Priorities for United Nations Reform, June 1994

The election of the Chrétien government to power in Ottawa on October 25, 1993 occasioned a return to the verities of Pearsonian internationalism. This did not come as a surprise to those who had perused the Red Book which outlined Liberal Party policy prior to the election. What was surprising was the eagerness with which the government appropriated the legacy of Lester Pearson.

One of the early efforts the Liberals made, in advance of the election, to outline their foreign policy came at a Vancouver conference, "Canada and the United Nations System in the 21st Century," held October 24-26, 1991. It was organized under the auspices of the National Liberal Caucus Committee on Foreign Affairs, chaired by Lloyd Axworthy, the M.P. for Winnipeg South Centre and Opposition critic on External Affairs, Mr. Axworthy's interest in the topic was well-known and dated at least back to his days as a doctoral student at Princeton University where his thinking was influenced by the scholar of international institutions, Leon Gordenker. The conference report also made special mention of the help of Ivan Head, the international affairs advisor to Prime Minister Trudeau and later President of the International Development Research Centre, who was then teaching law at the University of British Columbia.

The priorities for the UN that were outlined in the resulting Vancouver Declaration were: peace through preventive diplomacy, peace through collective action, peace through democratic development, and peace through the rule of law. For Canada, the priorities were simpler: to democratize foreign policy by elevating Parliament's review and advisory powers with respect to foreign affairs and by enhancing public access to information.

The Red Book, which served as the principal policy document for the Liberals during the 1993 federal campaign, repeated many of the same nostrums as the Vancouver Declaration. It highlighted the following view: "Liberals believe Canadians want their national government to play a more active, independent, internationalist role in this world of change....Canadians want a national government that takes pride in their tolerance, openness, and common sense, and that reflects those values in its foreign policy."[1] The chapter devoted to international affairs—entitled "An Independent Foreign Policy"— went on to declare that "Canada's role in the world can be strengthened by developing a secure multilateral context for countries like ours, within the framework of international law and the forum of the United Nations."

Among the new ideas broached in this chapter was a reorientation of defence policy and procurement practices to emphasize the key priority of international peacekeeping. "Consideration will be

given to creating a special peacekeeping brigade, comprising
Canadian volunteers with both military and non-military expertise...."
There was also concern expressed to improve the UN's policies on
peacekeeping.[2]

Another proposal was to hold a UN Charter Review Conference
in 1995, the 50th anniversary year of the founding of the world organization. The document laid out its aspirations clearly, but followed
them with a warning:

The UN is experiencing a renaissance in its authority and stature in the
world, much as its founders hoped it would.... However, a crisis of confidence in the UN's financial and political capacities is threatening to destroy
the chances for a new and stronger internationalism. Resolving this contradiction in favour of an improved UN will require vigorous and persistent
diplomatic initiative and negotiation. Canada's strong legacy of support for
the UN and the reputation we have built there give us a unique opportunity to help lead this effort.[3]

In the meantime, the United Nations Association in Canada (UNA-
Canada) had been setting up a process to mark the 50th anniversary.
Its origins date back to the fall of 1992. The concept was to have the
non-governmental sector and the Government of Canada working in
close cooperation to organize ways to mark the anniversary. Hence,
although the idea originated with a non-governmental organization
(NGO)—UNA-Canada—a strong government presence and involvement in every aspect of planning and implementation was envisaged
from the outset. The favoured approach was to conceive and implement a series of events across the country marking the fiftieth
anniversary and to indicate thereby both the breadth of concerns and
activity within the UN system and the many different ways in which
Canadians related to its work.

From the outset, substantive issues were emphasized, especially
by Douglas Roche, whom the UNA-Canada board approached in
August 1992 to act as Chairman of a putative Canadian Committee for
the Fiftieth Anniversary of the United Nations; this Committee was
selected over the next few months and formally launched in May
1993. It set up several satellite committees to deal with different
issues, one of which—the UN Reform Committee—was intended to
advise on policy research questions. It was chaired by Dr. Michael
Oliver, who doubled as the National President of UNA-Canada and

who strongly supported Roche's emphasis on substantive issues of public policy.[4] This satellite committee set up several working groups and attracted some important persons to chair them. These included retired diplomat Geoffrey Pearson to head the working group on *An Agenda for Peace*; Nancy Gordon, Deputy Executive Director of CARE Canada to head the group on human rights; and first Ted English, Emeritus Professor of Economics at Carleton University, and later Naresh Singh of the International Institute for Sustainable Development, based in Winnipeg, to chair the one on *An Agenda for Development*, the Secretary-General's laborious but less successful exercise to produce a statement on UN development activities of comparable significance to *An Agenda for Peace*.

As part of the Red Book's emphasis on democratizing the foreign policy process, the government launched a complete review of Canadian foreign and defence policy, first signalling its intention in the Speech from the Throne of January 18, 1994 that opened the first session of the 35th Parliament. Two special committees were established, both drawn jointly from the House of Commons and the Senate. The first, set up on March 15, 1994, was to consider, "Canada's foreign policy including international trade and international assistance," while the second, on Canadian defence policy, was organized on June 22, 1994—the first such comprehensive review ever undertaken in Canada. Each committee was co-chaired by a Senator and a Member of Parliament. For the foreign policy committee, the chairs were Senator Allan J. MacEachen, the former senior Trudeau cabinet minister and Deputy Prime Minister, and Jean-Robert Gauthier, the veteran M.P. for Ottawa Vanier, while for the parliamentary defence review, another Trudeau cabinet minister, Senator Pierre De Bané, co-chaired with Bill Rompkey, the longtime Liberal M.P. for Labrador.

To launch the foreign policy review process, a general debate on Canada's international relations was held in the House of Commons. The new Foreign Minister, André Ouellet, led off with a lengthy "tour d'horizon" in which he frequently alluded to the legacy of Lester Pearson and quoted from the book by his son, Geoffrey Pearson, *Seize the Day*, concerning Lester Pearson's time as External Affairs Minister in the 1950s. Among the responses the most thoughtful was that of Lucien Bouchard, the Leader of the Bloc Québécois, who quoted UN Secretary-General Boutros-Ghali at some length, to wit, "'To enter into a relation with someone else, you must first be yourself. This is why a sound globalization of modern life is based on strong identities, since the globalization of a standardized culture could crush other cultures and melt them together, something from which the world has nothing to gain.'"[5]

As a first step in the process, the government organized the first National Forum on Canada's International Relations, held on March 20-21, 1994, under co-chairs Janice Stein, a University of Toronto political scientist, and Pierre Pettigrew, vice-president of a Montreal consulting firm. The forum involved about 100 invited participants drawn from various relevant constituencies to discuss the entire canvas of Canada's international commitments and aspirations. It then reported its findings to one of the first sessions of the Special Joint Committee Reviewing Canada's Foreign Policy. At that meeting, the National Forum co-chairs reported seven priority areas identified by the Forum, including the UN itself and peacekeeping.

Peacekeeping was identified as an area of comparative advantage for Canada in view of the country's long historical experience. Accordingly, "there was a sense that Canadian forces could be restructured to emphasize a larger army, a smaller air force and a differently configured naval force..." The rationale for a larger army was not the existence of any direct threat of attack against Canada but because:

The rationale for a larger army is that we are now unable to meet the requests for peacekeeping that the international community directs to us, that our capabilities are stretched thin by the present deployment of forces in Bosnia, that this is an area again that the forum identified as one of comparative advantage for this country in a way [sic] that it contributes to the international community and toward international security.[6]

The upcoming 50th anniversary of the United Nations also gave National Forum participants "a sense that Canada could lead in the international effort to reform some of the creaking machinery of the United Nations."[7] Specifically, "in the case of United Nations agencies that are not doing an efficient job, it was suggested that Canada withdraw if this conclusion is confirmed by a study."[8] No such withdrawals have occurred in the subsequent interval and the built-in bureaucratic inhibitions against taking such action should not be underestimated. Each UN specialized agency acquires its own constituency within the federal government, which makes any objective assessment extremely difficult. Indeed, even the Food and Agriculture

Organization, which over the years could hardly be said to be one of Canada's favourite agencies, nonetheless came in for special largesse and attention from Canada through the Department of Agriculture when in October 1995 its own anniversary was marked in Quebec City, where it had been founded 50 years before.

A leading influence on both Parliamentary Joint Committee reviews was the Canada 21 Council. This initiative had been supported chiefly by the Walter and Duncan Gordon Charitable Foundation of Toronto and involved an impressive roster of notable Canadians. Its report, *Canada 21: Canada and Common Security in the Twenty-First Century,* appeared precisely at the time when the Joint Committees were beginning their own hearings in the spring of 1994. Partly because of the membership of Canada 21 (it included a generous sprinkling of well-known Liberals), partly because of the sophisticated professionalism of the product, and partly because of some new ideas and approaches it offered, Canada 21 had considerable impact on the deliberations of both Joint Committees.

The central thrust of Canada 21 was in support of a concept of common security: "the ability to create the conditions of tolerance and respect where a multiplicity of cultures and communities can flourish."[9] It offered a variety of prescriptions to achieve this end. With respect to peacekeeping, it focused on inadequate management of missions at the UN, and the complicated training requirements that would be needed if future UN operations were to span a range from traditional peacekeeping to quick deployment forces. However, although Canada 21 was keen for Canada to continue its involvement in UN peacekeeping, it proposed to exclude service in high-intensity operations against modern, heavily armoured forces.[10]

The parliamentary defence review committee was subtly antagonistic toward Canada 21's findings from the start, but used them as reference points to avoid. The foreign policy review was more sympathetic (indeed, at one point, Senator MacEachen observed that he had not yet heard anything that contradicted the group's main proposals—to the dismay of several onlookers).

Among the innumerable groups and witnesses who appeared before the committees, UNA-Canada and the Canadian Committee for the Fiftieth Anniversary of the United Nations made a joint appearance before the Joint Parliamentary Committee Reviewing Canada's Foreign Policy on June 15, 1994. There Douglas Roche and Michael Oliver presented a booklet, *Canadian Priorities for United Nations Reform,* which contained chapters on "An Agenda for Peace," "An

Agenda for Development," "An Agenda for Human Rights," and "An Agenda for Reform of the UN System," including 52 recommendations to the Government of Canada. The booklet was also presented to Prime Minister Jean Chrétien on June 16.

Its key recommendations included the following: an increase in the number of Security Council members from the current 15 to 21, with enhanced representation from Southern countries and an effort to reduce the significance of the veto power; value-for-money auditing and the appointment of a UN Auditor-General; tightening the standards of the UN's Register of Conventional Arms; the creation of a Sustainable Development Security Council and an International Development Advisory Council; greater coordination within the UN system on human rights questions; and the creation of international peace enforcement units to be deployed either as a quick reaction force or in other situations of high risk.[11]

The parliamentary joint committees continued to hear from witnesses across the country in a veritable orgy of consultation on every conceivable aspect of Canadian foreign and defence policy. After a series of trips both across Canada (from Whitehorse to St. John's) and out of the country (to Brussels, Washington and New York), the foreign policy committee concluded its work in November 1994 with its report, *Canada's Foreign Policy: Principles and Priorities for the Future*. The defence policy committee released its report, *Security in a Changing World*, simultaneously.

In both reports considerable emphasis was placed on issues relating to UN reform. The foreign policy review hedged on the vocabulary of common security, arguing it would be unhelpful to divide over security labels:

The task is collective—all states agree to renounce the use or threat of force among themselves and to assist any member under attack. The methods must be cooperative—seeking through multilateral methods to work *with* others, not against them. And the results should be shared in common—security as one dimension of the global commons.[12]

It did include a fairly detailed discussion of peacekeeping and asked a number of hard questions:

The UN cannot afford to do everything everywhere, and yet the UN has no agreed set of criteria to guide its decisions. We think there is a pressing need to establish clear and consistent criteria for intervention and for "exit strategies" so that missions do not get bogged down indefinitely with no resolution. Otherwise, there is a danger that the media will set the agenda (the CNN factor).[13]

The review also acknowledged the government's in-depth review of methods to strengthen the UN's rapid reaction capability (see below), although this was an afterthought, since the government did not wait for the Committee's report before launching that initiative. It set out a number of considerations to help guide decision making with respect to Canadian participation in peace operations. It also called for several changes in the way the UN mounted such operations. In general, the foreign policy review was cautious about an automatic embrace of UN peacekeeping, recommending "a more selective approach to Canadian involvement," while at the same time urging that training for such operations become a major thrust of Canadian policy.[14]

This cautious approach accurately reflected the increasing reserve on the part of many Canadians about the efficacy of UN peace operations, on which the experience of Somalia and former Yugoslavia cast considerable doubt. A January 1994 Gallup poll indicated that, while Canadians remained supportive of UN peacekeeping efforts, feelings were mixed about Canada's role in the former Yugoslavia. Nationally, 43 percent favoured either increasing (11 percent) or maintaining (32 percent) Canada's presence at its current level. An equal portion of the public, 43 percent, favoured either decreasing Canada's presence there (17 percent) or eliminating it altogether (26 percent). However, as the pollsters themselves pointed out, the 26 percent who favoured the complete elimination of Canada's presence in Yugoslavia was more than twice as large as the 12 percent who favoured the complete elimination of all Canada's global peacekeeping efforts.[15]

These misgivings on the public's part appeared to grow with time. A Gallup poll taken towards the end of the UN's fiftieth year (September 7, 1995) found that Canadians were losing respect for the world organization, in contrast to a similar poll taken in October 1990 when more claimed to be gaining respect. In the 1995 poll only nine percent of Canadians said they had increased respect for the UN as the years went by, compared to 34 percent in 1994. Conversely, 39 percent of Canadians in 1995 found that their respect was decreasing over the years (22 percent in 1990). Decreasing respect outweighed increasing respect in every region of the country, by a margin of roughly five to one in Quebec, Ontario and the Prairie provinces compared to a margin of three to one in British Columbia and the Atlantic provinces. If these polls were accurate, they demonstrated a fair degree of support for the UN, tempered, however, by a more realistic appreciation of the limitations of UN action in the current circumstances and conditions than was the case during the brief period of euphoria about the institution that followed the end of the Cold War.

Perhaps for this reason the government's own UN agenda during the anniversary year reflected two preoccupations which went to the heart of the UN's problems. One concerned the UN's inability to respond rapidly in military terms when threats to international peace and security arose. The other was the debilitating effects of the UN's ongoing financial crisis. These were identified as critical problems fairly early in the new government's mandate. Certainly by the time preparations were being made for Foreign Minister Ouellet's first address to the UN General Assembly in September 1994, the policy priorities were already sketched out, based in particular on the assessment of Louise Fréchette, Canada's serving Ambassador in New York at the time. Other issues—such as reform of the Security Council or the UN's social and economic agenda—were mentioned by government officials from time to time, but in a rather perfunctory way with no major leadership role for Canada either envisaged or undertaken.[16] The central issues in the government's eyes were credibility (hence the need to grapple with the question of rapid reaction) and survivability (requiring reform of the UN's finances and administration).

THE RAPID REACTION STUDY

On September 29, 1994, in his first address as Foreign Minister to the UN General Assembly, André Ouellet announced that the Canadian government would undertake a study of ways and means to improve the UN's capacity to respond rapidly to international crises. Above all else, it had been the frightful and first-hand experience of Rwanda that was the catalyst for the Canadian government's decision to press forward on the issue. The evident frustration of Major-General Roméo Dallaire, the Canadian commander of the United Nations Mission in Rwanda (UNAMIR), concerning his inability to do much more than stand at the sidelines of a blood bath, shook Canadian opinion and shocked the government into activity. Dallaire's own analysis was at the heart of the study:

In Rwanda, the international community's inaction ... contributed to the Hutu extremists' belief that they could carry out their genocide ... UNAMIR could have saved the lives of hundreds of thousands of people. As evidence, with the 450 men under my command during this interim, we saved and directly protected over 25,000 people and moved tens of thousands between the combat lines. A force of 5,000 personnel rapidly deployed could have prevented the massacres in the south and west of the country that did not commence in earnest until early May, nearly a month after the start of the war.[17]

The device the government chose for its pursuit of the matter was that of an in-depth review of the short-, medium- and long-term options available to strengthen the UN's rapid response capability in times of crisis. As Foreign Minister André Ouellet remarked in announcing the study in an address to the 49th UN General Assembly, "The international community cannot remain indifferent to the conflicts that threaten the lives of millions of innocent people and expose them to the worst violations of their most fundamental rights." Mr. Ouellet further noted:

some people are tempted to give up and wonder if the United Nations is wrong in trying to resolve essentially domestic conflicts that have numerous complex causes. Canada does not share this opinion.

We think that, despite these problems, the Security Council is on the right track, even though the steps it has taken have not always proved capable of solving all the problems.[18]

The study was a joint effort of two departments, Foreign Affairs and National Defence. Following the Minister's address, a Senior Steering Group of bureaucrats from both departments was appointed to guide the course of the study, while a Core Group of researchers and specialists drawn from outside the government was formed to oversee the preparation of background materials and the production of initial papers.

Two seminars were held, involving both of the above groups and a variety of additional experts, in Cornwallis, N.S. and Quebec City respectively. Among the most influential presentations made at these seminars were those of Major-General Dallaire, now Canada's Deputy Land Force Commander; Lieutenant-General (ret'd) J.K. Dangerfield, the former Director of NATO's International Military Staff; Major-General (ret'd) Andy Christie, the former commander of NATO's Ace Mobile Force (Land), and Sergio Vieira de Mello, a Brazilian UN official who was a key administrative official in the UN operations in Cambodia and Bosnia and who now serves as Director for Policy and Operations with the UN High Commissioner for Refugees.

Finally, a high-profile International Consultative Group was created under the co-chairmanship of Sir Brian Urquhart and Dr. John Polanyi, the University of Toronto professor and Nobel laureate in chemistry who had long been active in the Pugwash Group and other disarmament activities. They presided over an international roster of distinguished specialists, all of whom met as a group in Montebello, Quebec in early April 1995.

The next step was preparation of the actual report. This proceeded during the spring and summer, with the report being released by the Foreign Minister at the time of his address to the 50th General Assembly on September 26, 1995.[19] The report contained some 26 recommendations for action by the United Nations. The central recommendation, however, was that which called for the establishment of:

a permanent UN operational-level headquarters, which would be a standing, fully-deployable, integrated, multinational group of approximately 30 to 50 personnel, augmented in times of crisis, to conduct contingency planning and rapid deployment as authorized by the Security Council.

To ensure multidimensionality, the headquarters should contain a significant civil affairs branch with linkages to the key humanitarian and other agencies and the non-governmental sectors.[20]

Throughout the study emphasis was laid on the concept of a capability rather than a force. The stress was on a multi-disciplinary and multidimensional capacity, encompassing NGOs and humanitarian, human rights, political and legal elements as well as civilian police. Thus while the "instrument" at the sharp end of future UN action was hardly ignored (Dallaire's figure of 5,000 personnel became the benchmark for the military forces or "vanguard groups" involved), it was conceived as only part of the mechanism that would be needed.

The desirability of early treatment of an ailing body politic was a guiding metaphor for the Canadian study:

In certain parts of the world the society or nation-state is so afflicted that outside intervention is the only hope. In the body's case, this would mean active treatment by recognized medical authorities. Early on, before the body rebels absolutely, warning signals are sent out—perhaps a fever or another symptom. Doctors are consulted and decide whether and what treatment should be pursued. They are not always good diagnosticians, nor do they always possess the medicines required. But especially if they can identify a remedy that works, the chances are that they will prescribe it. This is the essence of an enhanced UN rapid reaction capability. It offers the United Nations a capability for effective intervention when the malady of the body politic reaches a crisis point or, better yet, when the disease is still containable. It remains up to the doctors (in this case, the Security Council) to decide how and if it should be used.[21]

"The time for moving towards fundamental improvements in the way the UN responds to crisis is now," declared Foreign Minister Ouellet when he presented the report to the 50th UN General Assembly in September 1995. "Follow-up is of key importance," he went on since, for Canada, "this report is only the first step in translating ideas into action." Hence he announced, among other things, that Canada would offer the UN the secondment or loan of civilian personnel "on a short-term, urgent basis to help in the development of a fully-trained capacity in the areas of human rights, legal advice, humanitarian assistance and other aspects of a rapid civilian response to crisis."[22]

The Canadian study was not the only one undertaken by a Member State; in addition, the Netherlands government prepared a "non-paper" on a UN rapid deployment brigade and the Danish government worked on a study of a multinational UN high readiness brigade. Both were completed in 1995, with the Netherlands holding a major international conference in March. Canada and the Netherlands co-chaired a meeting of the foreign ministers of 12 interested countries in New

York on September 27, on the sidelines of the General Assembly.[23] Out of that meeting a process has emerged at the level of the Permanent Representatives and Deputy Permanent Representatives to the UN, working under the title of "The Friends of Rapid Reaction." This group meets periodically to work out various details both among its members and in close consultation with Secretariat officials.

At the time of writing, according to a senior Foreign Affairs official, the aim is to hold another ministerial-level conclave by May or June of 1996, when it is hoped that an operational-level headquarters will be established, most likely in New York. There had been some hope, among Canadian officials at least, that such a headquarters might be created in Canada, especially if the Canadian government provided most of the resources, in order to maintain a kind of "firewall" between the UN's Department of Peacekeeping Operations and the standing operational headquarters. But UN officials have resisted the idea of a headquarters outside the Secretariat's control and since official circles in both Washington and London have sided with New York the idea of a Canadian location has essentially been shelved.

UNITED NATIONS FINANCES

The other set of issues that the Government identified early on as crucial for ensuring a viable future for the UN concerned finances. There were two aspects of the problem in Canada's view: the need to improve revenues and the need to manage the expenditure side more efficiently.

The costs of the UN system *per se* are relatively small. The UN's regular budget in 1995 was $1.35 billion. Peacekeeping costs, which are accounted for separately, reached $3.3 billion in 1994 and are expected to be almost as high in 1995. Voluntary contributions to UN specialized agencies account for approximately another $3 billion. This compares with Canada's federal budget (excluding debt) of Cdn. $114 billion for 1996, a Pentagon budget of $264 billion and military spending in developing countries of $125 billion.[24]

The biggest single difficulty is created by the chronic cash-flow shortages from which the UN suffers, largely because over half its members do not pay their dues on time. Currently, the UN is owed $2.52 billion in overdue assessments, 46 percent of it by the United States. In a bleak memo to staff in September 1995, Secretary-General Boutros-Ghali observed that "The high level of the cash short fall is unprecedented".[25]

The largest donor, the United States, is more concerned to find ways and means of reducing its aid bill still further, while a number of other countries enjoying fast-rising economies (notably China, Japan and the ASEAN countries) are paying considerably less than an equitable apportionment would suggest. Diplomatic circles at the UN in New York have not been keen to explore alternative sources of revenue because of the precedent it would set: in particular, member states have been determined not to let the United States off the hook. However, there is increasing concern about the multitude of demands on the global system and the uncertainty of revenues. This is one of the reasons that Canada has emphasized expenditures and the necessity to achieve economies of scale, closer coordination among different divisions and agencies, to create collective data banks, and to secure efficient personnel policies and elimination or delayering of duplicative structures within the bureaucracy.

At the same time, the government also spent some energy on considering alternative sources of revenue for the world body. Among the most prominent ideas that have been discussed is that of some sort of fee or levy on foreign exchange transactions, the best known of which was the concept of James Tobin, a distinguished Yale University monetary economist and Nobel laureate in 1978. Tobin proposed[26] a tax on foreign exchange transactions, the primary objective of which was to discourage speculative runs on the key world currencies. Although Tobin did not intend that such a tax would be used to raise revenues for the UN, the latter idea received some currency at the UN Conference on Social Development ("the Social Summit") in Copenhagen in March 1995, when it was broached by six heads of state or government, including Prime Minister Gro Harlem Brundtland of Norway and by François Mitterand of France in his last presidential appearance. Moreover, in the aftermath of the Mexican financial crisis, the Canadian government provided some leadership in raising the matter in advance of the Group of Seven Summit of the leading industrialized countries in June 1995, which Canada hosted in Halifax.[27]

In the end, neither the Tobin tax idea nor other alternative sources of financing were discussed at the Group of Seven summit, although issues of UN reform were covered and the closing declaration noted them. The Prime Minister has been described as keen to "back winners," that is, to support ideas that have some chance of success rather than float trial balloons with few immediate prospects.

Once it became clear, in early discussions with the other Summit members, that the Tobin tax idea elicited little interest, it was decided to minimize discussion of it at the Summit proper. Nevertheless, UN financial issues continued to concern both Mr. Chrétien and Mr. Ouellet, and the matter was repeatedly mentioned by UN Secretary-General Boutros-Ghali in meetings with the Prime Minister and Foreign Minister when he visited Ottawa in late November 1995.

CONCLUSIONS

The most obvious conclusion that can be drawn from the government's attitudes towards issues of United Nations reform is that they are characterized by continuity and caution. Continuity was maintained with the broad outlines of Pearsonian internationalism that have shaped Canadian foreign policy for the better part of the half-century that coincides with the UN's existence. These are too well-known to require description, the chief features being multilateralism and strong support for and defence of the United Nations, combined with an incremental and pragmatic approach to enhancing the functions and the fortunes of the institution. What has been striking in the current government's style is the frequency of references to the Pearson era, which had a slightly stale flavour and even stultified debate, if only because the goals were so unexceptionable. Indeed, the rhetoric seemed increasingly hollow at a time of profound national distemper, when the disparity between our foreign policy aspirations and our declining ability to realize them seemed as great as the incoherences in the UN itself.

At the same time, the rhetoric contrasted with the rather cautious practice that characterized the entire Chrétien government and closely reflected the Prime Minister's own managerial temperament. The caution was typified by the focus on process in dealing with the UN's financial and administrative inadequacies and even, to some extent, with rapid reaction as well. It is no doubt important to get the process right, especially in the eyes of the bureaucrats who drive that particular agenda, but it does not offer much by way of uplift to a Canadian public that increasingly seems starved of it. And it contrasts poorly with the strategic sense and breadth of experience of Lester Pearson himself. It was indeed a Chevrolet rather than a Cadillac approach to foreign policy, as another contributor to this volume has pointed out. The unfortunate aspect was that, at a time of national crisis, it was also not the approach of a Lincoln.

Minority views were expressed from time to time, chiefly finding a mouthpiece in the Reform Party in the House of Commons, which questioned a number of the assumptions underlying the government's view, pointing particularly to the government's diminished resources and calling for a leaner and rationalized approach to UN affairs and Canada's role in them. However, these views remained largely outside the liberal internationalist consensus that predominated. The other minority view, of course, was that coming from Quebec, represented in the House of Commons by the Bloc Québécois, which did not necessarily disagree with the government's UN initiatives, but which made it clear that it sought its own voice in international affairs; hence its interest in Canada's role would be rather perfunctory. Under these circumstances, it was easy for the Government to dominate the agenda, but debate tended to be rather flat and predictable.

In many respects, however, the government's caution was perfectly understandable. It arose largely from uncertainty concerning Quebec and the government's unwillingness to take on too much when energies needed to be conserved for the struggle at home. Another factor was the disjuncture between certain U.S. views on UN reform and those of the Canadian government. There were no major disagreements between Canadian official policy and that of the Clinton administration, but the outright antagonism of the Republican majority in both houses of Congress to the UN, to Boutros-Ghali in particular, and certainly to any efforts to improve the UN's capacity to do more, made even limited Canadian efforts seem rather quixotic. The UN has always had a much more mixed reception in the United States than in Canada and this is to be expected, given the nature of the two countries' histories and their place in the world. What was disturbing in the United States, however, was the increasingly visceral and vitriolic character of the attacks on international organizations and the xenophobia that lay behind them. There is a rising sense of America turning inward at a key moment in world history, which does not bode well for determined multilateralists like Canada. Harvard academic Stanley Hoffmann has sounded the warning bell:

Because of the difficulties experienced by liberal internationalism in the
new post-Cold War world and the inconsistencies in UN and U.S. actions,
one can now legitimately fear a discrediting of international organizations
comparable to the one that submerged the League of Nations in the 1930s,

even though the causes, this time, are the problems of chaos rather than the challenges mounted by a few major powers.[28]

Canada on its own cannot make the UN work—far from it. Our role, as always, is to offer a blueprint for action (for example, rapid reaction) and then gradually to build the coalitions that will support our ideas. Moreover, Canada must always proceed in a two-step action: advancing with ideas, but then falling back in order to convince our recalcitrant neighbours to the south that it is in their long-term interest too.

It is a minuet that defines Canadian diplomacy. If we are skilful, both steps can be executed simultaneously; if not, the dance becomes disjointed. That is the danger at present: there is a disconnection between our entirely justified determination to give the UN what it needs and the hostility of many in the United States towards anything of the sort. We are not about to change our minds; but whatever hopes we may have for the world organization, others must be encouraged to take our vision and transform it to make it theirs as well.

NOTES

1   *Creating Opportunity: The Liberal Plan for Canada*, September 1993, 104-05.
2   *Creating Opportunity*, 106.
3   *Creating Opportunity*, 108-09.
4   Douglas Roche, a journalist and editor by profession, had served as the Progressive Conservative M.P. for Edmonton South (1972-84); he was well-known in the caucus and beyond Parliament for his keen interest in international affairs. A strong and practising Catholic, he later served as Ambassador for Disarmament (1984-89) and also briefly as National President of UNA-Canada. Michael Oliver was semi-retired, but continued to be active in a variety of public pursuits after a long and distinguished career which included stints as founding President of the New Democratic Party in 1961, Director of Research of the Royal Commission on Bilingualism and Biculturalism during the 1960s, and later Vice-Rector of McGill University and President of Carleton University. Neither of these men could be said to be well-known for their Liberal Party connections, although both certainly espoused the same sentiments as those sketched in the Liberal Party Red Book.
5   *House of Commons Debates*, March 15, 1994, 2265.
6   "Minutes of the Proceedings and Evidence of the Special Joint Committee of the Senate and the House of Commons Reviewing Canadian Foreign Policy," April 18, 1994, Issue no. 2, 28.

7   "Minutes of the Proceedings and Evidence of the Special Joint
     Committee of the Senate and the House of Commons Reviewing
     Canadian Foreign Policy," April 18, 1994, Issue no. 2, 10.

8   "Minutes of the Proceedings and Evidence of the Special Joint
     Committee of the Senate and the House of Commons Reviewing
     Canadian Foreign Policy," April 18, 1994, Issue no. 2, 34.

9   *Canada 21: Canada and Common Security in the Twenty-First
     Century*, (Centre for International Studies: University of Toronto),
     1994, 12.

10   *Canada 21*, 57.

11   The Canadian Committee undertook several other projects related to
     UN reform, the most significant of which was, arguably, a major con-
     ference in Montreal in March 1995, billed as the First Canadian
     Conference on UN Reform. It boasted a wide range of internationally
     renowned speakers including José Ayala Lasso of Ecuador, the new
     UN High Commissioner for Human Rights; Sir Shridath Ramphal of
     Guyana, former Secretary-General of the Commonwealth and the
     Co-Chair of the International Commission on Global Governance; and
     General Philippe Morillon, Commander of the French Rapid Reaction
     Force and former commander of the UN Protection Force in ex-
     Yugoslavia. Canadians who spoke included Major-General Roméo
     Dallaire and Major-General (ret'd) Lewis Mackenzie, Foreign Minister
     André Ouellet and former politicians Flora MacDonald, Stephen Lewis
     and Ed Broadbent. Ouellet, in particular, used the opportunity to
     deliver a major address on UN issues.

12   Report of the Special Joint Committee Reviewing Canadian Foreign
     Policy, *Canada's Foreign Policy: Principles and Priorities for the
     Future*, Parliamentary Publication Directorate, November 1994, 12.

13   *Principles and Priorities*, 16.

14   *Principles and Priorities*, 19.

15   Gallup Canada, *Canada's Peacekeeping Role Assessed*, January 27,
     1994.

16   The government's official statement, *Canada in the World*, which fol-
     lowed the parliamentary reviews, identified five areas in which
     Canada was committed "to making the UN work better": its capacity
     for preventive action; economic and social activities; the functioning
     of its decision-making bodies; rapid reaction capability; and finances.
     But the emphasis was entirely on the latter two. See *Canada in the
     World*, Government Statement, Her Majesty the Queen in Right of
     Canada, 1995, 27.

17   Government of Canada, *Towards a Rapid Reaction Capability for the
     United Nations*, Report of the Government of Canada, September
     1995, 5.

18   Government of Canada, "Notes for an Address by the Honourable
     André Ouellet, Minister of Foreign Affairs, to the 49th General
     Assembly of the United Nations," New York, 94/55, September 29,
     1994, Department of Foreign Affairs and International Trade, 2.

19   There were a handful of persons whose contribution to the process
      of the review was absolutely vital, namely: Maxim Faille, a young
      Montrealer who had worked for the New York-based international
      NGO, Parliamentarians for Global Action, and who was a member
      of the Core Group; Michael Pearson, the Senior Policy Adviser to the
      Minister of Foreign Affairs; Michael Kergin, Assistant Deputy Minister
      (Political and International Security Affairs) in the Department of
      Foreign Affairs and International Trade (DFAIT); David Malone, a for-
      mer Deputy Permanent Representative to the United Nations and at
      the time Director-General of the Policy Staff, DFAIT; Daniel Livermore,
      the Director of the Regional Security and Peacekeeping Division,
      DFAIT; and in addition LCol. L.W. Bentley and LCol. J.P. Culligan
      from the Department of National Defence, whose technical expertise
      was essential.
20   *Towards a Rapid Reaction Capability*, 51.
21   *Towards a Rapid Reaction Capability*, 10-11.
22   Government of Canada, Notes for an Address by the Honourable
      André Ouellet, Minister of Foreign Affairs, to the 50th General
      Assembly of the United Nations, 95/53 September 26, 1995
      Department of Foreign Affairs and International Trade, 5.
23   The other countries represented at the foreign minister level were
      Australia, Bangladesh, Denmark, Egypt, Jamaica, Malaysia, New
      Zealand, Nicaragua, Poland, Senegal, Ukraine, and Zambia.
24   Paul Knox, "The UN in 2045", *The Globe and Mail*, October 7, 1995.
25   Paul Knox, "Unpaid Bills Have UN Brass Starved for Cash," *The Globe
      and Mail*, September 25, 1995.
26   James Tobin, "A Proposal for International Monetary Reform," *Eastern
      Economic Journal* 4, no. 3-4, (1978), 153-160.
27   A senior analyst in the Canadian Department of Finance has ascribed
      the original interest of governments in the tax as a device to influence
      the behaviour of international financial markets: there was less inter-
      est in it as a revenue producer. This analyst remarked that the more
      revenue that national governments are obliged to remit to the UN, the
      less incentive they would have to collect it (Canadian Centre for
      Global Security seminar, Ottawa, October 6, 1995).
28   Stanley Hoffmann, "The Crisis of Liberal Internationalism," *Foreign
      Policy*, no. 98 (Spring 1995), 176.

XII

Rethinking Peacekeeping: The Bosnia and Somalia Experience

DAVID B. CARMENT

In 1988, the Nobel Peace Prize recognized the continuing contribution of UN peacekeeping troops to international peace and security. In the five years following that high point in UN history the anomalous conditions created by the end of the Cold War allowed the Organization to achieve remarkable results: termination of the Iran/Iraq war, an agreement on Namibian independence, Soviet withdrawal from Afghanistan, a coalition government in Cambodia, and settlement of El Salvador's chronic civil war. While these old conflicts were mediated, civil wars, state failures and genocides created new and in some cases unprecedented demands for UN peacekeeping.

There is little doubt that peacekeeping has become more dangerous, more costly and more complex. Reactive and hastily applied measures have become a form of triage that sustains and exacerbates problematic and unjust situations. An assessment of the organization's multifaceted and overstretched activities generates several questions: is traditional peacekeeping appropriate in situations that require the feeding and protection of ordinary people, the use of force to separate belligerents and long-term political measures that address mutually incompatible dreams of self-determination? Can these combined tasks lead to a resolution of internal conflicts? Is humanitarian intervention likely to be effective in the midst of war? Finally, what are the implications for Canadian foreign policy?

This chapter responds to these questions in four parts. The first three examine the nature of the disputes and the mission objectives, operational clarity and the complexities of humanitarian intervention. The fourth and final part assesses these findings in light of Canada's defence and foreign policy interests. The chapter draws on evidence from Bosnia and Somalia.

CANADA'S COMPARATIVE ADVANTAGE IN PEACEKEEPING

Saadia Touval contends that the UN has no real impact as a facilitator or communicator, lacks sufficient diplomatic clout and does not constitute a credible deterrent for conflict prevention.[1] Once again the Organization is seen to be in crisis. At stake is its authority, identity and purpose. By extension, Canada's peacekeeping role is also seen to be diminishing, if not as a result of its tarnished image in the aftermath of the "Somalia affair," then because of its assumed reluctance to build on its peacekeeping strengths and successes.[2] Arguably, Canada's comparative advantage as a neutral and internationally respected peacekeeper is in decline. This has implications for Canada's status as a peaceful, liberal state specifically and the concept of impartial peacekeeping generally. Ironically, it is the failure to uphold the principle of impartiality in peacekeeping operations—the deaths of Shidane Aroni and several other Somalis being the most prominent examples—that has detracted from Canada's strong performance in recent missions.

These points of view should be interpreted with caution. First, focusing on two failed-state cases may bias the results of the analysis. A comparison of operations in a larger number of cases such as Cambodia, El Salvador or Haiti might lead to entirely different and more positive interpretations of UN effectiveness.[3] Second, setting aside the issue of whether there is a Canadian way of "doing peacekeeping," the more important debate focuses on the scope, the timing and the intensity of force required to achieve a mediated settlement. As will be shown in this chapter, there *are* specific instances in which a situation is ripe for effective coercive diplomacy. These are conflicts which tend to be complex, intrastate disputes, often equated with failed states. State failure is most closely associated with wholesale political assassinations, genocide and power transitions. The most extreme example is when an armed group operates outside the control of recognized political authorities and resists peacekeeping efforts: circumstances applying to both Somalia and Bosnia.

Ideally, multilateral force (and the commensurate loss of impartiality) should be enough to guarantee access to refugees, to protect aid workers, and to shield ordinary citizens. However, when consent cannot be obtained, justification for the use of force can be derived from ethical concerns: the need to quickly disarm militias in order to stop or prevent genocides and political assasinations. These are operations which tend to be directed against a clearly identified aggressor, where there is a victim at substantial risk without external support.

It is equally important to understand when collective force should be avoided, exploited as a deterrent, or, in specific situations, employed as a stabilizing mechanism early on in the life-cycle of a conflict.[4] A fundamental set of tasks for both policy makers and analysts is to better understand the underlying causes of violent conflict and to relate this knowledge to peacekeeping training and to preventive measures that ensure early and rapid de-escalation in tensions. These are areas where Canada has already taken the lead.

From a policy perspective, it is not all that meaningful to characterize either the Bosnia or Somalia peacekeeping missions as failures; the nature and complexities of the disputes were such as to ensure that both operations would not be successful in absolute terms. A measure of "goodness of fit" between stated operational objectives and political outcomes demonstrates this point. For example, the second of the two United Nations Operations in Somalia (UNOSOM II) was, in theory, to be carried out in four phases. Phase I would concentrate on the transfer of operational control from the U.S.-led Unified Task Force (UNITAF). Military support to relief activities and the disarming of factions would continue throughout the transition period. Phase II would consolidate UN operational control and would conclude when UNOSOM II was deployed and operating effectively throughout Somalia and the border regions.[5] In phase III, major efforts would be made to reduce UNOSOM II's military activity and assist civil authorities to exercise greater responsibility. That phase would end when a Somali national police force became operational and major UN military operations were no longer required. Phase IV would concern redeployment or reduction of the UNOSOM II forces. In fact, UNOSOM II never really extended beyond the end of Phase II, the point at which the operation was terminated.[6]

It is too early to determine if the Bosnian peace process will achieve its objectives. A sustained Western military presence, massive economic aid and attitudinal change among the belligerents will all be required to ensure success over the long run. Operationally, the UN Protection Force (UNPROFOR) did secure some positive results in the final year of its mandate, but with a considerable sacrifice of UN legitimacy. This is because without NATO support a politically viable outcome would not have been possible over such a short time. On December 15, 1995 the United Nations Security Council, acting under Chapter VII of the Charter of the UN, adopted Resolution 1031, which authorized the member states of NATO to establish the NATO Implementation Force (IFOR), under unified command and control and composed of ground, air and maritime units from NATO and non-NATO nations, to ensure compliance with the relevant provisions of the Dayton Peace Agreement.[7] On the one hand, the decision to deploy a 60,000 person force in Bosnia was the logical next step for NATO.[8] From the beginning of the Bosnian conflict, it carried out peace support operations on behalf of the UN through an enforcement of an embargo and a no-fly zone. On the other hand, the cost to the UN has been considerable. While the organization's disengagement from the Bosnian peace process is significant, the resolution of a more long-term set of issues turns on the credibility and capacity of the UN to intervene on behalf of beleaguered minorities. In Bosnia, mutual hatred among the three major ethnic groups is exceeded only by their collective distrust of the UN.

THE NATURE OF THE DISPUTES AND MISSION OBJECTIVES

The conventional wisdom holds that external influence, a blend of "dictatorial" interference, coercion and international law, is sufficient to manage a crisis. Consider those interstate situations where violence has broken out and escalation is imminent. Traditional rules would suggest that the optimal choice is to use overwhelming force against a single aggressor in a well-defined operation and to terminate the engagement as soon as the objectives of the operation have been fulfilled. While this strategy might have worked in a dyadic interstate war, it clearly is not applicable in situations like Bosnia and Somalia where a limited use of force may be necessary, where there are zones of both peace and war, where consent is not easily obtained and exit strategies are impractical and undesirable.

Intervention in failed states is messy, protracted and open-ended. Any measure of success is highly dependent on the characteristics of the adversaries, the nature of the dispute and its level of intensity. When vital interests are at stake, third parties are unlikely to be very effective in settling the conflict peacefully. The identity and characteristics of the adversaries are also important factors that can influence the effectiveness of third party mediation.[9] Ethnic leaders must choose either a settlement imposed on them by third parties or a negotiated solution. For the belligerents these choices must be preferable to continued fighting. Therefore, leaders must be able to convince their supporters to accept the alternative and they must enforce their followers' observance of it. The problem is that, in Somalia and Bosnia, disunity and lack of cohesion within the ranks of the adversaries made it difficult for the various factions and the UN to engage in any meaningful form of negotiation.[10] Clan and ethnic leaders lacked both the power and the authority to enforce their decisions and concessions.[11]

For third parties, there is a need to lay the political groundwork before committing forces to a peacekeeping operation. Once in place, peacekeepers are there to ensure that those groups that do find the terms of settlement agreeable are kept on board while those that do not are effectively isolated. Neither of these tasks could be properly carried out in Bosnia and Somalia because both missions began in the midst of war. Somalia's implosion was a lingering ten-year struggle between clans whose conflicts were deeply rooted in the country's thirty-year irredentist confrontation with Ethiopia. In contrast, Bosnia's collapse was abrupt, predictable and almost entirely due to Yugoslavia's disintegration; events that emerged only in the last few years of Yugoslavia's existence. Both conflicts had their origins in identity-based territorial claims. An important feature of both of them was the fragmented nature of political and military power. In each case, paramilitary activity was a response to the escalation of social conflict.[12]

In post-independence Somalia, political parties were formed along regional clan fissures, which served only to compound the problem of national unity. Somalia has always been a religiously and linguistically homogenous state whose clan-based struggles for identity shift according to the external pressures placed upon the country.[13] For example, in August 1989 Somalia's leader Siad Barre responded to growing clan pressures in two ways: repression against the civilian population and the development of a new constitution, emphasizing UN-monitored multiparty elections to be held in February 1991.[14] A constitution review process continued into late 1990, at which time Barre's support, already weakened severely by clan conflict, collapsed. On January 23, 1991 Barre's militia admitted defeat and his Darod party, the Somali National Front (SNF), was toppled.[15] Into this vacuum entered a coalition of United Somali Congress (USC), SNM and Somali Patriotic Movement (SPM) forces, which deposed the leader and replaced him with a "national salvation committee."

In November 1991, the most intense fighting since the fall of Barre broke out in the capital. Fighting persisted in Mogadishu and spread throughout Somalia, with heavily armed elements controlling various parts of the country. Some of the 15 sub-factions declared alliance with one or the other major factions, while others did not. Numerous marauding groups of bandits added to the problem. The struggles that have since ensued are a reflection of clan-based politics at its most basic level; that is, in the absence of any semblance of institutions, the struggle for power and survival has been determined by weapons and clan alliances.

In 1992, UN relief agencies were engaged in an operation to provide famine relief for Somalis caught in the disintegrating internal situation (UNOSOM I).[16] On 28 August 1992, Canada offered to provide 750 Canadian Forces personnel for UNOSOM. This was to be the start of Operation Cordon. The Canadian contribution was to consist of the Canadian Airborne Regiment, reinforced with engineers and support personnel. These troops were to be deployed in Bossaso in the northeast area of Somalia. HMCS Preserver was to provide logistic support and was on its way from Halifax when the situation in Somalia deteriorated rapidly. Beginning in December 1992, aid agencies were assisted in their mission by a U.S.-led 15-country peacekeeping operation, intended to keep the warring clans apart and to bring stability to the country. Led by the United States, the 37,000 strong UNITAF force was deployed in Mogadishu on December 9, 1992. In the following weeks UNITAF forces expanded their operations to major relief centres in Somalia, covering 40 percent of Somalia's territory.[17] On December 14, 1992 the advance party of the Canadian Airborne Regiment Battle Group arrived in Baledogle, Somalia. The main body of the Canadian Airborne took responsibility for the Belet Uen Humanitarian Relief Sector in Central Somalia in operation Deliverance. The total Canadian contribution to UNITAF numbered 1300.[18]

During this period, the Canadian mission was to establish a secure environment for humanitarian relief operations. In operational terms the Regiment escorted food convoys, conducted foot patrols and seized weapons from locals. Unlike the larger UNITAF mission the Airborne was not mandated to aggressively disarm local militias. It was, however, charged with the more permissive rules of engagement under Chapter VII of the UN Charter. In principle, this meant that the Canadian mission was not exposed to the problems of a transformed mandate (known as "mission creep"), as has happened in Bosnia.[19] Although the Canadian contribution was small in size, the peacekeepers did achieve their objectives.

In retrospect, the hasty preparation, inadequate reconnaissance, and robust rules of engagement could have combined to create a situation similar to that which befell Pakistan's peacekeepers.[20] A lack of infrastructure in Somalia and insufficient logistical support had already made the Canadian mission difficult. The Regiment was separated by almost 400 km from its supply line in Mogadishu during the entire operation.

The UN Operation in Somalia (UNOSOM II), established in May 1993, was the first explicitly authorized UN peace-enforcement mission since the Congo operation in the early 1960s. The phase-out of UNOSOM II from Somalia began in November 1994 and was completed in March 1995. Given the volatile situation prevailing in Somalia, it was an intricate operation involving the departure of the 15,000 UN troops then deployed in the country.

Although the Canadian Airborne fulfilled its mandate under UNITAF, the larger UNOSOM II mission failed to deliver on its promise to pick up where UNOSOM I left off. This is because UNITAF never achieved its goal of disarming local militias. It merely drove them away. In some areas, notably Mogadishu, UNOSOM II troops were faced with the combined tasks of protecting relief aid and disarming intensely hostile Somali clans. The inclusion of disarmament (as opposed to demobilization, which takes place after a negotiated settlement) in the UNOSOM II mandate meant that any level of impartiality was immediately forfeited.[21]

The conflict in Bosnia proved no less intractable but its onset and escalation occurred over a much shorter period. It is difficult to analyze the Bosnian conflict without reference to the larger war. In Yugoslavia, two factors provided an indication of whether latent animosities would become violent. The first was the question of who controlled the military and political structures.[22] The second was the development of more particularist identities and competing visions of the future among Yugoslavia's various ethnic group leaders. The latter process was underway in the decade immediately following Tito's death, in which the confederal structures instituted under his power gradually ceded more and more power to the republics.[23] In prewar Bosnia, the convergence of the interests of Croatian, Muslim and Serb leaders resembled a balance of power system, characterized by a shifting pattern of flexible coalitions. Eventually this balancing broke down and Bosnia was no longer a state based on an equilibrium engendered by decentralized constitutional arrangements. Coercion and ethnic intransigence became commonplace.[24]

As the conflict in Croatia wound down in January of 1992, Croatia's Serb party, the SDS, declared an independent "Serbian Republic of Bosnia-Herzegovina," made up of regions that it had taken over during the summer of 1991.[25] Around the time of the referendum on Bosnia's future, Serb and Croat forces began fighting in key regions of Bosnia. Serbian guerilla forces threw up roadblocks around Sarajevo and other cities and began a process of orchestrated terror against dissenters. The real concern for Yugoslav leader Milošević was to control the unpredictable zealotry of the Bosnian-Serb leadership, in order to reduce the possibility that their "ethnic cleansing" would bring outside military intervention.[26] This could be best achieved by having a controlling interest in the Bosnian conflict and by staking claims to much of Bosnia.[27]

In response to the disintegrating situation in Yugoslavia, United Nations Protection Force (UNPROFOR) was established in early 1992 as an interim measure to create the conditions of peace and security required for the EC-initiated negotiation of an overall settlement to the Croatian crisis. Eventually, the operation evolved into a traditional disengagement mission in Croatia, a humanitarian support mission in Bosnia and Herzegovina, and a small preventive deployment in Macedonia.

On the surface, Bosnia would seem to be a more robust variation of the Somalia peacekeeping effort. In execution UNPROFOR was very unmuscular. From the beginning of the conflict there was never a situation in Bosnia where a conventional peacekeeping mission would have been adequate. Heavy weapons were operated and used by groups that were not members of any regular army of a recognized government. These weapons were used on a large scale against civilians in clear violation of international humanitarian laws.

To ensure safe havens for civilians ensnared in the conflict, NATO, at the request of the UN Security Council, implemented plans for the military enforcement of a no-fly zone. On February 19, 1993 UN peacekeepers were given the mandate to use force if necessary to defend themselves, under Chapter VII of the UN Charter. NATO made several announcements, including the one of April 22, 1994, that, if any Bosnian Serb attacks involving heavy weapons were carried out on UN-designated safe areas, these weapons and other Bosnian Serb military assets would be subject to NATO air strikes.

During the lifetime of UNPROFOR, Canada's decision makers were concerned with the United States' unwillingness to participate in a conventional peacekeeping operation. From the outset of the Yugoslav crisis the U.S. administration considered most options except sending peacekeeping troops to Bosnia. Even with the 1995 decision to deploy IFOR there has been no political backing inside the American political setting for conventional multilateral peacekeeping.[28] Following the outbreak of the conflict in Bosnia, there was always much greater support to use air-strikes as a negotiating "tool" to force the Serbs to the bargaining table. This choice had considerable impact on Canada's peacekeepers already on the ground. Differences in strategy were most acutely felt in November 1994, when Canadian UN peacekeepers were detained by Bosnian Serb forces in retaliation for the NATO bombing of Serb-controlled airfields.

UNPROFOR's half-measures may have prolonged the conflict. Most certainly the biggest issue was the change in the peacekeeping mandate.[29] The decision to move UNPROFOR away from the principle of impartiality added confusion and ambiguity to an already complex mission. Peacekeepers and civilians were placed at considerable risk.[30]

OPERATIONAL CLARITY—MEANS AND ENDS

It is difficult to resolve internal disputes without the active involvement of third parties. Today, there is debate about what constitutes an appropriate multilateral response to an internal conflict.[31] This debate centres on the regulatory norms for the execution of an operation, and for determining who is to be involved and when and where specific action is deemed appropriate.[32] The presence or absence of consensus on long-term goals, objectives and means determines whether a negotiated settlement will be successful or not.[33]

There are two reasons for this. First, the more complex an operation is, the greater the need for operational clarity at the outset. The increased number and variety of contributors and the need for cooperation with divided local populations and authorities add uncertainty to a mission. Include the need for higher intensity operations and the virtual absence of effective government in host countries, and it becomes clear why an ambiguous mandate is to be avoided.[34] If leaders of NGOs, governments and international organizations are unclear on exactly how a mission is to accomplish its goals and, more significantly, what those goals are, there is greater potential for abuse of the procedures. The risk of playing favourites is high. Leaders of NGOs now realise that in humanitarian operations only armies are likely to have the resources necessary to save lives. In turn, peacekeepers who do not have special training may lack the sensitivity to and understanding of the local situation.

Second, the dynamics of the Bosnia and Somalia conflicts make it clear that "quick and dirty" peace enforcement doctrines, like those utilized in the Gulf, are not easily adapted to these later situations. While it is true that the first act of choice is critical no matter what the choice is, it is also true that peacekeeping operations in failed states are path-dependent. Once initiated they seem to take on a life of their own. Humanitarian situations in which consent is unobtainable or where the belligerents are not easily separated—as in Bosnia and Somalia—are not amenable to static exogenous solutions. Unless a peacekeeping mission quickly adapts to changes on the ground or is prepared to take pre-emptive action, the associated peace process is doomed to failure. Internal conflicts are dynamic, robust, and seemingly impervious to external influence once they have escalated into widespread violence. In reality, the dynamics of a violent intrastate conflict often have a greater impact on peacekeeping behaviour than the peacekeepers' efforts have on the behaviour of the belligerents.[35] Changes in hostilities at the local level—even those of moderate magnitude—can result in a completely different mode of peacekeeping, mission creep and unanticipated reverberations.[36]

To understand these arguments it is useful to identify those principles which have traditionally guided peacekeeping operations in the past. These are principles which have determined classical UN Chapter VI operations, including impartiality, consent and the use of force only for self-defence. Conventional standards are most effective in the management of disputes between member states of the international system. These are conflicts in which peacekeeping is essentially observation, the belligerents are safely separated and the peacekeepers themselves are not vulnerable to attack. Peacekeeping of this type most often occurs after a cease-fire is obtained and when force and interposition are deemed unnecessary (i.e., there is no need for armed troops or buffer). In essence, impartiality works best where intervention is needed least: where the belligerents have already learned through bitter experience and sheer exhaustion that they are ready for the negotiating table.

UNPROFOR fell between the techniques of peacekeepers and observers and those of enforcement. This kind of peacekeeping has been labelled "Chapter VI and half," second generation peacekeeping, robust or muscular peacekeeping. It constitutes a mythical and ambiguous halfway house between peacekeeping and peace enforcement. There are both negative and positive connotations associated with this hybrid.

Negatively, peacekeepers become targets rather than intermediaries when at least one antagonist becomes convinced that favouritism is at work.[37] The perception that the UN is not an impartial agent also has implications for effective mediation. It is a destructive misconception to believe that neutrality can be applied in situations where the belligerents have yet to be convinced that they have little to gain in fighting. When there is no peace to keep, third parties are faced with a decision to withdraw, as was the case with UNOSOM I. Alternatively, peacekeepers can escalate the intervention in order to isolate those who will not accept a negotiated settlement, as happened under UNITAF and UNOSOM II.

Of course, escalation alone does not guarantee success and mission creep itself is problematic. However, there is a greater chance of success if the parties to the dispute also recognize the limitations of using violence to resolve their differences and are open to the conditions for peace presented to them. When such acceptance and commitment is lacking, enforcement operations are likely to be ineffective at best and destructive at worst. Soldiers who are asked to operate under such conditions are more likely to be exposed to a variety of potentially conflicting requests. Peacekeepers can become another party to the conflict, responding to the situation rather than taking the initiative. It is simply not good enough to say to a commander that a mission is either Chapter VI or Chapter VII. These provide only the legal basis for engagement. Rules of engagement must also conform to the political and diplomatic requirements of the mission. In principle, force should be used only to facilitate the negotiation process.

The problem in Somalia was that some of the clan leaders would not sustain their commitment to the negotiation process, while the use of force served only to drive clan leaders from the negotiating table. Beyond the recognition by most parties of the need to initiate a cease-fire, there did not exist a solid set of political conditions that could be negotiated during the lifetime of UNOSOM II. The goals of imposing martial law, terminating Somalia's civil war and ensuring the country's return to a civilian-controlled society were almost entirely a foreign enterprise derived from the need to protect those delivering humanitarian assistance and the desire to pursue "nation-building."[38]

Moreover, the Somalia reconciliation process was not able to build on the support of local allies that would permit the maintenance of a military status quo. Indeed, General Aideed proved very adept at exploiting the increased U.S. presence in the country. He did so in order to tip the precarious clan balance in his favour. The implications of Somalia's clan-based society are significant. The basic characteristic of such a society is its inherent instability. Depending on the nature and context of a particular political matter the segments of a clan unify, temporarily, to deal with an imminent emergency, only to splinter off into antagonistic subsegments when the emergency abates. In the spring of 1992 UN Special Envoy Mohammed Sahnoun sought to exploit the decentralized structure of clan politics, securing cooperation from clan elders and some of the militias.[39] Initially, this tactic worked. For example, Sahnoun succeeded in getting the two major factions in Mogadishu to agree to an immediate cessation of hostilities and the maintenance of a cease-fire. During intensive negotiations, Interim President Ali Mahdi and General Aideed signed an "Agreement on the Implementation of a Cease-fire." This Agreement also included the acceptance of a UN security component for convoys of humanitarian assistance, and the deployment of 20 military observers on each side of Mogadishu to monitor the cease-fire. Several of the Somali de facto authorities refused to agree to the deployment of UN troops to secure delivery of aid in areas of greatest need.

Given the difficulties, the Secretary-General concluded that the airlift operations—already being carried out by the World Food Program (WFP) and the UN Children's Fund (UNICEF), as well as by the International Committee of the Red Cross (ICRC)—needed to be enhanced substantially, with priority given to central and southern Somalia. In addition, a "preventive zone" on the Kenya-Somali border was established for special deliveries of food and seed, in an attempt to reduce famine-induced population movements. The Secretary-General concluded that the UN did not have the capability to command and control an enforcement operation of the size required, and that there was no alternative but to resort to the enforcement provisions under Chapter VII of the UN Charter.

By 1993 there was an attempt to find agreement among the leaders of all of the 15 Somali political movements. On March 27, 1993, these 15 leaders signed an Agreement of the First Session of the Conference of National Reconciliation in Somalia. The agreement was unanimously endorsed by all the participants, including representatives of women's and community organizations, as well as elders and scholars. In the agreement, the Somali parties resolved to put an end to armed conflict and to reconcile their differences through peaceful means. They reaffirmed their commitment to comply fully with the cease-fire agreement signed in Addis Ababa in January 1993, including the handing over of all weapons and ammunition to UNITAF and UNOSOM II. By 1995, after the departure of UNOSOM II, there was still no effective functioning government in the country, no organized civilian police force and no disciplined national armed force.[40]

Of course, effective mediation is possible without resorting to offensive measures. The Somalia and Bosnia missions suggest divergent conclusions on the efficacy of force as a negotiating tool and stabilizing force. On the one hand, during the time frame set out by UNOSOM II, few of the parties recognized the benefits of the peace process as compared with the advantages of continued fighting. On the other hand, the Bosnian peace process exploited the military and political isolation of the Bosnian-Serb militia. This combined effort ensured that the momentum that began with the Vance-Owen plan would not be lost. The influence of ethnic allies, Milošević and Croatian leader Franjo Tudjman in particular, was integral to the process. Both leaders brought pressure to bear on ethnic militias in order to cajole and persuade them to accept a mediated settlement. For example, to escape the constraints imposed on Serbia (namely, sanctions and embargoes), Milošević had to find a new strategy to build support at home, which eventually resulted in withdrawal of support for the Serb breakaway leaders in Bosnia.

Events in Bosnia show that third party coercive diplomacy, even late in a conflict's life-cycle, can have a positive impact. It can help bring the belligerents to the negotiating table. However the situation in Bosnia was unlike that in Somalia, in that a comprehensive power-sharing agreement was already on the table before concerted coercive measures were implemented. In this case, coercive diplomacy was a means to a political end. For example, soon after the Serbs had an opportunity to consider and reject the terms of the Vance-Owen plan, the UN and its proxy peace enforcer, NATO, nurtured an alliance between Bosnian Croatians and Bosnian Muslims.[41] Over time, this pact became capable of tipping the balance against Serb aggression.

In combination with sanctions and an embargo, the Western powers proved reasonably effective in containing the conflict and directing its flow.[42] In effect, the combination of sanctions and retaliatory measures sent specific signals to Serbian leader Milošević, who held a tight reign on SDS leader Radovan Karadzić: resolve the conflict through negotiations or face the consequences. This sustained economic and political pressure on Milošević eventually did bear fruit. For example, on January 11, 1993, Bosnian Serb leaders dropped their demands for a separate state and signed a short-lived peace plan (Vance-Owen) giving each of the three ethnic groups control of ten nominally equal "provinces" within Bosnia. Sarajevo would become an open city.[43]

Even though the Vance-Owen plan was not successful (it did not meet with the approval of the Bosnian Serb "parliament" under Karadzić's control) it did provide the basis for the negotiated settlement that would be reached almost three years later. The subsequent 1995 Dayton Accord also came at a cost: exclusion of the Bosnian

Serb leaders from the negotiating table and substantial territorial gains for Bosnian Croats in comparison to what had been offered them under Vance-Owen. In essence, territorial boundaries gained through military means were legitimate. The Bosnian Serbs' territorial stranglehold was to be reduced to 49 percent of Bosnian territory, with the Bosnian Croat and Muslim coalition taking the balance. By most standards, the Accord merely reaffirmed what had long been recognized; Bosnia would be two effectively independent nations and the Bosnian Muslims, although a numerical majority, would be left in the political wilderness.[44]

THE COMPLEXITY OF HUMANITARIAN INTERVENTION AND THE USE OF FORCE

UN humanitarian operations are more complex than ever before. In the absence of a cogent international law on intervention, humanitarian goals will continue to be very imprecise. State failure is still approached too much as purely a political problem exclusive to one state. However, state failures also have an immediate impact on neighbouring countries, with refugee flows providing a prime example. Immediate tasks include the need to contain spillover effects and resolve specific humanitarian dilemmas within a regional context. Over the long term, third parties have an important role to play in restructuring a state's security institutions and in supporting specific civilianization tasks.

The peacekeeping operations in Somalia and Bosnia illustrate the importance of these commitments. First, in Bosnia and Somalia spillover control was a central task. NATO operations, Sharp Guard and Deliberate Force, and the deployment of 300 U.S. soldiers in Macedonia are examples of conflict containment in fullfilment of specific UN resolutions. Conflict containment requires a more active role for regional organizations and a higher level of cooperation and coordination among the great powers. Preventive deployment focuses on containment as well. Due to changing circumstances and the complexity of the situation it requires a force that is highly mobile and has reliable, protected communications.

The second set of tasks centre on establishing a stable and secure internal environment in order to create the conditions for a negotiated settlement and lasting peace.[45] These tasks include: guarantee and denial of movement, which requires large and well-protected forces (ground and air), cargo aircraft, increasing use of armour and substantial offshore facilities; protection of humanitarian relief through military operations; forceful separation of ethnic groups and counter-insurgency activities.

The third task is to establish the groundwork for a sustained peacebuilding process, to be initiated once the parties have demonstrated their commitment to the terms of a negotiated settlement. Peacebuilding is premised on a number of goals, the most important being the maintenance of a permanent cease-fire and the gradual return of power to a civilian government.[46] In Bosnia, long-term political strategies encompass a package of incentives, policies and techniques that encourage the deconstruction and demobilization of ethnic armies and democratization processes which separate civilian from military control.[47]

The constraints on implementing these tasks are twofold. First, existing decision-making regimes do not favour a coherent and timely military response to humanitarian disaster. Decisions by third parties to intervene militarily are characterized by two patterns of behaviour: they are often described as major policy shifts in which ground forces are inserted only after all other options are assumed to have failed; and further, this decisional shift exhibits considerable institutional pulling and hauling not only within the UN organization but within each state's bureaucracy.[48]

Second, there is a need to coordinate the self-interested activities of NGOs which may already be present in the conflict-zone. It takes strong and unified direction from outside actors to help the parties realize their mutual desire for peace. The competition for influence between and within institutions is a reality of any humanitarian intervention.[49] The implication is that justification for a significant policy shift and the subsequent debate over means must be pitched in a way that has broad cross-appeal to constituencies, interest groups and policy makers.[50]

CONCLUSIONS

Failed states are multifaceted phenomena that demand a multi-functional response. When states fail there is a need to respond quickly, efficiently and effectively. If policy makers and heads of state are not fully committed there is a tendency to rely on reactive measures which may prolong or at worst exacerbate tensions. There is an emerging consensus among policy makers that peacekeeping needs to be more proactive in its approach. In the past, Canada's strengths lay in contributing personnel and finances to peacekeeping missions. Even though these contributions continue to dwindle as a result of the Liberal government's budget cutbacks, there remains the need to improve the quality of peacekeeping in order to make peacekeepers more effective and efficient.[51]

Canada has chosen to improve the quality of peacekeeping in three ways. First, Canadian policy makers are beginning to realize the benefits of doing peacekeeping properly. The costs of failure (material, political and human) have led to sober second thoughts about the efficacy of ad hoc conventional peacekeeping and to a peacekeeping "chill." Bosnia and Somalia were less a failure of humanitarian principles than they were failures in forethought and planning. There is a need to improve the way the United Nations defines missions, peacekeeping mandates, force levels and budgets. Poorly implemented and ambiguous mandates in Bosnia and Somalia were derived from a basic misinterpretation of adversarial will, oversimplification of the disputes and underestimation of mission complexity.

Improving the quality of peacekeeping means more research, education and training. It also means recognizing those situations where conventional peacekeeping is best applied and where it is not. Canada's contributions in this area are two-fold: first, through significant contributions to peacekeeping training (specifically through the Pearson Peacekeeping Centre) and through a major study of UN response to failed state situations. In 1995, DFAIT released a report on a UN Rapid Reaction Capability. Among its main conclusions was the need to conform to principles of reliability and effectiveness.[52] Questions of risk were also central to the report. Early detection of crises is important but careful analysis of the situation is also crucial. Unsuccessful mediation in Somalia and, to a lesser extent, in Bosnia can be traced to a failure to accurately diagnose the situation on the ground prior to making a peacekeeping commitment.[53]

Second, and related to the first point, is the growing awareness that making peace is a holistic process. This view is reflected in the current government's recognition that CIDA, DFAIT and DND, as well Canadian NGOs, have a significant role to play in conflict prevention, peacekeeping and peacebuilding. We should probably think of peacekeeping less as the main instrument of conflict resolution and more as a means towards creating a stable environment within which a long-term peace process can be nurtured. Both military and development structures have a role to play in this process. In this era of diminishing defence budgets and deficit reductions, no Canadian institution can risk financial or political isolation. Public opinion is more likely to favour a mission that has a clearly defined foreign policy behind it.[54]

In its most expanded form, a holistic approach includes a full range of political, diplomatic and military instruments. Arguably, such a comprehensive list is beyond the scope of any single state. Thus, the third undertaking in which Canada continues to play a significant role is its continuing contribution to peacekeeping within multilateral frameworks.[55] Multilateral operations have the distinct advantage of exemplifying the cooperative security arrangements that have been a cornerstone of Canada's foreign policy. They also have the important task of developing and promoting stability among states during peacetime.

NOTES

I am grateful to Maureen Molot and Fen Hampson for helpful commentaries on the paper. I would also like to thank Michael Elliott for his able research assistance and insights on Canadian peacekeeping. This research was supported by funding from Carleton's GR6 Research Grant program and the Military and Strategic Studies Program of the Department of National Defence.

1   Saadia Touval, "Why the UN Fails," *Foreign Affairs* 73, no.5 (1994), 44-57.

2   Canada's recent peacekeeping contributions have been relatively small in terms of personnel and finances. This reduction does not automatically translate into diminished responsibility and influence. The reality is that Canada has taken several important initiatives in the areas of training and conflict prevention.

3   While it is true that a re-evaluation of international peacekeeping should focus on establishing workable mandates and preventive measures, a more fundamental challenge the Organization confronts is the fact that it is based on state sovereignty and relates institutionally to states. The UN is an organization of states, not of nations. It therefore has difficulty in relating to sub-state actors which have no legal personality and are the forces of war and peace in many intrastate disputes, ethnic conflicts and civil wars. International peacekeeping in internal conflicts has precedent. The list of major peacekeeping efforts of this sort includes the Congo (1960-64), Cyprus (since 1964),

Lebanon (since 1978), Namibia (1989-90) and Cambodia (1991-93). See: Adam Roberts, "The Crisis in UN Peacekeeping," *Survival* 36, no. 3 (1994), 93-120.

4   For a comparison of success and failures in peacemaking/peacebuilding see: Fen Osler Hampson, *Nurturing Peace: Why Peace Settlements Succeed or Fail* (Washington, D.C.: United States Institute for Peace, 1996).

5   Chester A. Crocker, "The Lessons of Somalia," *Foreign Affairs* 74, no. 3 (1995), 2-8.

6   The troubled outcome of the Somalia mission caused a rethinking of the feasibility of UN peace enforcement in a failed state. UNOSOM II was unsuccessful, not because of inadequate rules of engagement, but because of the multitude of political authorities with whom the UN was required to conclude agreements and the inability of the Organization to isolate those who defected from cease-fires and negotiated settlements. See Sergio, Ciano, "Some Thoughts on the Restoration of Somalia," *Canadian Defence Quarterly* 22, no.5 (1993), 25-28, and "A Role for the UN Still" in *Economic and Political Weekly*, November 6, 1993, 2425.

7   IFOR Canadian troops heading to Bosnia have been told not to abuse, torture or kill prisoners. Those instructions are spelled out clearly in the rules of conduct tucked in the pockets of each soldier assigned to Operation Alliance, NATO's peace enforcement mission in the war-torn Balkans. There will be a 1,000-strong Canadian contingent, mostly from CFB Petawawa, Ont., in Bosnia as part of the NATO-led, multinational force of about 60,000. Knowing how and when to use force is part of the training for Canadian soldiers preparing to leave for Bosnia. Canadians will staff headquarters of a multinational brigade under British command and, at Velika Kladusa, they will operate a supply depot, providing food and essential supplies to Canadian troops. See Donna Hooper, "Bosnia: New rules for engagement learned from Somalia," *Southam News*, January 8, 1996.

8   In the light of the peace agreement initialled in Dayton on 21 November, 1995, the North Atlantic Council (NAC), on December 1, 1995, authorized the Supreme Allied Commander Europe (SACEUR) to deploy Enabling Forces into Croatia and Bosnia-Herzegovina. All the NATO nations with armed forces (Belgium, Canada, Denmark, France, Germany, Greece, Italy, Luxembourg, Netherlands, Norway, Portugal, Spain, Turkey, United Kingdom and United States) pledged to contribute forces to IFOR. Iceland is providing medical personnel for it. The Peace Agreement (General Framework Agreement for Peace in Bosnia and Herzegovina) was formally signed in Paris on December 14, 1995. As of January 19, the following 16 non-NATO countries have been or will be considered for IFOR participation: Austria, Czech Republic, Egypt, Estonia, Finland, Hungary, Jordan, Latvia, Lithuania, Malaysia, Morocco, Poland, Romania, Russia, Sweden and the Ukraine. Sources: IFOR Coalition Press Information Centres in Zagreb and NATO Fact Sheet, January 18, 1996. Text of the Fact Sheet is

available on INTERNET via E-mail, on request (send requests to AFSOUTHSA@naples.dla.mil). It can also be found at the NATO gopher (gopher.nato.int) and on the World Wide Web (www.nato.int) on the IFOR icon.

9   The characteristics of the adversaries and the nature of the disputes are also similar. According to Ted R. Gurr the Bosnia and Somalia conflicts exemplify "communal contenders for state power." These are violent disputes consisting of "heterogenous assemblages of contending ethnopolitical groups; political power at the centre is based on intergroup coalitions. Institutional change opens up opportunities by which communal groups could more openly pursue their objectives." Ted R. Gurr, "People Against States: Ethnopolitical Conflict and the Changing World System," *International Studies Quarterly* 38 (1994), 347-78.

10 Samuel Makinda, "Somalia: from the Humanitarian Intervention to Military Offensive?" *The World Today*, (October 1993), 184-86. However costly and irrational it appears in human and material terms, the decision to resort to violence is a means of regulating behaviours, maintaining social order and ensuring favourable results. In short, a collectivity will pursue violence if by this means it safeguards advantageous and long-term political and economic outcomes. Violence can serve a functional and positive role for an ethnic elite and their followers. Leaders will use violence if it is a means of increasing cohesion among the group. Identification of a common enemy provides an opportunity for a group ridden with antagonisms to overcome them. Ted R. Gurr, "Resolving Ethnopolitical Conflicts: Exit, Autonomy or Access" in Gurr, ed., *Minorities at Risk: Origins and Outcomes of Ethnopolitical Conflicts* (Washington, D.C.: United States Institute of Peace Press, 1993), 290-313.

11 Collective action is the result of historical struggles for autonomy and self-determination or of current political processes. Collectively, ethnic conflict appears to be irrational because it leads to undesirable social outcomes over the short term, such as destruction of property and economic decline. Michael Hechter, "Explaining Nationalist Violence," *Nations and Nationalism* 1, no. 1 (1995), 53-68.

12 In general, ethnic wars are a function of low levels of institutionalization, narrow and ethnically defined elite bases of political support and high levels of ethnic consciousness due to repression by the regime, civil unrest and loss of civil liberties.

13 The clan fissures are important for four reasons. First, during the colonial period, most of the Somali population was divided into three distinct territories: the former Italian East African Colonies; Somaliland under British control and Somali areas in Ethiopia. The Somali struggle aimed at extending the boundaries of the new state to include missing Somali communities in Ethiopia, the French territories of Afars and Issas (Djibouti) and Northern Kenya. The idea of securing self-determination for all Somalis was born from the 1947 UN Human Rights Sub-commission on the Prevention of Discrimination and

Protection of Minorities, associated with the post-World War Two decolonization process. In 1949, at Somalia's urging, the country had been placed under UN trusteeship with Italy as the administering authority. Second, Pan-Somali nationalism was the country's unifying and legitimizing principle and "every Somali leader has been judged by his willingness and ability to pursue the goal of a 'Greater Somalia'." Samuel Makinda, *Security in the Horn of Africa*, Adelphi Papers no. 269 (London: International Institute of Strategic Studies, Summer 1992), 26. A sense of Somali "nationhood" developed out of the exigencies of colonial divide and rule policies. In turn, traditional animosities between Somali clans were set aside to face the perceived perils of foreign political control. Third, faced with potentially debilitating domestic divisiveness, Somalia's post-independence leaders set about framing a coherent foreign policy aimed at reclaiming Somali territory, in the belief that such action would be the best way to achieve internal unity. This policy culminated in an irredentist war with Ethiopia in 1977. The main effect of the war was to intertwine regional and domestic conflicts. At the regional level, the immediate post-war period was characterized by a series of important realignments in the region. The United States, though never openly committed to support for Somalia, sought to strengthen its relations with Mogadishu. Fourth, Somalia's internal situation was transformed as a result of the war. For example, the Barre regime was threatened by an abortive coup in April 1978. The coup signalled serious dissatisfaction among various clans with Somalia's humiliating defeat at the hands of the Dergue (the military revolutionary council which deposed Emperor Haile Selassie). Officers of the Majerteen clan who led the failed coup sought refuge in Ethiopia and subsequently formed the Somali Salvation Democratic Front (SSDF). Somalia's spiral into disintegration through the actions of clan leaders is clearly a legacy of this failed coup. See Samuel Makinda, *Security in the Horn of Africa*, and John Drysdale, *The Somali Dispute* (New York: Praeger Press, 1964).

14   Somalia's social and economic activities, and its political organizations, have traditionally stemmed from lineage systems based on one of the six major clan families—Darod, Digil, Dir, Hawiye, Issaq and Rahaniwan. The six groups are further split into smaller clans and patrilineal kinship groups. These groups are divided even further into *dia-paying* or family-based sub-clans varying in size from a few hundred to few thousand. In 1988, under great pressure from the United States, Somalia signed a peace accord with Ethiopia. The accord called for the demilitarization of the common border and effectively amounted to Somalia's renunciation of its claims to the Ogaden region. When the accord was signed, a guerilla challenge to the Barre regime, mounted by the Issaq-dominated Somali National Movement (SNM), signalled the onset of Somali civil war in the north (on May 18, 1991, the SNM leadership openly declared a secessionist "Republic of Somaliland"). Samuel Makinda, *Seeking Peace from Chaos:*

Humanitarian Intervention in Somalia, (Boulder, CO.: Lynne Reinner Press, 1993).

15   See note 14 for a discussion of Somalia's clan structure.

16   Almost 4.5 million people in Somalia—over half of the estimated population—were threatened by severe malnutrition and malnutrition-related disease, with the most seriously affected living in the countryside. It was estimated that perhaps between 300,000 people had died since November 1991, and 500,000 by December 1992. At least 1.5 million lives were at immediate risk. Almost one million Somalis sought refuge in neighbouring countries. Jonathon Stevenson, "Hope Restored in Somalia?" *Foreign Policy*, no. 91 (Summer 1993), 138-54; Jonathon T. Howe, "The United States and United Nations in Somalia: The Limits of Involvement," *The Washington Quarterly* 18, no. 3 (1995), 49-62.

17   UNITAF's principal goal was to establish a secure environment for urgent humanitarian assistance. Once that was accomplished, the military command would then be turned over to the UN. The U.S. decision to send troops to the country focused on three competing concerns: humanitarian assistance, the strategic value of potentially large Somali oil reserves and a potentially important strategic military installation at Berbera.

18   On March 27, 1993, the Belet Uen sector was declared secure. On May 24, 1993, the Battle Group was redeployed. See Deputy Chief of the Defence Staff, National Defence Headquarters, Ottawa, "Operation Deliverance: Final Report of Lessons Learned" Reference 33501 (COS J3) July 7, 1994.

19   The more permissive rules of engagement under Chapter VII of the UN Charter are considered more effective, less time-consuming and less dangerous to troops than those rules which are susceptible to gradual creep. See "Operation Deliverance: Major Lesson Learned - Subject: Rules of Engagement" B-15/21-B-16/21 National Defence Headquarters, Ottawa July 7, 1994; Bruce D. Berkowitz, "Rules of Engagement for UN Peacekeeping Forces in Bosnia," *Orbis*, 38, no. 4 (Fall 1994), 635-46.

20   On June 5, 1993, 25 Pakistani soldiers were killed, 10 went missing and 54 were wounded in a series of ambushes and armed attacks against UNOSOM II troops throughout south Mogadishu carried out by Somali militiamen, apparently belonging to Aideed's USC coalition. "On the Attack," *Macleans*, June 28, 1993.

21   The clan leaders also had difficulty in accepting UN neutrality. Although disarmament was to be applied universally, some clans were targets of more aggressive UN operations, specifically the forces of General Aideed. Located 300 km from Mogadishu, the Airborne was less exposed to the risk of appearing partial. See: Deputy Chief of the Defence Staff, "Operation Deliverance: Final Report of Lessons Learned."

22   The 860,000 strong Territorial Defence Force was designed to counter outside attack and would be joined by the 200,000 strong regular

armed forces. As Slovenia and Croatia prepared to secede, the Serb-dominated army handed out heavy weapons, including artillery, to Serb irregulars. Though the United Nations imposed an arms embargo in 1991 the number of weapons showed no sign of drying up. Major external suppliers of arms included Germany (arms manufactured in both East and West Germany), and many weapons from the U.S. (from a 1951-57 aid program), Czechoslovakia (pistols), and Russia (tanks). *The Globe and Mail*, July 14, 1992.

23   The subsequent inability of the leaders of these republics to develop national policy consensus, can be traced to the rise to power of Serb nationalist leaders and the failure of the other republics to pursue policies that would balance this domination. Reformists who held fast to the view that Yugoslavia's constitution and economy could be restructured in accordance with existing political arrangements were discredited by their failure to respond to Yugoslavia's economic collapse. P. Ramet Sabrina, "War in the Balkans," *Foreign Affairs*, 71, no. 4 (Fall 1992), 79-98; Misha Glenny, "What is to be Done?" *New York Review of Books*, May 27, 1993, 14-17; Misha Glenny, *The Fall of Yugoslavia: The Third Balkan War* (New York: Penguin Books 1992).

24   Of Yugoslavia's three crisis theatres, Bosnia-Herzegovina is the most complex. Bosnia is the one state in which Slav Muslims make up most of the population. Although the Muslims are a numerical majority (44 percent of the population) they never possessed the equivalent political clout and military power of their numerically smaller Serbian and Croatian counterparts. At crisis onset, Bosnia was led by a coalition government comprised of representatives of all three ethnic groups. Operating outside this coalition the Bosnian SDS, a Serb breakaway group led by Radovan Karadzić and armed with Federal Army equipment, had already proved successful in stalling any political solution to the future of Bosnia. This stalling tactic was aided by the fact that the major part of the Federal Army was stationed in Bosnia-Herzegovina prior to the conflict and the republic was the site of most of the Army's weapons factories, *The New York Times*, March 3, 1992.

25   In an agreement reached March 18, 1992, Bosnian Muslims, Serbs and Croats agreed to a plan that would transform Bosnia-Herzegovina into an independent country divided into three ethnically defined regions, *The New York Times*, March 19, 1992. On April 7 the agreement fell through as air strikes on predominantly Croatian-held territory were ordered by the Federal Army, *The New York Times*, April 8, 1992. At the same time, Bosnia mobilized its Guard and reserves and President Izetbegović (a Bosnian Muslim) assumed command of the Guard, *The New York Times*, April 4, 1992.

26   For example, by portraying itself as the sole arbiter of Serbian politics, inside and outside Serbia, Milošević's party, the Serbian Socialist Party (SPS), could justify its continuation and the preservation of the existing power structure. Since Serbia itself is only 65 percent Serbian, the SPS, by bringing the 30 percent of Bosnian Serbs into the political fold, would be able to increase the total Serbian proportion

substantially (aided by the expulsion of Albanians from Kosovo). A key ingredient in Milošević's ability to consolidate his power within Serbia was his ability to appeal to nationalist sensibilities and control the hypernationalism of his allies in Bosnia. Milošević's SPS was the source of supply for the Serb's mobilizing efforts in Bosnia, providing them with money, weapons and strategic advice. See Glenny, "What is to be done?"

27   It is important to note that a year earlier, on March 18, 1991, Croat, Serb and Bosnian Muslim leaders met in Lisbon and had already agreed to a set of ethnically based cantons which might have turned Bosnia into the entity envisioned in the Vance-Owen plan 18 months later. Under pressure from Serb hard-liners the Bosnian leader, Izetbegović renounced that agreement. When an overwhelming number of Bosnians chose independence in that state's March 2, 1992 referendum, the act had the simultaneous effect of triggering foreign policy crises for both Croatia and Serbia and signalling a shift in the winds of the larger Yugoslav war. In the referendum, Muslims, Croats, and Serbs outside Serb-controlled areas, voted overwhelmingly for a "democratic" independent Bosnia, an act that suited neither the interests of Croatia's leader Tudjman nor those of Milošević.

28   On May 3, 1994, President Bill Clinton signed Presidential Decision Directive 25 (PDD-25), a policy directive outlining the administration's position on reforming multilateral peace operations. PDD-25 sets forth several stringent requirements that must be satisfied before the U.S. will participate in future international peacekeeping operations and suggests ways in which the UN could improve its management of such operations. The Directive defines "command" by the United States' armed forces and "operational control" of those forces, distinguishes the two, and maintains that although the President never relinquishes "command" over United States military personnel, he may place United States military personnel under the "operational control" of a non-U.S. commander for limited and defined purposes.

29   There still remains a "rift" between the U.S. military and other contributors to peacekeeping on the question of the use of ground forces as an impartial element in the peacekeeping process. In contrast to the American military, the European states, for example, approach the issue of peacekeeping from a completely different starting point derived from historical experience. Those with colonial experience— such as the United Kingdom, France, and the Netherlands—are more likely to respond to an internal conflict rapidly with effective direct strategies, which limit casualties while achieving basic objectives. The Europeans have long recognized the need for local superiority on the ground.

30   NATO eventually altered its constitution so that it could provide military assistance to non-military multilateral organizations (leading to the July 1992 deployment of naval forces in the Adriatic Sea to assist in the use of sanctions against Serbia.)

31   The legal basis for operations is the mandate of each separate mis-
      sion. In general, Security Council resolutions and agreements between
      the UN and individual nations are the legal basis for the initiation and
      implementation of peacekeeping operations. A coalition of forces may
      have the de facto right to intervene once the Security Council labels
      events as aggression (although that term is not clearly defined in the
      Charter) and any state that has ratified the Charter agrees to its inter-
      pretation by the Security Council.

32   In essence, peacekeeping is an improvised technique that has no
      legal basis in the UN Charter. The rules surrounding peacekeeping
      have been built by practice over the years, much like common law.
      Six criteria apply: (a) whether a situation exists and the continuation
      of which is likely to endanger, or constitute a threat to, international
      peace and security; (b) whether regional or subregional organizations
      and arrangements exist and can readily be used to resolve the situa-
      tion; (c) whether a cease-fire exists and whether the parties have
      committed themselves to a peace process intended to reach a political
      settlement; (d) whether a clear political goal exists and whether it can
      be reflected in the mandate; (e) whether a precise mandate for a
      United Nations operation can be formulated; (f) whether the safety
      and security of United Nations personnel can be reasonably ensured,
      and in particular whether reasonable guarantees can be obtained from
      the principal parties or factions regarding the safety and security of
      United Nations personnel. Alan James, *Peacekeeping in International
      Politics*, (New York: St. Martin's Press, 1990).

33   The failure of traditional criteria to find a home in the post-Cold War era
      is due to a continuing desire for flexible mandates and to a doctrinal
      void. Decision makers are leery of formulating policies in too dogmatic
      a fashion. In the past, flexibility and pragmatism were constructive in
      those interstate situations in which limited and impartial operations were
      not undertaken to make peace but to monitor cease-fires accepted by
      the adversaries. The doctrinal void has proved more problematic. It can
      be traced to past restrictions on activities in internal conflict and the
      debate over the kinds of measures required in these situations.

34   For example, the mandate of UNOSOM II, covering the whole
      territory of Somalia, would include the following military tasks:
      (a) monitoring respect by all factions for the cessation of hostilities
      and other agreements to which they had consented; (b) preventing
      any resumption of violence and, if necessary, taking appropriate
      action against any faction that violated or threatened to violate the
      cessation of hostilities; (c) maintaining control of the heavy weapons
      of the organized factions, which would have been brought under
      international control pending their eventual destruction or transfer to
      a newly constituted national army; (d) seizing the small arms of all
      unauthorized armed elements and assisting in the registration and
      security of such arms; (e) securing or maintaining security at all ports,
      airports and lines of communication required for the delivery of
      humanitarian assistance; (f) protecting the personnel, installations and

equipment of the United Nations and its agencies, the International
Committee of the Red Cross (ICRC) as well as NGOs, and taking such
forceful action as might be required to neutralize armed elements that
attacked, or threatened to attack, such facilities and personnel, pend-
ing the establishment of a new Somali police force which could
assume this responsibility; (g) continuing the program for mine-clear-
ing in the most afflicted areas; (h) assisting in the repatriation of
refugees and displaced persons within Somalia; (i) carrying out such
other functions as might be authorized by the Security Council.
Source: UN WWW Home Page, "Peacekeeping Missions Current and
Past." For an analysis of lessons learned see: Rafael Moreno and Juan
José Vega, "Lessons from Somalia," *Peacekeeping and International
Relations*, 23, no. 3, May/June 1994.

35   This dynamic and interactive process results in a situation in which
the peacekeepers are influenced by occurrences at the local level.
While a military presence may improve the humanitarian situation in
a starving country, for example, the local population may find that
over time they depend on the foreign soldiers for their survival.
Consider, for example, General Aideed's exploitation of the increasing
U.S. presence. Aideed insisted on UN neutrality but sought U.S. support for his clan in order to tip the scales of balance in his favour.
See Jonathon Stevenson, "Hope Restored in Somalia?."

36   Gottfried Mayer-Kress, Centre for Complex Systems Research (CCSR),
Beckman Institute, Physics, University of Illinois at Urbana-Champagne
(UIUC), Paul Diehl, Political Science, UIUC, and Holly Arrow,
Psychology, UIUC "The United Nations and Conflict Management in a
Complex World: Technical Report of the Center for Complex Systems
Research, CCSR-94-31," WWW Hypertext Document, University of
Illinois at Urbana-Champagne (ongoing project).

37   An array of factors, primarily sanctions and the threat of intervention
were developed to discourage Serb leaders from coercive policies.
None of the restrictions, however, appears to have succeeded in fully
deterring Serbian expansionism or frustrating most of its objectives.
The failure of the international community to fully enforce sanctions
permitted Serbia to press its advantage. However, the threat of international involvement does appear to have presented Serbian leaders
with a second-best solution. If Serbia could not maintain command
of an integrated Yugoslavia, then at least it would control all of the
territory with significant Serb populations through proxy-militia
established in Serb-held enclaves.

38   Apart from the breakaway Somaliland (which has not gained international recognition) territory was not an issue in Somalia. The primary
issues were ending a civil war and imposing martial law on two
major factions and fifteen political movements. For the 500 poorly-
armed Pakistani soldiers stationed in Mogadishu these tasks were
beyond their capacity.

39   For example, Mogadishu's airport was made secure, which enhanced
the logistic capabilities of the NGOs. During and after Sahnoun's

tenure, malnutrition and disease figures improved in four of the nine sectors occupied by peacekeepers (including that eventually patrolled by Canada's Airborne Regiment). See: Crocker, "The Lessons of Somalia" and Stevenson, "Hope Restored in Somalia?".

40 This ceasefire was short-lived. On October 3, 1993, United States Rangers launched an operation in south Mogadishu aimed at capturing a number of key aides of General Aideed who were suspected of complicity in the 5 June attack, as well as subsequent attacks on UN personnel and facilities. The operation succeeded in apprehending 24 suspects, including two key aides to General Aideed. During the course of the operation, two U.S. helicopters were shot down by Somali militiamen using automatic weapons and rocket-propelled grenades. Patrick J. Sloyan "Mission in Somalia" *Newsday*, December 7, 1993.

41 For example, NATO made several announcements, including the one of April 22, 1994, that if any Bosnian Serb attacks involving heavy weapons were carried out against UN-designated safe areas, including Bihać, these weapons and other Bosnian Serb military assets, as well as their direct and essential support facilities—including but not limited to fuel installations and munition sites—would be subject to NATO air strikes, in accordance with the procedural arrangements worked out between NATO and UNPROFOR following the Council decisions of August 2 and 9, 1993. A further decision of November 19, 1994, authorized air strikes in response to attacks against, or threatening, the UN safe areas in Bosnia-Herzegovina; these strikes were launched from the UN-protected areas in Croatia. Sources: Various NATO Fact Sheets, available from NATO Office of Information and Press, Brussels.

42 Earlier in the year the United States had rejected the Vance-Owen Peace Plan as being unfair to the Muslims. Under the new Clinton administration that policy was reversed. Meanwhile the UN deployed 1172 troops to Macedonia in an effort to prevent the outbreak of hostilities there, *The Globe and Mail*, December 15, 1992.

43 The concessions coincided with the arrival of Milošević at the Geneva Peace Talks. The proposed map of the new Bosnian state showed that both the EC and the U.S., which was then party to the talks, were willing to allow Bosnia to be redrawn along ethnic lines, with the Serbs controlling almost 70 percent of the former Yugoslav territory. As before, the Bosnian Croatian leader Mate Boban and the Muslim leader Izetbegović were receptive to the idea of the plan, comprising a ceasefire plan, a political agreement and a map reorganizing the former Yugoslav republic into 10 separate regions under a central government. Karadzić's willingness to sign the agreement came only after immense pressure from Milošević, *The Globe and Mail*, January 10, 1993.

44 Clearly, UN imposed sanctions (including a naval blockade) and condemnation of Serb involvement were necessary but not sufficient conditions for achieving a negotiated settlement. Even after sanctions,

oil continued to get to Serbia and heavy armaments were still being used by both sides. However the sanctions did have the important effect of bringing Milošević and the Bosnian Muslims on side.

45   Protecting refugees and internally displaced peoples is more problematic, because it raises the question of whether the use of force as self-defence should be extended to peoples caught in the conflict. On these grounds, the Somalia mission can be considered much more successful. Despite the deliberate attempts to prevent UNOSOM II from performing its tasks, the overall situation in Somalia underwent a major transformation: humanitarian assistance was reaching its destinations, protected from attacks and banditry; starvation was largely eradicated; nutrition programs were successful in reducing the number of deaths; return and repatriation programs for refugees were initiated; schools, closed for three or four years, were reopened. See: Crocker, "The Lessons of Somalia."

46   Key roles to be played by the UN and other third parties are assistance to the interim civil community; logistic effort to establish cantonment sites; supervision of the handing over of weapons and demobilization; ensuring the safe return of displaced populations and training local cadres to clear the war zone.

47   The military tasks include: to ensure self-defence and freedom of movement; to supervise selective marking of boundaries and Zone of Separation (ZOS) between the parties; to monitor and—if needed— enforce the withdrawal of forces to their respective territories, and the establishment of Zones of Separation; to assume control of the airspace over Bosnia-Herzegovina and of the movement of military traffic over key ground routes; to establish Joint Military Commissions, which will serve as the central bodies for all Parties to the Peace Agreement; to assist with the withdrawal of UN forces not transferred to IFOR. The deployment of the IFOR should also eventually create a secure environment which will facilitate the work of humanitarian organizations and the accomplishment of the non-military aspects of the settlement. Sources: IFOR Coalition Press Information Centres in Zagreb and NATO Fact Sheet. Text of the Fact Sheet is available on INTERNET via E-mail, on request (send requests to AFSOUTHSA@naples.dla.mil). It can also be found at the NATO gopher (gopher.nato.int) and on the World Wide Web (www.nato.int) on the IFOR icon.

48   Debates over command and control between third parties is problematic: it can lead to a vacuum of inaction or indecision when each pushes responsibility on the other. For example, on March 12, 1994, after a mortar attack from Serb tanks against French Blue Helmet positions in the south of Bihać, the UN called for intervention by NATO aviation. However, at the last minute the attack was cancelled. The UN explained that this was because of local atmospheric conditions and the fact that the Serb cannons had stopped firing. Such intervention would have been the first allied close air support action in favour of UNPROFOR. The NATO version is somewhat different. In

AFSOUTH, Naples, a spokesman pointed out that the attack had not been cancelled because of bad weather but simply because of the fact that UNPROFOR had not confirmed its request for an air strike. See North Atlantic Council, Sub-Committee on Defence and Security Co-operation Between Europe and North America, "NATO, Peacekeeping and the Former Yugoslavia" (May 1994).

49 This kind of approach is not likely to result in early and pre-emptive action unless consensus-building is pursued at the outset. Leaders of the coalition forces are usually at a loss to explain to their publics why ground forces are necessary on purely political grounds. This difficulty is more keenly felt in the post-Cold War era, when the term "lack of political will" is often used to explain the absence of a coherent response to a humanitarian conflict.

50 Regional organizations can play a helpful role, as is shown by the Association of Southeast Asian Nations (ASEAN) in Cambodia and by the Contadora Group in Central America.

51 Reconciling the decreasing size of the Canadian Armed Forces and a governmental desire to continue to be a significant player on the world stage means that others within Canada and the world at large will be required to take up the slack. Canada's challenge is to ensure that these states, institutions and individuals are as well trained as possible.

52 Department of Foreign Affairs and International Trade, *Towards a Rapid Reaction Capability for the United Nations*, the Government of Canada, September, 1995.

53 From a policy perspective, decision makers must have exact knowledge about the costs of not being involved, coupled with awareness that a conflict will probably escalate. Accurate information is essential to the process of finding an appropriate fit between strategy, the problem at hand and resources available. Decision makers must then develop an active and effective response to the conflict. Finally, they must ensure a comprehensive follow-through program to prevent recurrences. All these activities are indispensable to any successful pre-emptive action.

54 Joseph, T. Jockel, *Canada and International Peacekeeping*, (Center for Strategic & International Studies, Washington D.C. and Canadian Institute of Strategic Studies, Toronto, Ontario, 1994).

55 "Department of Foreign Affairs and International Trade Policy Staff Documents," May 18, 1993. Internet WWW page at URL. Discussion papers include: "Managing International Conflict," "Conflict and the Regional Option" and "Beyond Emergency Assistance."

XIII

NGOs and the International System: Building Peace in a World at War

KENNETH D. BUSH

The broad objective of this chapter is to provide a critical analysis of non-governmental organizations (NGOs) and the international system, with some discussion of Canadian NGOs and their varied and intensive involvement in a range of activities and responsibilities.[1] This chapter takes up this challenge through an examination of a conspicuous feature of the Canadian NGO community in 1995: the efforts of NGOs to define their peacebuilding role in regions of latent and manifest violence. "Peacebuilding" is being used to refer to efforts to foster and support those structures and processes which strengthen the prospects for peaceful coexistence and decrease the likelihood of the outbreak (or reoccurrence) of violent conflict.[2] The chapter is divided into two main sections. The first section contains a broad discussion of NGOs in war zones, and the evolving relationship between military and non-governmental actors; the second provides a more specific discussion of the peacebuilding activities of Canadian NGOs, in particular the transformation of the security environment, political reconstruction, human rights and democratic development, and social reconstruction and local empowerment.

It is important to stress that peacebuilding is not a specific activity, but a function or consequence of an activity. Consequently, a very wide range of NGO activities may fall with the scope of our concern. The peacebuilding contributions of NGOs therefore include projects and activities which are not conventionally viewed as being "peace-related." These are the initiatives of NGOs which often find themselves quite literally on the front lines of violent conflict, managing projects in agriculture, irrigation, health, education, urban poverty alleviation, and so on. Realistically, NGO activities alone cannot resolve the protracted social conflicts which are so prevalent in the world today. However, they possess the potential to significantly contribute to conflict management and resolution in those areas in which the NGOs have direct experience. What is equally important is that their activities have the potential to exacerbate tensions and inhibit conflict management.[3] The capacity of NGOs to influence events must be evaluated carefully since it varies considerably from case to case.

One indication of the increasing prominence of the peacebuilding role of Canadian NGOs was the holding of three separate conferences in Ottawa on this theme in late 1995: "NGOs and Peacebuilding: Lessons Learned and Next Steps," organized by the Ad Hoc Group on NGOs and Peacebuilding; the "Peacebuilding Contact Group" Meeting of the NGO Division of the Canadian International Development Agency (CIDA); and the Horn of Africa Policy Group Annual Meeting organized by the Canadian Council for International Cooperation (CCIC).[4] In some ways, these meetings were the culmination of a three-year process of workshops, roundtables, and conferences sponsored by a variety of agencies and organizations, including CIDA, the International Development Research Centre (IDRC), the Department of Foreign Affairs and International Trade (DFAIT), the Parliamentary Centre, CCIC, and numerous NGOs. The gatherings provided opportunities for all interested parties to assemble and share their ideas and experiences with each other. As a result of this regular contact, the governmental, military and NGO communities are now able to begin asking the questions that need to be answered if Canada is to play a constructive peacebuilding role. The importance of this process cannot be over-emphasized. The questions that are asked are even more important than the provisional answers that are provided. The wrong questions will inevitably lead to the wrong answers, no matter how elegant, sophisticated, or practical such answers might appear to be.

NGOS ON THE FRONT LINES

It is not new for NGOs to work in conditions of social tension and violence. The Canadian government is increasingly turning its attention to the NGO sector, asking it to undertake tasks previously performed by governments, such as the delivery of significant portions of humanitarian and development assistance, as was done in apartheid South Africa, Rwanda, and Sri Lanka. A related phenomenon is evident even in the world of international financial institutions, where the International Monetary Fund (IMF) and the World Bank are turning more and more to NGOs to help offset the attendant dislocations of structural adjustment programs. Ironically, while the significance of the NGOs in the international system is increasingly recognized,[5] the Canadian NGO community was savaged by the 1995 Federal Budget, which was a continuation of a trend of decreased government commitment to the non-governmental sector.

Increasingly, NGOs are choosing to continue their activities when faced by levels of violence which would have previously led to their suspension of operations until the situation stabilized; examples are CARE Canada in Somalia, OXFAM in the Horn of Africa, World University Service of Canada (WUSC) and Sri Lanka-Canada Development Fund (SLCDF) in Sri Lanka and Save the Children Fund (SCF) in Mozambique, as well as Médecins Sans Frontières Canada in various conflicts. Under such conditions, NGOs have often been forced into a humanitarian and relief mode at the expense of longer-term development objectives. There is little doubt that this illustrates the recalibration of development assistance to the exigencies of changed circumstances. However, it also suggests that Official Development Assistance (ODA) and NGO activities may play a role that is broader than relief in violent or volatile situations by actively cultivating the preconditions and structures for peace.

NGOs are especially well-suited to play a peacebuilding role. Not only are they intimately familiar with the social, political and economic context within which peacebuilding must be undertaken, but they also possess a wealth of hands-on local expertise in activities which are crucial to this process, such infrastructural development, education, and cooperative projects. It is equally important that NGOs typically occupy a strategically pivotal position in conflict situations, located as they are between societal and state actors. As Francisco Solis and Pauline Martin point out in the case of El Salvador, "the presence of NGOs in the polarized context of civil war established a kind of mediation between the unsatisfied needs of the population and the social and economic policies of successive governments."[6]

One final caveat is necessary. It may strike the reader as naive to suggest that peacebuilding activities may be undertaken in the midst of protracted violence. However, it is essential to recognize that even in the most extreme cases, violence is neither undifferentiated nor impenetrable. Even in the most severe conflicts, cooperative events occur alongside those that are conflictual. In some cases or areas cooperative events may even be more prevalent, but, it is the conflictual events that tend to capture the attention of policy makers and the public. The point to be emphasized is that even within severe conflicts the space exists for peacebuilding, spaces which are often dangerous, tenuous and fluid, but very much in existence.[7]

Military-NGO Collaboration: Shotgun Marriages

The presence of NGOs in war zones frequently puts them in direct contact with military actors, both combatants and international peace-keeping or peace enforcement troops. The evolving relationship between military and humanitarian NGOs has been described as a "shotgun marriage."[8] This is an apt description because it recognizes that the union of these two types of actors is demanded by the immediate predicament in which they find themselves. The short-term situation completely eclipses consideration of the longer-term implications of the union.

Some NGOs are speaking of the need for closer cooperation between the military and the development community in conflict situations. This sentiment has been fuelled by the immediate threat to the lives of NGO workers and the continued operation of projects in war zones and shaky "post"-war zones. John Watson of CARE Canada has been especially vocal in suggesting what this type of cooperation should look like. The new role required of the military in "armed humanitarian interventions" requires new thinking, new training, and a new modus operandi.[9] According to Watson, more appropriate peacekeeping intervention might be undertaken by specially trained military "minimalists," individuals able to work with NGOs in the ways that NGOs work—with locals, with local resources, with appropriate technology, and with low dependence on institutional support. What is needed is a military technical assistance which can function within an "inefficient" environment. NGOs need "peacekeeper trainers," for example, who can set up security and distribution systems in camps for refugees and displaced people (to prevent bottlenecks, riots, and breakdowns in order) and who can support certain progressive elements within society as part of their larger mandate and standard operating procedure. Watson's vision is less one that refines the military-NGO relationship, than one which transforms peacekeeping into a function of development and humanitarian efforts.

This view is not shared by Major-General Lewis Mackenzie, who argues simply that "good soldiers make good peacekeepers." Interestingly, this corresponds with the position of some NGOs. Mackenzie recognizes there is a clear division of labour between military and humanitarian actors, based on their respective skills and capacities. According to Mackenzie, the task of the "peacekeeper" is to create and ensure the security conditions that will enable NGOs and other agencies to get on with their work. He cautions against direct linkages between the peacekeepers and aid-givers because they may taint the perception of NGO impartiality.

While more effective military-NGO coordination may indeed be necessary under certain crisis conditions, this paper argues that it should be bracketed within the larger development and peace problematic; that is, it should be explicitly harnessed to the means and ends of development *and of peace* activities. Failure to take this step raises a serious problem: the immediate military "security" requirements of the short-term may foreclose or inhibit the ability to pursue both short-term humanitarian goals and longer-term development objectives. This was the case with the operations of the Unified Task Force (UNITAF) and the UN Operation in Somalia (UNOSOM) II, where military intervention so skewed the allocation of available resources that the subversion of humanitarian and development objectives was almost inevitable.

The failure of large-scale interventions in Somalia to take account of the developmental objectives of humanitarian intervention led to a situation in which the immediate (military) security requirements (as defined by the principal intervening state) prevented the pursuit of both development and peace in the short-term and long-term. Jan Eliasson, the UN Undersecretary-General for Humanitarian Affairs, observed in July 1993, that the international community "was spending ten dollars on military protection for every dollar of humanitarian assistance," and that "unless sufficient funds [were] provided for rehabilitation activities, there [was] a risk that the military operation [could] be perceived as an end in itself."[10] Even higher estimates are suggested by Mohammad Sahnoun, the former UN Special Representative in Somalia,[11] who also points out that between April and December 1993 "an estimated 6,000 Somalis and 83 UN Peacekeepers may have died in clashes between UN forces and Somali armed groups since the UN took over the American-led UNITAF mission."[12] Sahnoun's assessment echoes that of many NGOs and Somalis: "the perception that the role of the UN presence has shifted from a humanitarian one to that of an 'occupying force' is widespread among Somalis."[13] It is increasingly clear that the development community, no less than the military community, needs to develop new analytical and policy tools in order to take effective action, both individually and collectively, within the so-called new world order.

Recently, Canadian Forces Base Cornwallis was converted into a Canadian International Peacekeeping Training Centre, with a mandate "to provide research and education on peacekeeping in all its forms, while also serving as a uniquely Canadian point of contact for peacekeeping information."[14] It is a positive sign that the Centre "will [also] support non-governmental organizations, and provide assistance where possible to the academic community and other private interests in matters germane to peacekeeping... [Additionally] it will offer short courses in peacekeeping, conflict resolution and related issues [which will be] open to other nations with an interest in peacekeeping operations."[15] Significantly however, it is not within the Centre's mandate "to conduct the military training required by Canadian Forces personnel assigned to peacekeeping duties." In other words, as it is currently constituted, the Training Centre is not meant to "train" peacekeepers operationally; it is meant to facilitate research and provide courses *about* peacekeeping. If the Centre lessened the risk to Canadian peacekeepers through training, and if it were open to officers and troops from other peacekeeper nations, Canada would have created the opportunity to make a significant contribution to the operational skills and capacities of peacekeepers in UN operations. Such tasks, however, are not within the mandate of the Centre.

There is no doubt that research on peacekeeping is important, given the complexity of the environment within which Canada will be asked to contribute to future "missions for peace" or large-scale peacekeeping operations.[16] However, peacekeeping is but one component of the peace process. To overemphasize this component is to weaken other equally crucial factors (such as peacebuilding, peacemaking, and preventive diplomacy) and actors (NGOs, community organizations, political leaders, and private actors). There remains the need for a centre to undertake or coordinate research that would consider the full breadth of the issues underpinning the peace-nurturing process. In the absence of such a centre, research is undertaken, more often than not, in an uncoordinated or disconnected manner.

PEACEBUILDING ROLES OF NGOS

NGOs perform a wide range of peacebuilding activities. This section will examine Canadian NGO experiences in four particularly important areas of activity: transformation of the security environment; political reconstruction; human rights and democratic development; and social reconstruction.

NGOs and the Transformation of the Security Environment

A significant feature of both CIDA-sponsored and other peace-nurturing projects is the frequency with which non-governmental organizations have come to play a central role in a variety of initiatives aimed at transforming the security environment of violence-prone regions. NGOs have undertaken activities as diverse as: (1) a project to financially support the Commission on Illegal Armed Groups in El Salvador; (2) human rights training programs for Armed Forces and Police in Haiti and Sri Lanka; (3) support for the International Resource Group on Disarmament and Security in the Horn of Africa; (4) community-based non-violent defence; (5) support for an Organization of African Unity (OAU) conference on conflict prevention for African leaders; (6) police monitoring and liaison; and (7) vocational training for ex-combatants.[17]

In 1995, the "landmine crisis" served to galvanize concerted action by Canadian NGOs. In late 1994 they created an ad hoc coalition,

"Mines Action Canada," to press for action on the "landmine crisis." The coalition seeks a total ban on the production, stockpiling, trade, and use of antipersonnel mines including a Canadian moratorium on the production, export and transfer of these weapons, their component parts and the related technology. Additionally, the coalition endorses recent Canadian initiatives and calls for additional assistance to humanitarian mine-clearance activities, asking the Canadian government and public to increase support for, and participation in, unilateral, bilateral, multilateral and NGO programs providing assistance to the victims of landmines.[18]

Individual NGOs have also responded to the land mine crisis directly on the ground. For example, in Cambodia, the Banan Agriculture Returnee Reintegration project (World Vision Canada) addresses the issue of land shortages due to widespread mining, and facilitates community efforts to locate, mark, and map mined areas, as part of an effort to assist reintegration by enhancing community participation and capabilities in the agricultural, economic and social service sectors. Similarly, in Laos, the Mennonite Central Committee Canada (MCCC) has been working with the Mines Action Group (UK) to develop the local expertise necessary to clear the millions of mines and bomblets that litter the country and inhibit the development process ("Unexploded Ordnance Project"). This capacity-building approach is similar to that of the Cambodian Mine Action Centre (CMAC) in Cambodia, currently operating under the auspices of the United Nations Development Program (UNDP). The advantage of this type of approach is that it draws on local resources and expertise, creates a sense of ownership among participants, and allows for the indigenization of the de-mining process. This stands in stark contrast to the competing model of mine clearance—the commercial model which hires highly trained and expensive experts (often from the same companies who manufacture landmines) who are bungeed in and out of an area. In this model there is little, if any, dissemination of technical expertise; it is extremely expensive; and it is not especially cost-effective in terms of the number of mines cleared. Approaches which encourage participation are likely to be more sustainable and effective in the long run.

A number of other, broader, projects are especially noteworthy for their efforts to encourage indigenous efforts to transform the local security environment. Two examples, drawn from Somalia, focus on the societal disjuncture that has developed between legitimacy,

authority and power, thereby allowing the coercive authority of war-
lords to become a dominant force in Somali social relations. The
power of the gun has displaced those traditional, and legitimate,
forms of elder-based authority that were based on discussion and
compromise. However, war lordism has not erased the authority of
elders. These initiatives should serve as important examples of efforts
to push gun-based power to the margins while recentring traditional
sources of social relations. The first project, nurtured by the
Mennonite Central Committee Canada, is the series of the Borama
and Sanaag elders' conferences.[19] These meetings in early 1993
brought together hundreds of Somali elders and thousands of advi-
sors for a period of almost five months. The national conference was
the culmination of a series of multilateral conferences at the regional
level, which in turn developed from a series of bilateral peace conferences. After this period of extended discussion, the participants
arrived at a consensus on how to govern Somaliland and how to
resolve inter-clan conflict in that region. Specifically, the conference
adopted a countrywide security framework, laid down a national
constitutional structure, and enabled a peaceful change in government to take place. While this marks the beginning of a solution,
rather than a solution per se, it is most notable for its support of an
indigenous Somali peace effort, and its willingness to use indigenous
methods of conflict management.

The second initiative which warrants attention is the process leading up to the signing of the Hiraab Treaty in January 1994, an
eight-point peace agreement reached by 310 delegates from five
Hawiye clans. The fact that this was a treaty brokered directly by clan
leaders rather than by their politicians and military leaders is very significant for other peace efforts. If the treaty holds, it will serve to
demonstrate the peace-making capacity of the indigenous Somali
social system.

These types of approach require that Canada, and other members
of the international community, accept a long-term commitment to
nurturing indigenous conflict management structures and processes,
possess a thorough understanding of, and sensitivity to, cultural factors relevant to conflict resolution, and display a willingness to build
a relationship of trust between indigenous partners, based on significant and long-term involvement in the country.[20] The building of the
political space within which indigenous groups can work out their
own solutions to their own problems is not a quick or easy process.

However, if solutions are to be sustainable, this may ultimately be the most essential phase of a successful peacebuilding effort.

Such an innovative, bottom-up strategy need not, indeed should not, be pursued in isolation from other conflict-resolution efforts, undertaken at other levels and involving other actors. In other words, a multitrack approach is likely the most efficacious course of action. That may, however, entail coordination problems and the danger that parallel efforts may "jump track" and stymie the overall peace nurturing process. It might be possible to reduce such problems by anticipating them in advance.

Political Reconstruction

Canadian governmental and non-governmental actors have been very much engaged in the broad field of political reconstruction. Their initiatives have varied widely in scale and impact. In the area of public sector reform and management, for example, the non-profit Institute on Governance has been active in Canada and internationally, having performed a training and consultation role for officials from the Association of Southeast Asian Nations (ASEAN), Vietnam, Indonesia, South Africa, and Kenya. Similarly, the IDRC is sponsoring projects to strengthen research and policy institutions in Cambodia and Laos, including the Mekong Development Research Network, which encourages cooperation among the countries bordering the Mekong. In South Africa, Canadian actors were involved extensively in a wide variety of initiatives during the apartheid era. Especially noteworthy have been the CIDA-funded projects developed and implemented by NGOs. These include: substantial projects assisting victims of apartheid; alternative media projects; election monitoring; citizenship education projects; voter education and monitoring programs; legal and humanitarian aid; education for democracy campaigns; educational projects for the South African judiciary; peace monitor training; a program to strengthen the national civic movement; and a variety of human rights projects.[21]

In the transition towards a post-apartheid era, Canadian governmental and non-governmental actors have made significant contributions to South African efforts to build democratic institutions and structures of governance. The federal parliamentary system of Canada is seen by some South Africans as model from which they might draw insights relevant to the particular set of political challenges they face. There was, for example, a notable degree of consultation between Canadians and South Africans concerning the framing of the post-apartheid constitution, a consequence of which is the resemblance of the South African Bill of Rights to the Canadian Charter of Rights and Freedoms.[22] In an effort to support a peaceful process of political and social transition, the IDRC has created three projects in the fields of public administration, education, and macroeconomic policy development. The public administration project has supported a variety of governance-related initiatives involving the newly constituted national and provincial governments in South Africa, including a legislative cooperation project which brings together members and staff of legislatures from both countries to exchange experiences and ideas.

While the South Africa-Canada Legislative Cooperation Project of the Parliamentary Centre focuses on the political reconstruction of the formal political structures of governance, there are many other initiatives in existence which contribute to this process by strengthening the capacity of civil society to participate effectively in the political process. They include education projects for Third World nationals here in Canada, and similar ventures in violence-prone regions, such as those undertaken by WUSC, Canadian University Services Overseas (CUSO), and the South Africa Education Trust Fund. There are also broader research and development projects which provide a degree of protection, or a temporary exit option, for professionals who otherwise might be killed or who would lose the ability to maintain their professional skills under conditions of latent and manifest violence. The survival and encouragement of such professionals will help to sustain a level of leadership capacity which might otherwise be decimated. While they may be in a position to contribute to the reconstruction process in their home land, the phenomenon of brain drain is a debilitating reality for many countries in the South. Almost by definition, an immediate postwar environment is characterized by a lack of those structures which would induce professionals to return and accommodate their requirements. This is often enough to inhibit all but the most intrepid, the most entrepreneurial or the most committed from returning home. In thinking through this facet of the peacebuilding process, we must consider the need to support persons in this category both during violent phases of a conflict, and—what is equally important—during the short and medium term of the transitional and post-conflict phase.

Canada has clearly contributed much to political reconstruction and democratic development in wartorn societies. However, past initiatives and current trends need to be highlighted in order to adequately assess their overall impact. On the one hand, Canada has encouraged democratic development and respect for human rights around the world. Yet, where the human rights objectives of foreign policy have conflicted with commercial and economic interests, we have seen a disturbing trend towards giving the latter priority over the former. An example is the so-called "Team Canada" venture in China in late 1994. The record of this expedition, consisting of the Prime Minister, the premiers of all the provinces (except Quebec) and an army of business people, suggests that the promotion of Canadian prosperity and employment may take precedence over the abstract and perhaps less economically lucrative issues of human rights and democratic development, cornerstones of the peace nurturing process.[23] The same aspect is glaringly evident in the Canadian development assistance policy towards Indonesia,[24] a major beneficiary of Canadian aid despite the well-documented reality of systematic, pervasive human rights abuses including arbitrary arrest, protracted detention without trial, torture, and extra-judicial killings. Indeed, Canadian assistance jumped dramatically following the 1975 Indonesian invasion of the former Portuguese colony of East Timor, where it is estimated that one-third of the population has perished as a result of starvation and indiscriminate killings by the occupying army.[25]

Some observers have suggested that Canada has not necessarily abandoned completely its stated commitment to the promotion of human rights; they point to this country's continued diplomatic pressure on the Nigerian military regime in response to its rejection of the results of a general election in 1993 and its subsequent crackdown on political opponents. However, such observers argue that different Canadian responses to human rights abuses in different countries are attributable to national self-interest, narrowly defined in terms of Canadian trade interests and geopolitics.[26] As Keenleyside writes, regarding Canada's significant trade relationship with China and its muted response to the Tiananmen Square massacre and subsequent arrests, torture, and executions: "clearly, Canada was not prepared to allow government repression to disrupt investment, especially when other countries were moving to restore full economic relations."[27]

The Canadian government's effort to juggle economic self-interest and the promotion of human rights has become even more awkward recently, in light of the announcement by former Foreign Affairs

Minister André Ouellet that "Canada has expressed, through this new [Liberal] government, our desire to vigorously pursue a series of [trading] initiatives in a number of countries irrespective of their human rights records."[28] If this statement accurately reflects the Liberal imprint on Canadian foreign policy, then it is a radical departure from the past, when at least token reference was made to the links between trade and human rights. This shift contradicts two decades of Canadian foreign policy towards South Africa, in which an emphasis on human rights and social transformation superseded commercial interest. It would therefore appear that the approach which was central to political and social change in South Africa is no longer a privileged option in the Canadian foreign policy repertoire. An unsettling conclusion is that the lessons we might cull from the South Africa experience may well have little relevance to or bearing on the formulation of current Canadian foreign policy. Despite the inherent danger of counterfactual reasoning, this paper's focus on peace-building efforts compels us to reflect on the possibility that South Africa might not be where it is today if Canada and the rest of the world had not for more than twenty years pursued a principled foreign policy giving human rights priority over trade.

Human Rights and Democratic Development

Some of the most active contributors to human rights research, advocacy, education, monitoring, and so on, have been NGOs such as the Human Rights Internet, the Canadian Human Rights Foundation, the Canada-Asia Working Group, Amnesty International (Canadian Section), the Canadian Lawyers Association for International Human Rights, and conflict-specific shoestring NGOs like the East Timor Alert Network or the Bougainville Network (Canada), as well as development NGOs, notably, church-based organizations and coalitions such as the Canadian Council of Churches, the Inter-Church Coalition on Africa, the Primate's World Relief and Development Fund of the Anglican Church, Développement et Paix/Peace and Development of the Roman Catholic Church, Centre Missionaire Oblats, the United Church of Canada, the Mennonite Central Committee of Canada, the YM/YWCA, Quaker Peace and Service, and World Vision Canada. The types of contributions are as varied as the NGOs involved, and have helped to create human rights partnerships in areas such as: relief and rehabilitation; socio economic development; the promotion of civil society; and collaboration with governments, the UN and other multilateral agencies, and women's and other grass-roots organizations. A project of the Sri Lanka-Canada Development Fund of South Asia Partnership (which was cut along with Partnership Africa Canada in the 1995 budget) is noteworthy for its efforts to develop the analytical and practical skills of NGOs so as to enable them to incorporate human rights directly into the formulation, implementation, and evaluation of their development work.[29]

Also noteworthy is Canadian participation in what are called "peace team activities," which include: the physical accompaniment programs like those undertaken by Peace Brigade International, in which persons from outside a wartorn country accompany individuals who are in life-threatening danger back to their home country; visits by Canadian delegations to violence-prone regions to show solidarity with non-governmental peacemakers and peacebuilders; and election monitoring (for example, Canadian participation in the Ecumenical Monitoring Program in South Africa, April 1994, and the Canadian church and NGO participation in the monitoring efforts in Namibia, El Salvador, Mexico, and Sri Lanka).[30]

Many NGOs, in collaboration with their partners overseas, have actively contributed to the dialogue with Canadian officials concerning Canadian foreign policy.[31] However, NGO work to increase the Canadian public's understanding of global human rights issues and the international role of Canada has been negatively affected by the decision of the present government to cut 100 percent of its funding for development education. In the area of peace nurturing, and international development in the broader sense, such cuts make it more difficult to link domestic and international concerns and to develop the capacity of the Canadian public to participate in discussion of Canadian foreign policy.[32]

Social Reconstruction, Local Empowerment, Capacity Building
The variety of activities undertaken by Canadian non-governmental actors in the social reconstruction of wartorn societies is vast. It includes the gamut of health-related projects, ranging from the immediate interventions of Médecins Sans Frontières Canada through the "health-initiatives-as-peace-initiatives" approach of McMaster University's Health Reach project and the humanitarian/immunization cease-fire initiatives supported by the Centre for Days of Peace to the Canadian Public Health Association's International Program's focus on primary health care, immunization, and AIDS. However, there are

special health challenges in the immediate postwar environment, such as the need to deal with the physical and psychological scars of torture, rape, and abuse, and post-traumatic stress disorder. In a number of cases, Canadian embassies or high commissions have provided monies from the Canada Fund to support local efforts to address these types of problems. For example, in the Gaza Strip, the Canadian Embassy in Israel contributed to an international effort supporting a local initiative to set up the Gaza Community Mental Health Program, which has a particular focus on traumatized children and families.[33] In Sri Lanka, the Canadian High Commission provided funds through a Canadian NGO for a substantial Family Rehabilitation Centre which will identify, treat, and care for traumatized victims from all sectors and communities, including youths, orphans, remand inmates, detainees and ex-detainees, and refugees.

One of the most debilitating legacies of violent conflict is the paralyzing uncertainty and distrust which characterizes social relations. The sociopsychological barriers may be as formidable as the physical ones. Rebuilding trust and reducing uncertainty may involve activities directed at both the collective and the individual levels. At the collective level, it may be necessary to conduct truth commissions in an impartial, fair, and above all, public manner in order to begin the healing process.[34]

At the individual level, in a smouldering post-conflict environment, uncertainty might be reduced by such programs as the Canadian Red Cross Society's "Tracing and Reunion Service," which helps to re-establish contact between Canadians and immediate family members that had been broken as a result of conflict or disaster.[35] Groups, such as women and children, which are particularly vulnerable or affected by the conflict should receive particular attention. Thus, for example, MATCH International Centre has supported women's groups in the South and in Canada in their work to eliminate violence against women. Activities have included sensitization campaigns, awareness-raising, assertiveness and para-legal training, popular theatre, action research, counsellor training, advocacy, and community organization. Some of these MATCH activities are similar to the women's encounter groups organized by INFORM, a local NGO in Sri Lanka, to bring together mothers and wives and daughters from both sides of the ethnic divide in order to increase understanding, break down stereotypes, and cultivate empathy and practical support linkages. A small example, focusing on children, is the UNICEF-sponsored puppet show for Hutu and Tutsi children located in a camp for displaced Burundians in the Bujumbura district of Ngagara in early 1995. Two puppets fight like cat and dog until they settle their dispute and live happily ever after, a small effort to help the children to overcome the ethnic rivalries that have led their parents into bloodshed. While such initiatives at the street or field level may not have immediate, large-scale results, they do contribute to a gradual, bottom-up process of reconciliation.

During the 1994 massacre in Rwanda radio broadcasts were used to whip up communal hatreds and coordinate the slaughter of hundreds of thousands of children, women and men. While this points to the role of the media in exacerbating violence, it also highlights the need to develop the capacity of those same media to play a constructive role in the rebuilding process. It was noted above that a portion of Canadian Official Development Assistance to South Africa was specifically directed towards the alternative press in South Africa, as a means of countering apartheid propaganda. This type of activity appears to have played a useful role both in initiating change and in the ongoing process of rebuilding the social system. A number of NGOs have also directed their attention to the media in Canada, in an attempt to improve Canadian journalists' understanding and coverage of development issues. Thus, for example, South Asia Partnership (SAP) has produced a journalist's guide to South Asia complete with contact names and story ideas, and both SAP and the Philippine Development Assistance Program have organized development education tours for Canadian journalists. Such initiatives have resulted in improved media coverage by those who have participated.

CONCLUSION

This paper has argued that NGOs have an important peacebuilding role to play in areas of latent and manifest violent conflict. An emphasis on these organizations is a necessary corrective to the general neglect of their contributions in this broad area of activity. However, they are not the "silver bullet" for attacking all the problems and challenges that characterize the peacebuilding process. While it is increasingly recognized that they have played a constructive role in bringing about the peace, it is also true that overemphasis on this sector may help to weaken the capacity of government to fulfil its necessary functions, and may prevent the development of problem-solving and self-governance capabilities in communities. The challenge is to develop a set of skills that will bring together government actors, NGO workers, and appropriate representational levels of the community. This will lead to negotiated objectives which have relevance for the community they affect and will increase the chances of building a sustainable peace.

In light of the overall tenor of the current volume, in particular the chapters by Evan Potter and Hal Klepak, this chapter concludes by echoing a call I have made elsewhere.[36] Canadians must move beyond a discourse of scarcity towards a discourse of potential and opportunity.[37] In other words, as long as we view the world through a set of analytical lenses that confines the definition of all problems and the consequent responses to the context of scarcity and cutbacks we hobble ourselves intellectually, politically, and perhaps morally. By impoverishing our collective imagination and limiting our creativity, the discourse of scarcity stifles the development of the two most important qualities that are needed if we are to begin the staggering task of peacebuilding. Never before has the need been greater to recast our understanding of both problems and solutions in a way that allows us to discern the potential for change and regeneration.

NOTES

1   There is not the space in this chapter to launch into an extended discussion of the competing definitions and descriptions of NGOs. With literally hundreds of thousands of such actors in the developing world alone, it is a daunting task to identify, let alone define, the full scope of the NGO sector. Even a narrow focus on Canada soon reveals that there are over 70,000 registered charities in this country. One the best recent discussions of NGOs may be found in Ian Smillie's *The Alms Bazaar: Altruism Under Fire—Non-Profit Organizations and International Development* (Ottawa: International Development Research Centre (IDRC), 1995). Following Smillie, this paper adopts David Korten's structural and operational definition of an NGO. An NGO is an organization which possesses the following characteristics: (1) *formal existence*: the organization is institutionalized to some extent; it is formalized in terms of regular meetings, office bearers, and some degree of organizational permanence; (2) *private status*: the organization is institutionally separate from government, although it may receive some government support; (3) *non-profit-distributing modus operandi:* while the organization may generate a financial surplus, this does not accrue to the owners or directors; (4) *self-governing administration*: able and equipped to control and manage its own

activities; and (5) *voluntary character:* there is some meaningful degree of voluntary participation in the conduct or management of the organization. This does not mean that all or most of the income of an organization must come from voluntary contributions or that most of its staff must be volunteers. The term "NGO" is employed throughout this paper despite its rather generic quality. Specificity is added where required, for example, Northern/Southern NGOs, development/relief NGOs, Church-based NGOs, and human rights/peace NGOs.

2 For a more detailed discussion of "peacebuilding," see: Michael Harbottle, "The Strategy of 3rd Party Intervention in Conflict Resolution," *International Journal* 25, no. 1 (1979); Boutros Boutros-Ghali's *Agenda for Peace*, (New York: United Nations, 1995); Stephen Ryan, *Ethnic Conflict and International Relations*, (Aldershot, England and Brookfield, Vermont: Dartmouth Publishing Co., 1990); and Kenneth D. Bush, "Fitting the Pieces Together: Canadian Contribution to the Challenge of Rebuilding War-Torn Societies," a paper prepared for the International Development Research Centre, Ottawa, 1995.

3 See for example David Gillies' discussion of the negative impact of the CIDA-sponsored Madura Oya project in "Principled Intervention: Canadian Aid, Human Rights and the Sri Lanka Conflict," in Robert Miller ed., *Aid as Peacemaker: Canadian Development Assistance and Third World Conflict* (Ottawa: Carleton University Press, 1992), 33-50.

4 All of these meetings were held in the third week of November 1995.

5 For example, in the UN Report on Global Governance, *Our Global Neighborhood* (Oxford and New York: Oxford University Press, 1995).

6 Francisco Alvarez Solis and Pauline Martin, "The Role of Salvadorean NGOs in Post-War Reconstruction," *Development in Practice* 2, no. 2 (June 1992), 104.

7 These are precisely the spaces which catalyze the activities of a variety of community groups in conflict situations around the world: citizens committees like the Batticaloa Peace Committee in Sri Lanka; "mothers' groups" campaigning for the end of disappearances, like the Mothers of Acari in Brazil; intercommunal groups like PACE, Corrymeela, the Cornerstone Community, and the Peace People in Northern Ireland; and many others. These are crucial points of intervention and islands of peace. They exist, but to fully exploit them requires sensitivity, creativity and diplomacy.

8 Major General (ret'd.) Lewis Mackenzie, IDRC Development Forum, "Peacekeeping, Peacemaking and Aid," Ottawa, 6 April 1994.

9 "Peacekeepers must understand and work with these groups [NGOs] in a manner that has not been required of them in the past. In the field, we need smaller units and secondments of individuals to work with us in such areas as refugee camp management, convoy escort, communications, logistics and water supply. Rather than being self-contained and bringing in everything from the outside, peacekeepers must be able to use and build locally available resources, both human and material, as much as possible. Above all they must concentrate in the area in which they are already specialists—security." See John

Watson, "Peacekeeping Troops Often Misused", *The Ottawa Citizen,*
January 20, 1993, D7.

10   Quoted in Samuel Makinda, *Seeking Peace from Chaos: Humanitarian
Intervention in Somalia,* (Boulder, CO. and London: Lynne Rienner,
1993), 185.

11   Mohammed Sahnoun argued that peacekeeping costs in Somalia
"dwarfed" humanitarian aid costs. In his estimation, it cost $2 billion
in "peacekeeping" to protect less than $50 million of "effective emer-
gency relief." (Presentation to the IDRC Roundtable on Peacebuilding,
May 1995.) Sahnoun offers some of the most penetrating criticism of
the UN operation in Somalia. He is reported to have said that the failure of relief operations was due to "an overwhelming United Nations
bureaucracy that, in contrast to the Red Cross, is made up of civil servants more interested in careers and perquisites than in the job at
hand" New York Times, September 7, 1992, A3.

12   Sahnoun, "An Environment for Peace," IDRC Reports 22, no. 3
(October 1994), 4-6.

13   Mohammed Sahnoun, quoted in *The Ottawa Citizen,* August 15, 1993.

14   Department of National Defence, "Cornwallis: A Canadian
International Peacekeeping Centre," *Backgrounder,* February 22, 1994.

15   Department of National Defence, "Cornwallis."

16   A workshop at the Centre for Conflict Studies of the University of
New Brunswick identified four tasks that the Canadian military forces
could be called upon to perform: 1) international enforcement operations (mid- to high-intensity conflict, e.g., the Korean and Gulf Wars);
2) peace and security operations (low- to mid-intensity operations,
e.g., Somalia and Bosnia); 3) traditional peacekeeping operations
(e.g., Cyprus); and 4) national security and sovereignty operations
(aid to civilian power, search and rescue, counter-narcotics operations). See Centre for Conflict Studies and the Military and Strategic
Studies Program, University of New Brunswick, "Defence Policy for a
New Century," The University of New Brunswick Report for the
Defence Policy Review, June 1994.

17   For a rich overview of NGO initiatives, see "Peace Interventions in
Regions of Conflict: Options for Project Ploughshares," A Report
Submitted to Project Ploughshares by Moira Hutchinson, October 12,
1994, revised October 19, 1994.

18   See Celina Tuttle, "Canadian NGOs Campaign Against Landmines,"
Turning Point (Physicians for Global Survival (Canada) 1, no. 2
(Spring, 1995).

19   I use the term "nurtured" because although the MCCC and other
external NGOs helped to finance the conferences (for a total cost of
U.S. $100,000), they did not play a direct role in the deliberations. For
details see Mennonite Central Committee Canada, "Submission of
MCCC to the Canadian Council for International Co-operation Foreign
Policy Review: A Framework for Our Common Future," by Chris
Derksen Hiebert and Joanne Epp, (MCCC: Ottawa, November, 1993).

See also, Rakiya Omaar, "Somaliland: One Thorn at a Time," *Current History*, 93, no. 583 (May, 1994).

20   MCCC, "Submission of MCCC."

21   See Linda Freeman, "Canada, Aid and Peacemaking in Southern Africa," Robert Miller, ed., *Aid as Peacemaker: Canadian Development Assistance and Third World Conflict*, (Ottawa: Carleton University Press, 1992) 33-50.

22   I am grateful to Ms. Liebeth Turbati, First Secretary to the High Commission for South Africa in Ottawa, for bringing this to my attention.

23   The same concerns were expressed during the same type of "Team Canada" Mission to South and Southeast Asia in early 1996.

24   As Keenleyside points out, Indonesia ranked fourth among Canadian aid recipients (ranking based on bilateral disbursements over the three fiscal years from 1984-85 to 1986-7). T.A. Keenleyside, "Aiding Rights: Canada and the Advancement of Human Dignity," in Cranford Pratt, ed., *Canadian International Development Assistance Policies* (Montreal and Kingston: McGill-Queen's University Press, 1994) 245.

25   For recent incidents and accounts see: Amnesty International, *East Timor: Continuing Human Rights Violations*, (London: Amnesty International, 1995), February, AI ASA 211095; and *The Liquiza Killings*, (London: Amnesty International, 1995), February, AI ASA 211595.

26   See for example: Paul Knox, "Canada's Blinkered Diplomacy," *The Globe and Mail*, July 1, 1995, D1; and Keenleyside, "Aiding Rights," 257-58.

27   Keenleyside, "Aiding Rights," 258.

28   This statement came only three weeks after the Liberal Party signed an international declaration on human rights and democratic development stating the need to pursue trade and human rights simultaneously. See: "Canada puts Trade Before Rights," *The Globe and Mail*, May 12, 1995, A1. See also, "Ouellet Assailed for Remarks on Rights," *The Globe and Mail*, May 13, 1995, A3.

29   South Asia Partnership, "The Practice of Linking Development and Human Rights in Sri Lanka: Training Workshop for Canadian NGOs— Final Report," sponsored by the Sri Lanka-Canada Development Fund, Ottawa, 12-14 June 1994.

30   Interestingly, Peace and Development of the Catholic Church invited the Mexican NGO election-monitoring alliance to monitor the Quebec elections, and is expected to extend the same invitation for the Ontario election. See Project Ploughshares, "Peace Interventions in Regions of Conflict: Options for Project Ploughshares," A Report Submitted to Project Ploughshares by Moira Hutchinson, October 12, 1994, revised October 19, 1994, 5.

31   See for example, the Canadian Council for International Co-operation's discussion paper entitled "Human Rights in Canadian Foreign Policy" (Ottawa: CCIC, December 1993).

32   While such cuts decrease the Canadian public's capacity to critically examine and understand international issues which have direct political,

economic and social effects on the lives of every Canadian, the government asserts in the 1995 Foreign Policy White Paper, *Canada in the World*, that: "more than ever before, it is important that foreign policy making broadly involves Canadians," and that "the government will ensure that it engages Canadians in all aspects of foreign policy on a systematic basis by conducting an annual foreign policy forum." Department of Foreign Affairs and International Trade, *Canada in the World: Government Statement* (Ottawa: Canada Communication Group 1995), iii.

33   Robert Semeniuk, "War Babies: Trauma Stalks Kids Growing up in the Gaza Strip," *Equinox*, no. 79 (January/February, 1995), 36-49.

34   For a recent discussion of this issue, see Neil J. Kritz, *Transitional Justice: How Emerging Democracies Reckon with Former Regimes*, Volumes I, II & III, (Washington: United States Institute of Peace, 1995).

35   As part of this program the Red Cross will also help in cases where persons have been promised entry visas by Immigration Canada and are unable to join their families in Canada because they have been refused exit visas. The Canadian Red Cross Society will send a letter of intervention on behalf of the family in Canada to the Red Cross or Red Crescent Society in the country involved, for presentation to the appropriate government authorities.

36   Kenneth Bush, "From Peacekeeping to Peace Nurturing: The Challenge of Rebuilding Wartorn Societies," (under review).

37   This observation was made by Dr. Necla Tschirgi of the International Development Research Centre at one of the November 1995 peace-building meetings in Ottawa.

XIV

International Financial Institutions: Beginning of the End or End of the Beginning?

ROY CULPEPER

Today's global economy is as yet in its infancy, and has brought in its wake many problems as well as opportunities. The International Financial Institutions (IFIs),[1] which have done much to facilitate the birth of the global economy over the last five decades, can make an important contribution towards the resolution of these problems. Inequity, instability and uncertainty are increasing in the global community. Global markets are increasingly obsessed with the short term.

Against this backdrop we must consider the future role of the IFIs. The globalization of the economy has accelerated since the end of the Cold War, but support for the IFIs seems to be faltering among their erstwhile strongest supporters, the G-7 industrial countries,[2] including Canada. In this chapter, these points are illustrated by events leading to and following the 1995 Halifax Summit.[3] The chapter also addresses Canada's role in the evolution of the IFIs as they adapt to new global realities. As the subtitle suggests, however, the international community is at a critical juncture. It is up to Canada, and other member countries which have always actively supported the IFIs, to ensure that these organizations play a growing rather than a diminishing role in an increasingly volatile and uncertain global economy.

SOME BACKGROUND ON THE IFIS

It is now commonplace to say that the multilateral edifice, so carefully built up by far-sighted individuals half a century ago to promote international peace and economic prosperity, is under siege. Indeed, the future of the UN system is questioned increasingly by those who judge its meagre achievements in resolving recent regional conflicts, or simply by those who observe the failure of member states, particularly the U.S., to pay their dues.[4]

The IFIs have always stood apart from the UN system[5] because of their different political architecture and their relative financial autonomy. The IMF and the World Bank, the first two IFIs, were born at a historic conference in Bretton Woods, New Hampshire in June 1944. The IMF was created to foster monetary co-operation, and to establish an open international trade and payments system after World War II. To this end, it encourages currency convertibility and helps maintain exchange-rate stability, by providing short term credit (repayable in three to ten years) to countries experiencing temporary balance of payments deficits.

The World Bank, in contrast, had *longer*-term purposes: to provide investment capital (repayable in 15 to 40 years) for reconstruction by war-torn countries during the decade following World War II, and thereafter for developing countries, many of which became independent during the 1950s and 1960s. (That is why the World Bank's formal title is still The International Bank for Reconstruction and Development.) Funds from World Bank loans are now used for agriculture, education, health, water and sanitation, power and transportation, as well as longer-term balance of payments adjustment problems. Over the past five decades, both the IMF and the World Bank have grown considerably in size and complexity. In 1994/95, the IMF made commitments totalling over U.S.$24 billion, while the World Bank's commitments were some U.S.$22.5 billion.[6] By mid-1994, 178 countries—virtually all the countries in the world, including almost all the countries of the former Soviet bloc—belonged to "the Fund" and "the Bank."

The regional development banks were all created more or less in the image of the World Bank: the Inter-American Development Bank (IDB), which lends to Latin America and the Caribbean, was established in 1959; the African Development Bank (AfDB) in 1964; the Asian Development Bank (AsDB) in 1965; and finally the European Bank for Reconstruction and Development (EBRD, which lends to Eastern Europe and the former Soviet Union) in 1991. In 1994, these four banks together committed U.S.$13.3 billion (the IDB, $5.3 billion; AsDFB, $3.7 billion; EBRD, $2.9 billion; and AfDB, $1.4 billion), so that the multilateral development banks (MDBs) collectively (the regional banks and the World Bank) made loan commitments in 1994/95 of about U.S.$35.8 billion.[7] Most of the loans of the MDBs are made to, or guaranteed by, governments of borrowing member countries (i.e. developing countries).

The IFIs have been relatively autonomous financially because, from the beginning, they have been given a large capital base by their member countries. For example, by 1994/95 the IMF's member countries had subscribed "quotas" of about U.S.$227 billion; while at the World Bank, members' cumulative capital subscriptions amounted to U.S.$166 billion, plus U.S.$93 billion in contributions to the Bank's soft-loan affiliate, the International Development Association (IDA). It is this fairly large capital base which has enabled IFIs to mount large lending programs on a multi-year basis, in contrast to the UN family, whose organizations lack a capital base and are typically dependent on annual and much smaller financial allocations from member countries. The IFIs' capital base and financial autonomy, in turn, issue from their political architecture, which is modelled on a modified form of the modern joint-stock corporation, with the member governments as shareholders whose voting power is dependent on their relative shares or quotas. As a rule, richer countries willingly take larger shares because they confer greater voting power; it is only somewhat exaggerated to say that whereas at the UN the rule is "one country, one vote," in the IFIs it is "one dollar, one vote." But it is precisely this feature which has led historically to the richer industrial countries supporting the expansion of the IFIs. Developing countries, on the other hand, have sometimes viewed the IFIs as agents of a neocolonialist world order in which financial power rules the day.

Until recently the IFIs were preserved from the multilateral contagion spreading through the UN, principally because the leading industrial powers (the G-7) were collectively able to exercise a dominating influence over these institutions,[8] which they could not wield in the UN and its other specialized agencies. The G-7 felt the IFIs were doing a good job, and accordingly they usually paid their bills on time. But all this has been quickly changing. In the past two years, the IFIs have come under increasing scrutiny by the G-7. After years, even decades, of resisting calls from developing countries to reform the IFIs, the G-7 suddenly became persuaded that the time for IFI reform had indeed arrived.

THE ROAD TO HALIFAX

The first indications that searching questions were being raised by the G-7 about the IFIs appeared a year before the June 1995 Halifax Summit. The 1994 Naples Summit occurred during the 50th anniversary year of the Bretton Woods Conference, which created the World Bank and the IMF. The Naples Summit also took place during the sixth year of a spectacular boom in private capital flows to developing countries, which increased from a low of U.S.$25.2 billion in 1987 to almost U.S.$173 billion in 1994.[9] Some U.S.$78 billion of this took the form of foreign direct investment; U.S.$56 billion was in the form of loans; and, most phenomenal of all, North-to-South portfolio equity investment, which was virtually nil until the late 1980s, accounted for U.S.$39 billion in 1994, having reached U.S.$47 billion in 1993.

Besides appearing to signal the end of the Third World debt crisis of the 1980s, the resurgence of private flows in an increasingly integrated global financial market also prompted some critics to question the very need for the multilateral institutions, such as the World Bank, which were created in 1945 specifically to facilitate the resumption of international trade and capital flows after the economic collapse of the Great Depression and World War II. These critics, coming from the conservative end of the political spectrum, feel that the IMF and World Bank now inhibit, rather than facilitate, private markets, principally because they channel their assistance primarily through governments, which are assumed always to act inimically towards the private sector.[10]

These critics were joined, in an "unholy alliance," by others from the opposite end of the political spectrum, who claim that globalized markets are the problem, and that the Bretton Woods institutions are implicated by cajoling member countries into adopting destabilizing "neo-liberal" policies which open their economies to the global marketplace.[11] Moreover, the devastating environmental impact of certain development projects funded by the World Bank and other aid agencies made the Bank a frequent target of environmental Non-Government Organizations (NGOs), which became adept at sensational exposés of the Bank's operations.

The middle ground between these two camps has become sparsely populated. A recent exception was a blue-ribbon commission[12] of "elder economic statesmen," in the middle of the political spectrum and very friendly to the Bretton Woods institutions. However, even this Bretton Woods Commission brought down a report in July 1994 which was quite critical, particularly of the World Bank group. The report agreed in many respects with the conservative critics who argue that development is best left to the private sector. Rather than eliminating the World Bank, however, the report—presaging the Halifax Summit communiqué—recommended re-orienting the Bank's activities to complement and catalyze private-sector efforts. The Bank subsequently made some efforts in this direction, although, as others have pointed out, it faces a dilemma in trying to serve public objectives at the same time as supporting private interests.[13]

At the subsequent 1994 annual meetings of the IMF and World Bank held in Madrid, a high-level Task Force on the Multilateral Development Banks was set up, primarily at the behest of the leading industrial countries. This initiative was given impetus by a series of recent reviews of their lending portfolios undertaken by four of the five MDBs.[14] These exercises all demonstrated that the MDBs were sacrificing quality in favour of quantity lending, that is, a higher priority was being given to meeting annual lending targets than to identifying and delivering projects with a sustainable development impact.[15]

Among the regional banks, the African Development Bank was experiencing particularly acute problems of its own. Some of its poorest members were not servicing their debts to the Bank and therefore plunging it into a deepening financial crisis. This was compounded by differences between the African and the non-regional members as to how to remedy the situation, and by a loss of confidence in the management which eventually led to the departure of the President and the election of a successor during the summer of 1995.

Until late 1994, most of the critical attention was focused on the World Bank and the regional banks. The IMF managed to escape the same degree of scrutiny or criticism until the very end of 1994, when the Mexican peso crisis broke out. The peso crisis, in turn, ushered in a period of turmoil in the international currency markets in the first half of 1995. The U.S. and Canadian dollars were also caught up in a bout of speculation which drove the currencies down to historic lows against the yen and the mark.

Emergency funding of about $8 billion which had been set aside in April 1994 by the three NAFTA partners as provision against such a currency crisis was suddenly felt to be inadequate to withstand the might of international speculators. The U.S. mounted an aggressive international campaign to put together a peso-defence fund of some U.S.$50 billion. The IMF was a participant in this package, but it took the Fund's Executive Board a few weeks to agree to an U.S.$18 billion credit for Mexico on an exceptional basis,[16] and even then ran into bickering from the Europeans, who felt that they were being unduly pressured by the Americans for "special favours" to their Mexican neighbours.

While the peso crisis was at full boil, Baring Brothers, one of London's most venerable merchant banks, went into bankruptcy because of unauthorized and excessive derivatives trading by one of its brokers in Singapore. This episode capped a series of developments which seemed to suggest that global financial markets were spinning out of control. Finance Ministers of the G-7, meeting in Washington in late April 1995, uncharacteristically took the markets to task for exchange rate movements which had "gone beyond the levels justified by underlying economic conditions."[17]

By April, in other words, fallout from the peso and Barings crises had the effect of pushing aside the problems of the MDBs and catapulting the IMF and the stability of world financial markets to the top of the Halifax Summit agenda. This was perhaps not only a case of short term firefighting displacing longer-term issues; the financial issues were also much closer to home for the G-7 countries than the issues of poverty reduction and sustainable development.

THE HALIFAX SUMMIT: WHAT WAS ACCOMPLISHED?

The IFI reform agenda was first articulated at the Naples G-7 Summit of 1994. The Naples Summit declaration stated that in Halifax G-7 leaders would focus on two questions: First, how can we ensure that the global economy of the 21st century will provide sustainable development with good prosperity and well-being for the people of our nations and the world?; and second, what institutional changes may be needed to meet those challenges and ensure the future prosperity and security of our people?[18] This was the first time in the 20-year history of the economic summits that the reform of the international institutions was put on the agenda (although it could be said that the transformation of the GATT into the present World Trade Organization resulted from a G-7 initiative, in which Canada had a central role).

Did the Halifax Summit live up to its promise? The short answer has to be "No," but under the best of circumstances it would have been hard for Halifax to live up to the expectations created at Naples and subsequently. At Naples it was hoped that the problems of the World Bank, and perhaps those of the regional banks, would be centre-stage at Halifax, but (as mentioned) in the six months prior to the Summit the Mexican peso crisis and financial turbulence had pushed the governance of the currency markets and the role of the IMF to the top of the agenda.

The G-7 has been unable to resolve the problem of currency instability ever since it began to meet formally as a group in 1975. It is no coincidence that the group was formed soon after the breakdown in 1973 of the Bretton Woods system of fixed exchange rates which had existed *de jure* since 1945 and *de facto* since about 1960. It could even be argued that the G-7 was formed as a reaction to the breakdown of the Bretton Woods exchange-rate regime, in an attempt to foster stability and growth, at least in G-7 countries themselves, through greater economic policy co-ordination. The quest to stabilize currency markets through G-7 decree reached its apogee in the Plaza agreement of 1985 and the Tokyo Summit and the Louvre accord in the following two years.[19]

These attempts by the G-7 to dictate to the currency markets proved to be futile in the long run. Currency markets have simply marched to their own drummers and have increasingly ignored the pontifications of the G-7. The particularly intense bout of currency volatility in the fall of 1992, which led to the unhinging of the European exchange-rate mechanism, was a further indication that attempts to achieve currency stability, even within closely-knit regional groupings, could be foiled by the markets.

Thus, by the time of the Halifax Summit, the G-7 had plenty of frustrating experiences upon which to reflect when contemplating reform of the international financial system. This is why much more radical ideas, such as the Tobin tax on international currency transactions,[20] were being discussed, at least informally, in the run-up to the Summit. If the G-7 could not exert moral suasion on the markets, could they use their taxation powers to bring the speculators to heel? There were rumours that such measures were being contemplated when Prime Minister Chrétien was reported to have chided the proverbial young men "in red suspenders,"[21] who populate the international trading rooms of banks and other financial institutions, and whose collective actions determine the course of the increasingly volatile currency markets.

The Tobin tax and similar proposals[22] were, apparently, broadly discussed at Halifax. But there were severe technical problems of implementation; there would have to be measures to prevent evasion and major trading centres, inside and outside the OECD, would have to be persuaded to adopt the tax. Furthermore, the Tobin tax derived much of its support from labour and NGO constituencies who perceived that the tax could generate sizable amounts of revenue (all estimates indicated amounts well in excess of $100 billion per year) and thereby relieve ubiquitous budget constraints on domestic and international spending. This revenue potential, rather than the deterrent effect of the tax on speculators, became its central attraction for its supporters. But while at least some G-7 central banks and Finance ministries may have been attracted by its revenue possibilities, they would also have had to contend with the general opposition to new taxes in their business constituencies, and the unpopularity of the Tobin tax in the financial sector in particular.

In the end, the Halifax Summit did very little to come to grips with increasing speculation on the financial markets. The Background Document to the Halifax Summit sternly asserts that "Administrative measures, such as selective taxes or controls on capital transactions, are an ineffective and very costly means to attempt to limit exchange market volatility ... Controls would also tend to hamper investment and capital flows that are productive for growth and reinforce stability."[23] In other words, far from throwing sand in the wheels of international finance to slow down speculation, as Tobin and others had recommended, the Halifax Summit sent out a signal that any obstacles to open capital markets constituted bad policy. Instead, emphasis was placed by the G-7 on early warning systems (meaning better statistics and financial reporting by member countries), improved surveillance, and emergency financing mechanisms.

The IMF was accorded an important role in each of these areas, but the G-7 held back in several important respects from giving the IMF the backing sought by its management and many of its developing country supporters. For example, neither an early and substantial increase in IMF quotas, nor a new allocation of Special Drawing Rights (SDRs),[24] was given high priority by the G-7. Instead, most of the additional "muscle" in the G-7 declaration, insofar as new financial mechanisms were concerned, was put into an expansion of the General Arrangements to Borrow (GAB) from the G-10 countries (actually a group of 11, comprising the G-7 plus the Netherlands, Belgium, Sweden and Switzerland).[25] The meeting also endorsed initiatives already underway, including an Emergency Financing Mechanism and funding for the Enhanced Structural Adjustment Facility. But the emphasis given by the G-7 to expanding the GAB betokens a less than fully multilateral approach, which essentially says, "We (the powerful industrial countries) will give the resources only if we think the financial crisis is bad enough, and then on conditions we will decide."

Given the rapidity with which the financial markets have evolved, there have been suggestions—from the Government of Canada, among others[26]—that there needs to be more supervision and regulation of international transactions, analogous to that undertaken by domestic monetary and banking authorities. But in this area too the G-7 chose to put their faith not in the IMF but elsewhere: the G-10, the Basle Committee on Banking Supervision of the Bank for International Settlements (BIS), and the International Organization of Securities Commissions, all of which were exhorted to intensify and co-ordinate their work on regulation and supervision,[27] with little suggestion that a new *systemic, global* regulatory framework needs urgently to be put in place. None of the particular bodies asked to co-ordinate is democratic, universal or accountable even in the limited fashion of the Bretton Woods institutions; and they all reflect industrial power and capital market interests. As in the case of enhancing the GAB, the G-7 seemed to be signalling that, if any initiatives need to be taken at all, the G-7 wish to determine their nature and scope.[28]

So much for international financial issues. What about sustainable development, which was at the top of the agenda for the Halifax

Summit before the peso crisis blew up? It is important to set the discussion of this set of issues in context. The election of Republican majorities in both Houses of the U.S. Congress in 1994 quickly brought the legislative and executive branches of the American government into opposition on a range of issues, generally centred on expenditure priorities. Early among the Republican offensives was a move to slash by 50 percent the U.S. appropriation for existing commitments to the International Development Association (IDA), the World Bank's soft-loan aid agency.[29] On top of that, there were rumours that the Republicans would seek to lower or even eliminate the U.S. contribution to the next replenishment[30] of IDA, scheduled to begin in mid-1996.

Since IDA is the flagship agency, among all the multilateral development banks, for lending to the poorest countries and indeed is one of the three largest sources of Official Development Assistance (ODA, or foreign aid), this threat by the U.S. could sound the death-knell for the soft-lending operations of the banks, besides inflicting a mortal blow on the overall flow of aid from rich to poor countries. Possibly because the members of the G-7 are too polite to air their differences in public, there is only an oblique reference to this issue; the Summit document simply urges "all donor countries to fulfil promptly their commitments to IDA" in order to support "efficient and effective multilateral institutions."[31]

As if nevertheless anticipating a negative outcome of this momentous struggle in the U.S., the Halifax Summit document placed emphasis on greater rationing by the MDBs of their increasingly scarce resources. It suggested that the banks give priority to certain countries ("those that need [resources] most and have a demonstrated capacity to use them effectively") and to certain sectors (producing "public goods" such as primary education, health care or protection of the environment). There is also a strong suggestion that the MDBs should give lower priority to countries whose military expenditures are excessive in comparison with their own development expenditures. Most important, however, G-7 leaders emphasized that sustainable development and poverty reduction should be the overarching objectives of the MDBs.[32]

These priorities are unexceptional, as far as they go. However, in the face of possibly drastic cuts to the funding of IDA and to aid programs generally in most donor countries, the donor community needs to do more than simply reassess priorities for dwindling aid flows. It must find ways of salvaging the entire enterprise of development assistance, as we presently know it. After all, if aid is to concentrate on the production and delivery of public goods (whose benefits are widely distributed), and leave the rest to the private sector, deep cuts to aid budgets, along with expenditure reductions by developing country governments, will only result in a smaller output of public goods.

Summit leaders also felt that traditional lending for capital projects, in contrast to education, health and the environment, should be left to the private sector, and the role of the MDBs should be to complement, rather than compete with or displace, the private sector. The rationale of this approach is clear. The private sector is seen as increasingly willing and able to meet the needs of developing countries for financing. The rapid growth since the late 1980s of private flows to the developing countries has been mentioned; in 1994, private flows of $167 billion dwarfed those from the World Bank and the IDA, totalling $5.3 billion, a ratio of 31:1.[33] Naturally, private capital may be expected to have a much more significant role in financing development in the 1990s.

But two cautionary notes are needed. First, the explosion of private flows should be put in perspective. Some 80 percent of private flows went to just 12 out of 154 developing countries, primarily the largest countries in East and Southeast Asia and Latin America. Virtually none are flowing to the poorest countries or to sub-Saharan Africa. Second, many private sector investors appreciate the role the MDBs have played in financing capital projects, particularly infrastructure. Even though there are a growing number of ways in which the private sector can finance and operate infrastructural works, such projects do typically qualify as public goods for which public financing (both domestic and international) is as justifiable as for health or education.

There is no question that financing must be widely shared by a variety of public and private agencies: the World Bank estimates that developing countries' annual capital expenditures on infrastructure are now running at $200 billion.[34] While the MDBs can only finance a very small proportion of this amount, quite often their involvement is key to ensuring the financial and economic soundness of infrastructural investment, not only in the microeconomic feasibility analyses they commission, but more importantly, through the policy dialogue they undertake with member governments to encourage the latter to take appropriate measures for project sustainability.

Moreover, there has been increasing sensitivity to the environmental impacts of large-scale infrastructural investments in developing countries. It seems unlikely that as much attention would be paid to environmental issues without the involvement of the MDBs,[35] which should give pause to those who propose the total withdrawal of MDBs from infrastructural financing in favour of the private sector.

There was one other issue on the table at Halifax concerning both the IMF and the World Bank as well as the other MDBs—that of multilateral debt. Briefly, debt to the multilateral institutions is the principal remaining vestige of the debt crisis of the 1980s. While important initiatives were taken by the commercial banks (through the Brady Plan of 1989) and by bilateral creditors (through the Paris Club from 1988 until 1994), little has been done to relieve the burden of debt to the multilaterals, which have refused to entertain partial writedowns or even reschedulings, like the other creditors. Moreover, debtors go to great lengths to avoid defaulting on their debt to the multilaterals since the latter are international lenders of last resort. As a result, servicing their multilateral debts has become very burdensome, particularly for the poorest countries, for which multilateral debt service now accounts for a third of the total.

While the G-7 belatedly addressed this problem for the first time at Halifax, little progress was made. The UK, which has developed a reputation for being the most far-sighted of the G-7 on developing country debt issues, went to Halifax with a proposal to sell some of the IMF's $40 billion in gold stocks (valued only at $5 billion at the official rate), to create a multilateral debt-refinancing facility. The proposal seemed to get little support from other G-7 members other than Canada.[36] The Background document referred vaguely to the "flexible implementation of existing instruments, and new mechanisms where necessary." Shortly before the IMF-World Bank Annual Meetings held in Washington early in October, 1995, a leaked World Bank document suggested establishing a trust fund of some $11 billion to refinance the debt. The source of the funds was not identified, but the proposal was in any case hurriedly withdrawn because it turned out that the IMF had not been sufficiently consulted.

AFTER HALIFAX

It may only be a slight exaggeration to assert that at the Halifax Summit the G-7 "damned the IFIs with faint praise." Notwithstanding repeated reaffirmations at the Summit of the IFIs' roles and mandates, the G-7, if they had been truly serious about revitalizing and reforming these institutions, would have exercised more leadership in preparing them for the 21st century. Instead, they have hedged their bets, preferring an incrementalist path to reform. Given the major threat of disengagement emanating from the United States, the decisions taken at the Halifax Summit may weaken these institutions and reduce their potential to play a fuller role appropriate for the future.

But what should be the roles for the IFIs in the coming decades—how, in other words should they be reformed? In order to do justice to this question we must go back to more fundamental questions. What are the most pressing issues posed by the global economy for the world community? Three words suffice: inequity, instability, and uncertainty. Rising *inequity* is manifest in widening income disparities between rich and poor countries, and within all countries, both rich and poor. According to the United Nations Development Program, the richest 20 percent of the world's population now enjoy 85 percent of world income, while the poorest 20 percent have to struggle with less than 2 percent;[37] this poorest one-fifth of humanity (over a billion people) still lives on the equivalent of $1 a day. Increasing *instability* is manifest in world currency markets, in which daily turnover is now estimated to be a staggering $1.3 trillion[38] and rising. Finally, in a world of incessantly fluctuating exchange and interest rates, *uncertainty* seems only to deepen—despite information technology, which often serves to feed the rumour-mill with false or largely short term impressions.

It must also be said that today there is an excessive degree of faith on the part of the leading industrial powers in the ability of global markets to solve these problems. It is sobering to see how financial markets perceived Mexico—both before the recent crash, when they were much too positive in their assessment, leading to a speculative boom, and after, when they were too negative, precipitating a disorderly capital flight.

There is a long literature on "market failure," a literature which scarcely gets mentioned, or perhaps even read, today.[39] Now it is necessary to add to the lengthy list of reasons why markets fail: their prevalent obsession with the short term. The Halifax Summit recommended the strengthening of current economic reporting by developing countries, ostensibly to improve surveillance by the IMF and to design early warning systems to prevent future peso-type crises. While such a measure is defensible simply for better domestic economic management, it might only reinforce the myopia of the markets. It is hoped that better current data will permit a more orderly response from markets and will prevent financial stampedes. But more frequent data could also intensify the propensities to panic if, for example, market agents are simply comparing interest rate differentials between countries in their search of the highest short term return, rather than basing their actions on long term fundamentals. It is no accident that the peso crisis was preceded by a doubling of the U.S. Federal Reserve Board's discount rate in the nine months prior to the crash.[40] Mainstream economists are fond of talking about long-run market equilibrium, but such concepts seem remote from the realities of today's global market economies.

It is against this backdrop of increasing inequity, instability and uncertainty in the global economy, and the obsession of markets with the short term, that we must consider the future role of the IFIs. Stated simply, global problems require global solutions, and global solutions require global, public institutions with the resources and mandates they need to do their job.

Let us start with the role of the World Bank in dealing with global inequities. Over the past five years, the World Bank has undergone a substantial transformation from a large, bureaucratic institution, mostly concerned with big projects and moving money, to a more people-oriented agency. It has restored poverty reduction to its rightful place as its overarching objective, after more than a decade of preoccupation with rectifying balance of payments deficits and designing structural adjustment policies. It has instituted quasi-judicial mechanisms whereby citizens can halt any project which they feel infringes their rights.[41] It has also established an access to information policy. The Bank still has a way to go in many respects, but Mr. James Wolfensohn, its new President, promises to accelerate the pace of change.

The World Bank, along with the regional development banks, should be in the forefront of the global struggle against poverty. But it will be difficult for the MDBs to continue the fight without the necessary resources. This is largely, but not entirely, a question of the G-7 (and other countries) putting their money behind commitments made at Halifax and elsewhere.[42] The most glaring example is the funding crisis at IDA. At the October 1995 annual meetings of the IMF and World Bank in Washington, there were many outspoken, though polite, criticisms of the U.S. by its G-7 partners and others, for not upholding its existing pledges to IDA and for threatening to reduce the next replenishment to abysmally low levels. But behind all the moral indignation on the part of other donor countries one detects notes of both resignation and relief. Because of the practice of "burden-sharing," whereby the U.S. (still the largest donor to IDA) contributes around 20 percent, Canada 4 percent and so forth, the U.S. in effect sets the size of the replenishment and the other donors fall into line. If the U.S. cuts its contribution deeply, other donors, including even Canada, are likely to follow suit. The donors will plead the principle of burden sharing, even though they may have been prepared to contribute more,[43] but it will be too tempting for many donors to use this as a windfall expenditure reduction to set against deficit-reduction targets.

There is an additional problem arising from the disengagement of the major donors from IDA. The net transfer of finance from the World Bank group (net of principal and interest payments) is now negative, and becoming increasingly so.[44] That means the developing countries are, in the aggregate, providing resources to the World Bank's bondholders, who are among the richest individuals or institutions in the world. The World Bank was created to transfer resources to the developing countries, not vice versa, at least, not until its job is done, and the borrowing countries are (like Japan, Finland, New Zealand and Korea, all former borrowers) in a position to pay back their loans. The net transfer from South to North through the World Bank will only intensify with a drop in IDA funding.

This brings us squarely back to the problem of multilateral debt. It will be necessary to find ways of writing off some of this debt—especially if IDA funding dries up—using the Bank's loan-loss provisions and other reserves, rather than getting bilateral donors (whose own aid budgets are also being decimated) to foot the bill, as has happened in the past. All the MDBs will need to come to grips with the multilateral debt problem in this way, regardless of the outcome of current development fund replenishment negotiations.[45]

With respect to instability and uncertainty, and generally, the financial issues, the IMF needs more than it got from the G-7. It cannot undertake more than two emergency operations, such as it organized for Mexico in early 1995, without a substantial increase in its *own* resources. It is interesting that many developing countries are now stronger supporters of increasing the IMF's resources than are the industrial countries. They viewed the principal outcome of Halifax (an increase in the GAB) with suspicion, believing that borrowed resources are not a substitute for an early and substantial quota increase. Likewise, the developing countries have also pressed for a substantial allocation of SDRs, and have expressed caution about the proposal to review the future role of the SDR as a reserve asset.[46]

The IMF should be (but is not) well-positioned to play a significant role in overseeing the world's financial and monetary system. Since the end of the Cold War, virtually all countries have joined, making the Fund (as well as the Bank) a truly universal institution. The IMF has the potential to take on the regulatory and supervisory functions which were deflected by the G-7 to the Bank for International Settlements, the G-10 and other bodies. In the longer run, it may even take on some of the functions of a world central bank, issuing world currency (in the form of SDRs) in response to the liquidity needs of member countries, just as central banks do for domestic banking systems. This idea is actually not as far-fetched as it sounds; it was part of the original concept of the IMF, advanced by Keynes in the discussions leading up to Bretton Woods. Moreover, it has more recently attracted some noted authorities on international monetary affairs.[47] Certainly, when the SDR was created in 1967, the intention was clearly to make it, ultimately, the principal reserve asset in the international monetary system. But because of opposition by key G-7 members to any new allocations over the last 15 years, the SDR is steadily atrophying as a reserve asset.

It is evident that, as far as oversight and supervision of the financial markets is concerned, a two-tier system has come into effect. In the top tier are the major industrial countries (represented by the G-10 rather than the G-7), their central banks, and the BIS. This tier of institutions is responsible for determining the "rules of the game" to be followed by financial market actors, for example private banks. The top tier will also mobilize emergency financing on a very short term basis if needed. The lower tier consists of the IFIs, with the IMF playing the principal role, but the MDBs also playing supporting roles. It is the responsibility of the lower tier to support the overall framework put in place by the G-10 by providing resources to eligible countries on a medium- to long-term basis.

Perhaps one should be thankful that any co-ordination mechanisms exist at all to deal with international financial crises, be they under the aegis of the G-10, the BIS, or anyone else. But in whose interest do these bodies make their decisions? Why are they not subject to scrutiny by the public, as are the IMF, the World Bank, and, increasingly, the G-7? To whom are they accountable? Why are developing countries excluded from this "inner sanctum?" These are questions that are likely to loom larger when the world is subjected to renewed bouts of international financial instability and is unable to make sense of institutions such as the G-10 and the BIS, which work largely behind the scenes, though presumably in the public interest.

CANADA'S ROLE

Canada has traditionally taken a prominent part in the deliberations of the IFIs. A key manifestation of its interest is that it is the only member country, other than the United States, to be represented by its own national on each of the IFIs' Executive Boards, which exercise day-to-day oversight at the institutions. This distinction has reflected significant financial contributions to the IFIs from Canada, amounting to about C$17 billion since the establishment of the World Bank, an amount corresponding to about 19 percent of its overall aid budget.[48]

In recent years, Canada's prominent role at the IFIs has come under intensive scrutiny and some criticism from Parliamentary Committees and the Auditor General of Canada.[49] The Parliamentary Committees in particular have heard testimony from a large number of witnesses, many of whom (particularly members of the NGO community) expressed concerns about the policies of the IFIs.

In the run-up to the Halifax Summit, the House Standing Committee on Foreign Affairs and International Trade produced a report on the issues involved in reforming the international financial institutions for the Agenda of the 1995 Halifax Summit.[50] The Government responded to the Committee four months after the meeting, putting forward its view of what had come out of the Summit.[51]

The parliamentary committees have generally taken very forward-looking positions by challenging the IFIs, and Canada's representatives thereto, to respond to the emerging issues of the day. The most recent report of the Standing Committee on Foreign Affairs and International Trade urged that a process of far-reaching, systemic reforms be launched at Halifax, which would make the IFIs more effective in supporting poverty reduction and sustainable human development, and bring about greater stability in international capital and currency markets. It also pressed for the inclusion among the IFIs objectives of respect for universal human rights, democratic "good governance" and demilitarization. Like the reports of previous committees, it advocated more transparency, accountability and democratic scrutiny of the operations and policies of the IFIs.[52] The report carried the unanimous support of all parties (the Liberals, the Bloc Québécois, and Reform), which was in itself an important achievement.

In its response[53] the Government agreed with many of the committee's recommendations (on greater efficiency, transparency and accountability, and the pre-eminence of the objective of poverty reduction, for example), pointing out that they were reflected in the Halifax Summit communiqué and that a process of ongoing reform was evident at the IFIs. It also reiterated Canada's support of the proposal—originated by the U.K.—to address multilateral debt problems via a sale of some of the IMF's gold reserves, although agreement had not been reached on this item.[54]

The endorsement by Canada (and by other G-7 donors) of the multilateral institutions' anti-poverty strategies as their "overriding priority"[55] is particularly to be welcomed. Indeed, the missionary zeal with which donors have promoted poverty reduction abroad might provoke some observers to wonder whether, in the face of rising poverty and inequality at home, domestic economic policies might also benefit from similar, visionary objectives.

Some issues were conspicuously absent from both the report of the Standing Committee and the Government Response. Primary among these was the question of the *resources* Canada intends to allocate to the IFIs in the current climate of fiscal retrenchment. This question is particularly acute in the case of the MDBs, which have absorbed a growing portion of Canada's total ODA budget in recent years, principally because of cutbacks in the bilateral aid program.[56] Canada's share of IDA, which had historically been between 5 and 6 percent, was reduced under the Conservative Government to 4 percent for the tenth replenishment, and reductions of up to 40 percent in allocations to the regional banks were announced by the Liberals in the February 1995 budget. It now seems imperative for Canada to announce clearly its intentions on the IFIs. With falling contributions to the MDBs, does it intend to maintain its seat at each of the Executive Boards? A selective withdrawal would mean a clear departure from its oft-repeated strong commitment to multilateralism.[57] However, there is probably some "room" for Canada to reduce its contributions without losing its claim to any seats, since by comparison with other G-7 countries (although not with the Nordics or the Netherlands) it has been more generous to the IFIs.[58]

Retaining Canada's seats and its influence at the MDBs is important at this juncture. Given its role as an "honest broker" between the industrial powers and the developing countries, Canada can play an important role in helping to steer a course for the MDBs over the next few years. It could display some moral leadership in coming months if an impasse is reached over the next (the eleventh) IDA replenishment. This will mean overriding the principle of burden-sharing. By allowing its *share* in IDA to rise (without spending more than it has already decided it can afford), even as the U.S. share falls, Canada would send a signal to donor countries and recipients alike that some priorities, like the fight against world poverty, are more important than others (such as burden-sharing principles). However, this is a stand that Canada should not take alone. It will need to deploy all its powers of diplomacy to convince at least some other donors to take similar action.

While the Standing Committee Report was somewhat reserved on the question of resources for the IMF—as part of a reform proposal—it advocated studying and perhaps increasing its capacity to intervene in currency-exchange crises effectively—the Government *Response* was not. The Government expressed the somewhat astonishing belief that "individual governments are better positioned to stabilize foreign exchange markets" than is the IMF, for which "a more direct role in stabilizing exchange rate movements," going beyond its surveillance function, "is clearly beyond [its] scope."[59]

This seems to go beyond merely downplaying the potential role of the IMF alluded to above, an impression which is reinforced when one notes the contrasting positions taken by the Standing Committee Report and the Government's *Response* on the more general issues of the oversight and governance of the international financial markets. The Standing Committee recommended examining the role played by central banks, and by the poorly understood, Basle-based Bank for International Settlements, which unlike the IMF is not a formal intergovernmental institution. The Committee's report expressed some misgivings about the growing role of the BIS in the discussion and resolution of financial crises and co-ordination, largely because of its lack of transparency and universality.[60] The Government's *Response*, however, expressed satisfaction with the current role of the BIS, which it saw primarily as improving the supervision and regulation of international banks, and its division of responsibilities with the IMF. During crises, it asserted that "the BIS essentially functions as a convenient channel through which the G-10 countries can assist countries...until medium-term financing from the IMF and other sources becomes available."[61] As also noted in the Halifax Summit documents, the G-10 and the BIS are to play a key role in reviewing financial market regulations and procedures for the resolution of financial crises, to be discussed at the Lyon Summit next year.[62]

Finally, while the Government Response to the Standing Committee expressed the view that existing structures and accountabilities for the IFIs are broadly appropriate[63] (a view which is contestable), accountability structures do not exist at all for the G-10 or the BIS. The lack of universality and accountability of this "top tier," as well as the overall rationale of the two-tier system, are likely to be the subjects of future Parliamentary inquiries in Canada and discussions surrounding prospective G-7 Summits.

Is it possible for Canada to support the position of most developing countries favoring an *early* quota increase (i.e., before March 1998, when the current quota review process is scheduled to end) and a new SDR allocation? More generally, should Canada press for a more central role for the IMF in world monetary affairs, and take the position that discussions on the functioning, supervision, regulation and reform of the international financial system must be undertaken with the full and substantive participation of the developing countries? In the ongoing review of the future role of the SDR, should Canada press to restore its original objective, namely, to make the SDR the world's foremost reserve asset? Such positions seem unlikely, given the articulation of the Government's current positions in its *Response* to the Standing Committee. But perhaps they are worth advancing in any case, given the problems and contradictions inherent in those positions.

CONCLUSION: THE ROAD TO LYON

Let us return to the question posed in the subtitle of this chapter: are the IFIs facing the beginning of their end, or the end of their beginning? It should be clear by now that this author's preference inclines strongly toward the latter, "Churchillian" position. The global economy is at an important crossroads in its evolution, and the world community desperately needs competent institutions through which it can exercise governance over global markets.[64] There is much vital work ahead for the World Bank, the IMF, and the regional banks, as long as they can be given the resources and the mandate to do their job.

However, the reality is that the IFIs may be facing the other fate. Even though the G-7 seemed to endorse an agenda for change, their approach is clearly an incrementalist one. Indeed, the October 1995 IMF Interim Committee meeting in Washington expressed some satisfaction over the management of the peso crisis, now that the ashes are settling and the systemic shock has been absorbed. (To its credit, however, the communiqué admitted that "the social costs of the crisis have been severe in some countries."). While the G-7 are *not* undertaking a wholesale or sudden abandonment of the IFIs, the evidence from the IDA negotiations, and the attitudes to an IMF quota increase and SDR allocation, suggests the possibility of a slow and steady attrition.

However, it is not too late. The issue of IFI reform is on the agenda for next year's Summit at Lyon, suggesting a continuing interest by the G-7 in these institutions. The host of the Lyon Summit, President Chirac—in a celebrated, if colourful remark[65]—has expressed his low opinion of financial market speculators. By next summer there should be much firmer indications on the state of the IDA replenishment, on the treatment of the multilateral debt question, and on the IMF quota review and SDR allocation. Hopefully Canada will work closely with sympathetic countries inside and outside the G-7 to ensure that these milestones truly do mark "the end of the beginning," rather than the alternative.

NOTES

An earlier version of this paper was presented at the October 1995 annual meeting of the Canadian Council on International Law in Ottawa. For helpful comments I am grateful to my colleagues Andrew Clark and Gail Anglin; to editors Maureen Molot and Fen Hampson; to Dr. Gerald Schmitz; and to officials at the Department of Finance in Ottawa. The views expressed here are my own.

1   "IFIs" is a term which usually refers to the Bretton Woods twins (the World Bank and the International Monetary Fund [IMF]), plus the four

regional development banks: the Inter-American, African and Asian Development Banks, and the recently-created European Bank for Reconstruction and Development. The term sometimes includes the General Agreement on Trade and Tariffs (GATT) and its successor born in the Uruguay Round, the World Trade Organization (WTO). However, since the WTO deals primarily with trade matters, which are related to but distinct from financial issues, it is *not* included in this discussion, nor are other organizations which sometimes deal with financial policy issues, such as the Organization for Economic Co-operation and Development (OECD) in Paris.

2   The United States, Japan, Germany, France, the United Kingdom, Italy and Canada.

3   This chapter takes a rather more sombre view of what was achieved at the Halifax Summit and of subsequent prospects than that advanced by Gordon Smith in Chapter 4 of this volume.

4   According to Secretary-General Boutros Boutros-Ghali, the UN is owed $4.3 billion, nearly half of which is due from the United States.

5   Indeed, while the IMF and the World Bank are recognized as special agencies of the UN, the regional development banks are not formally affiliated with the UN.

6   All financial and other data in this section are from the IFIs' most recent annual reports.

7   These figures do not include the loans and investments of affiliates which specialize in lending to the private sector, such as the International Finance Corporation (IFC), part of the World Bank Group. Total financing by IFC amounted to $4.5 billion in 1994. Affiliate and similar financing at the other MDBs was much less, however.

8   The G-7 collectively account for about 45 percent of the voting power at the IMF and World Bank; the OECD (industrial countries) collectively account for close to 60 percent.

9   Figures are from the World Bank, *Annual Report* 1995, Appendix 11, 3.

10   An articulate representation of this view may be found in Doug Bandow and Ian Vásquez (eds.), *Perpetuating Poverty: the World Bank, the IMF and the Developing World*, (Washington D.C.: the Cato Institute, 1994); or Jude Wanniski, "An IFI Question: Are Multilaterals the Solution ... or Part of the Problem?" *The Wall Street Journal*, October 12, 1995. For a Canadian version, see Patricia Adams, *Odious Debts: Loose Lending, Corruption and the Third World's Environmental Legacy*, (London and Toronto: Earthscan for Probe International, 1991).

11   See Kevin Danaher, (ed.) *50 Years Is Enough: The Case Against the World Bank and the International Monetary Fund*, (Boston: South End Press, 1994), and Bruce Rich, *Mortgaging the Earth: The World Bank, Environmental Impoverishment and the Crisis of Development*, (Boston: Beacon Press, 1994).

12   *Bretton Woods: Looking to the Future*. Report of the Bretton Woods Commission, (Washington, D.C.: 1994).

13   Richard W. Richardson and Jonas H. Haralz, *Moving to Market: The World Bank in Transition*, (Washington D.C.: Overseas Development Council Policy Essay No. 17).

14   The most famous of these was the World Bank Report of the Portfolio Management Task Force entitled, *Effective Implementation: Key to Development Impact*, (Washington D.C., September 1992), the so-called "Wapenhans report" (after the name of the head of the Task Force). The only MDB not to undertake a portfolio review was the EBRD, because it had only just been established.

15   "Sustainable development" is, of course, one of the fuzzier terms in the development lexicon. Here it is intended to mean what most users of the term infer: that is, development which is not beyond the financial and human delivery capacity of the local community, or the carrying capacity of environment, and whose benefits therefore do not require additional infusions of external resources.

16   The amount is about six times Mexico's Fund quota, and greatly exceeds the credit normally extended to Fund members experiencing balance of payments problems.

17   Quoted in Halifax Summit, "Review of International Financial Institutions: Background Document," (Halifax, June 15-17, 1995), 3.

18   Nicholas Bayne and Robert Putnam, "The G-7 Summit Comes of Age," in Sylvia Ostry and Gilbert R. Winham, eds., *The Halifax G-7 Summit: Issues on the Table*, (Halifax: Centre for Foreign Policy Studies, Dalhousie University, 1995), 11.

19   Bayne and Putnam, "The G-7 Summit," 11.

20   James Tobin, "A tax on international currency transactions," Special Contribution in United Nations Development Program, *Human Development Report 1994*, (New York: Oxford University Press, 1994), 70. Tobin, the 1981 winner of the Nobel Prize for Economics, suggested a 0.5 percent tax on international currency transactions to deter short term speculators. Since daily currency transactions now exceed $1 trillion and the tax would be levied on each transaction, Tobin estimated that such a tax would also generate in excess of U.S.$1.5 trillion in revenues yearly.

21   Editorial, *The Globe and Mail*, May 22, 1995. Mr. André Ouellet, Minister of Foreign Affairs, confirmed the Government's interest in measures such as the Tobin tax when he appeared before the Standing Committee (Report of the House of Commons Standing Committee on Foreign Affairs and International Trade, *"From Bretton Woods to Halifax and Beyond: Towards a 21st Summit for the 21st Century Challenge,"* Ottawa: Canada Communication Group, May 1995, 56-57.)

22   See B. Eichengreen, J. Tobin and C. Wyplosz, "Two Cases for Sand in the Wheels of International Finance," *Economic Journal*, vol. 105, no. 428 (January 1995), 162-72. The authors suggested placing deposit requirements on loans in domestic currency to non-residents, which would have the same impact as a tax against potential nonresident currency speculators.

23   Halifax Summit, *Review of International Financial Institutions:
     Background Document*, (Halifax, June 15-17, 1995), 3.

24   The SDR was created in 1967 by the IMF as a new medium of
     exchange, with a view to supplementing international liquidity. In the
     1970s, an amendment to the IMF's Articles of Agreement enjoined
     member countries to make the SDR the world's principal reserve
     asset. But there have only been two allocations of SDRs, and none
     since 1981. Further allocations have been favoured by most develop-
     ing countries and many industrial countries, including Canada, but
     opposed by the largest industrial countries, especially the United
     States and Germany. These countries have felt that there is already
     too much world liquidity and that additional SDRs would only add to
     world inflation. Apart from a "one-time special allocation" to cater to
     the needs of recently admitted members of Eastern Europe and the
     former Soviet Union, plus the poorest countries, the G-7 could not
     agree to an allocation in Halifax. Additionally, the future role of the
     SDR was designated as the subject of a separate study by the IMF's
     Interim Committee. And discussions on a new IMF quota review were
     also supported. The emergency financing mechanism proposed for
     the IMF is simply a procedure to facilitate IMF credit more quickly
     and in larger quantities than current rules permit.

25   The GAB is a special supplement to the IMF's envelope of resources,
     outside its normal quotas. It provides a channel for the provision of
     additional short term resources from the richer countries, principally
     for emergency purposes. It was created to obviate the need for a
     larger IMF, which some industrial countries (particularly the U.S.) have
     increasingly opposed, notwithstanding their large influence. Actually
     the doubling of the GAB proposed at Halifax was based, in part, on
     "other" countries outside the G-10, including some of the newly
     industrialized Asian economies. On the creation of the GAB in the
     1960s, see A.I. MacBean and P.N. Snowden, *International Institutions
     in Trade and Finance*, (London: George Allen & Unwin, 1981), 43,
     which indicates that the IMF would not be allowed to use GAB
     resources at its discretion but only with the approval of the G-10.

26   This is contained in the Government's Foreign Policy Statement,
     issued in response to the Report of the Joint Parliamentary Committee
     Reviewing Canada's Foreign Policy. "We will explore with our OECD
     partners whether the systems that regulate financial markets and insti-
     tutions domestically should be replicated internationally to strengthen
     global financial stability." *Canada in the World: Government
     Statement*, (Ottawa: Supply and Services Canada, 1995), 18.

27   Halifax Summit, *Background Document*, 9.

28   This is at odds with the notion that "the G-7 does not seek to dictate
     mandates to international organizations, regional banks or national
     governments," (Gordon Smith in this volume). The preferred strategy
     of the G-7 is to withhold resources which would make international
     action possible until the initiatives are consistent with G-7 needs and

priorities. This strategy has always been implicit in the weighted-voting structure of the IFIs, as noted above.

29   When the ensuing debate between the U.S. House of Representatives and the Senate (the House favoured even deeper cuts than the Senate) was finally settled in October 1995, the proposed reduction in the IDA-10 appropriation was around 48 percent (i.e., only 52 percent of the scheduled payment would be permitted). However, uncertainty on the appropriation continued into 1996 with the impasse over the Budget between Congress and the Administration.

30   Each of the MDBs' "soft funds," such as IDA in the World Bank, must be replenished, generally every three years, with new contributions from the donor countries. The latter meet to negotiate a replenishment agreement with each other and with the MDB management, since there are typically policy issues on the negotiating table as well. In recent years, donors have used replenishment negotiations to advocate greater emphasis on poverty reduction, the gender dimension of development, and environmental sustainability.

31   Halifax Summit, *Background Document*, 11.

32   Halifax Summit, *Background Document*, 11-12.

33   In 1986, in contrast, the figures were $27.5 billion and $11 billion respectively, a ratio of only 2.5:1.

34   World Bank, *World Development Report*, 1994, 89.

35   Two examples of projects are the Sardar Sarovar projects in India, and Three Gorges in China. The former, to which the World Bank was scheduled to contribute over $900 million, elicited much criticism by NGOs and led to a now famous review by Bradford Morse and Thomas Berger (*Sardar Sarovar: The Report of the Independent Review*, [Ottawa: Resource Futures International, 1992]), and finally to a decision by India not to proceed with World Bank funding. The latter has attracted so much criticism that the World Bank has refused any involvement in the project apart from supervising a feasibility study financed by CIDA.

36   The G-7 have traditionally been slow to acknowledge the intractability of debt problems for many Third World countries and therefore to find remedies, except in cases where their own interests were threatened, as in the case of commercial bank-related debt in the 1980s. The debt of the poorest countries in no way threatens industrial country interests. To this has been added a dogmatic resistance against debt forgiveness. The interesting exception has been the UK government under John Major, which has exercised considerable leadership since 1988 in pressing for debt reduction for the poorest countries through the Paris Club, the forum in which government-to-government debt is renegotiated. To its credit, Canada has been a key supporter of these initiatives but other G-7 countries have been much slower to come around. See Percy Mistry, *Multilateral Debt: An Emerging Crisis?*, (The Hague: FONDAD, 1994).

37   United Nations Development Programme, *Human Development Report 1994*, (New York: Oxford University Press, 1994), 63.

38 *The Economist,* Survey on the World Economy, October 7, 1995, 10.
    The survey goes to some lengths to show that financial volatility
    measured on a monthly basis has not changed over the past three
    decades, but admits that volatility on a daily basis has increased since
    the late 1970s.

39 The literature is strongly associated with the Great Depression, when
    markets failed to produce full employment. Subsequently a literature
    arose to address the economics of pollution and other externalities
    not accounted for in market decisions. Markets fail, in other words, to
    bring about optimum social welfare. A modern proponent of the
    importance of market failures in developing economies is Joseph
    Stiglitz, "Economic Organization, Information and Development," in
    Hollis Chenery and T.N. Srinivasen, (eds.), *Handbook of Development
    Economics,* vol. 2, (Amsterdam: North Holland, 1988).

40 The United States Federal Reserve Board ("the Fed") is the country's
    central bank; it affects interest rates in the U.S. economy by increasing
    or lowering its discount rate, the rate at which it makes short term
    loans to U.S. banks. The great boom in emerging market equities was,
    not coincidentally, accompanied by a decline in the Fed's discount
    rate to about 3 percent, the lowest level since the Great Depression.
    This "pushed" much portfolio investment out of the U.S. market, in
    search of higher returns, only to precipitate a reverse flow when the
    Fed altered course in 1994.

41 The mechanism at the World Bank is called the Inspection Panel.
    Recently it held hearings on the Arun III dam project in Nepal,
    resulting in the cessation of Bank support for the project.

42 It is also true that the MDBs could enhance their effectiveness (partic-
    ularly their impact on poverty reduction) with their current resources.

43 Thus, Canada may be prepared to pay U.S.$600 million of a $15 bil-
    lion IDA replenishment, but if the U.S. is only prepared to pay $2
    billion instead of $3 billion, and is only willing to contribute 20 per-
    cent, the replenishment total gets pulled down to $10 billion. Canada
    must then choose between contributing $600 million (which it can
    presumably still afford) and allow its share to rise to 6 percent, and
    cutting its contribution by a third to $400 million to maintain its share
    at 4 percent.

44 See Percy Mistry, *Multilateral Development Banks: An Assessment of
    their Financial Structures, Policies and Practices,* (The Hague: FON-
    DAD, 1995), 13-17.

45 Some experts, including Jeffrey Sachs (*Financial Times,* October 6,
    1995, 4), have called for the creation of an international bankruptcy
    court analogous to existing domestic institutions, in which creditors
    and debtor countries can settle their differences. See also Roy
    Culpeper, "A Note on the Multilateral Creditors and the Debt Crisis,"
    World Development, vol. 21, no. 7 (July 1993), 1239-44.

46 Communiqué of the Intergovernmental Group of Twenty-Four on
    International Monetary Affairs, Washington D.C., October 7, 1995.
    The so-called "G-24" is the coalition of developing countries at the

IMF-World Bank forum, analogous to the G-77 at the United Nations. The developing countries are pressing for a doubling of quotas (100 percent increase), thus supporting IMF management, while the G-7 are believed to favour an increase of around 50 percent.

47   See Azizali Mohammed, "Transforming the IMF into a World Central Bank," in Roy Culpeper and Caroline Pestieau, (eds.), *Development and Global Governance* (Ottawa: IDRC and The North-South Institute, forthcoming 1996); and Richard N. Cooper, "A Monetary System for the Future," in R.N. Cooper, *The International Monetary System*, (Cambridge, Mass: MIT Press, 1987).

48   Roy Culpeper, *Canada and the Global Governors*, (Ottawa: The North-South Institute, 1994), 4-6. The cumulative figure was $16.7 billion down to 1992.

49   *Securing our Global Future: Canada's Stake in the Unfinished Business of Third World Debt.* Report of the Standing Committee on External Affairs and International Trade (Ottawa: Supply and Services Canada, June 1990); *International Financial Institutions: Nineteenth Report of the Standing Committee on Finance,* (Ottawa: Supply and Services Canada, June 1993); Report of the Joint Parliamentary Committee Reviewing Canada's Foreign Policy, (Ottawa: Canada Communications Group, November 1994); and Report of the House of Commons Standing Committee on Foreign Affairs and International Trade, *From Bretton Woods to Halifax and Beyond: Towards a 21st Summit for the 21st Century Challenge,* (Ottawa: Canada Communications Group, May 1995). Also the 1992 Report of the Auditor-General of Canada to the House of Commons, Chapter 11 (on the Regional Development Banks) and Chapter 12 (on the Bretton Woods Institutions and the EBRD), Minister of Supply and Services.

50   *From Bretton Woods to Halifax.*

51   Minister of Finance and Minister of Foreign Affairs (Ottawa: Supply and Services Canada, October 5, 1995). *From Bretton Woods to Halifax and Beyond: Towards a 21st Summit for the 21st Century Challenge—Government Response to the Report of the House of Commons Standing Committee on Foreign Affairs and International Trade.* Hereinafter termed *Response.*

52   *From Bretton Woods to Halifax,* xiii-xiv.

53   The *Response* is broadly consistent with the exposition of Gordon Smith in Chapter 4 of this volume.

54   *Response,* 15.

55   *Response,* 11.

56   Culpeper and Clark, *High Stakes and Low Incomes,* (Ottawa: The North-South Institute, 1994), 43-46.

57   Repeated in the foreign policy statement, *Canada in the World,* 6.

58   Auditor General's Report 1992, 278, 305; Culpeper and Clark, *High Stakes,* Table 5, 17.

59   *Response,* 16. Recent events have shown that, while individual governments have been forced to intervene to stabilize their exchange rates in the face of speculative attacks, they have had to adopt

extreme measures (such as sharp escalations in domestic interest rates) which in effect destabilize domestic investment and employment.

60   *From Bretton Woods to Halifax*, 58-60.

61   *Response*, 18. As noted above, the G-10 also plays a key role in providing emergency resources to the IMF via the GAB. It is curious that the Standing Committee devoted virtually no attention to the G-10 in its Report.

62   *Response*, 15, 17.

63   *Response*, 8.

64   See also Culpeper, *Canada and the Global Governors*, and Culpeper and Clark, *High Stakes*.

65   "La spéculation est 'la Sida de nos économies,', selon Jacques Chirac," Agence France-Presse, (Halifax, June 16, 1995).

XV

Canada and the OAS:
Terra Incognita

JOHN W. GRAHAM

Canada joined the OAS in January, 1990 after a half a century of dithering. Why did we join and why then? The Americans wanted us because we would help pay the bills. They also anticipated our support on a range of policy and administrative issues. Many of the Latin Americans wanted us as a counterweight to the Americans and the English-speaking Caribbeans wanted Canada as a counterweight to the Latin Americans. The immediate reasons were none of these.[1] Nor was the Mulroney government impelled by internationalist zeal to convert the Organization into a more effective and professional instrument of hemispheric interests. Canada joined essentially for political and symbolic reasons. It appears to have been a decision taken from above, even though for the first time in eighty years a Canadian Prime Minister's positive view of the Pan-American system coincided with that of his foreign minister (Joe Clark) and many of his senior officials.

The decision about the value of the OAS to Canada and, for some, about assigning increased priority to Latin America had been made in the face of some domestic scepticism. Accordingly, an effort was required to put a convincing face on it and market it. The challenge to be met in improving the Canadian public's view of the OAS lay in changing the image of somnambulance and irrelevance, as well as in demonstrating that Canada was not joining a tropical version of the Warsaw Pact which would rubber-stamp unattractive U.S. policy actions (e.g. the 1965 intervention in the Dominican Republic).

The Canadian government's first initiative, very shortly after joining, was to propose that the OAS revitalize its priorities and launch itself into the area of governance and democratic consolidation, an unthinkable proposition only a few years before. The initiative was successful and the Unit for the Promotion of Democracy (UPD) was formed, with the mandate "to provide a program of support for democratic development which can respond promptly and effectively to member states, which in the full exercise of their sovereignty request advice or assistance to preserve or strengthen their political institutions and democratic procedures."

This initiative was followed the next year at the OAS General Assembly in Santiago, Chile by vigorous Canadian advocacy of Resolution 1080 (the Santiago Resolution), designed to confer on the OAS means for leveraging states back into constitutional democracy "in the case of any event giving rise to the sudden or irregular interruption of the domestic, political institutional process or the legitimate exercise of power by the democratically elected government in any of the Organization's member states." In December, 1992 a special General Assembly of the OAS was convened in Washington to insert the substance of Resolution 1080 into the Charter of the OAS. Included in the amendment to the Charter was the specific sanction that "a member of the Organization whose democratically elected government is removed by force will be suspended from participation in the Organization" on the basis of a two-thirds vote. The amendment is not yet in force as two-thirds of the member states have not yet provided formal ratification.

There have been obstacles and setbacks. Like Columbus, the OAS was venturing into Terra Incognita, suffering from inadequate funding, corporate bickering and political back-stabbing. Although the Organization was formally committed by its 1948 Charter to uphold both democracy and sovereignty, through most of the intervening

half-century the first part of the commitment had been largely
ignored and the second part erected into the principal doctrine of the
Organization. And while considerable positive change has taken
place in the past years, movement forward in both governance and
conflict resolution is resisted by those who see it as cutting away the
protective walls of sovereignty. Mexico and Brazil are in this category. Mexico was the one country that did not support the December
1992 Washington amendment.[2]

While we now regard the Latin American tradition of taking
refuge behind thick walls of sovereignty as the means by which
governing élites in many countries have traditionally maintained
authoritarian power against liberalizing external pressure, there is
another less pejorative explanation. For one hundred and fifty years,
the principal source of external pressure has been the United States.
Mexico particularly considers that it has historical reasons to employ
whatever non-military device it can to insulate itself from outside
interference. While NAFTA has pulled down a large part of this wall,
a rigid approach to sovereignty remains a frequently used foreign
policy strategy.[3] It also represents a challenge to Canadian objectives
aimed at bending the OAS into a more effective instrument for the
preservation of constitutional democracy and the development of
governance.

Some academic and NGO communities (particularly in the United
States) would, however, like to see preventive democracy and conflict resolution fused with more assertive policies of governance
development under the UPD. It is disconcerting to see that the new
Secretary-General of the OAS, Cesar Gaviria, is moving tentatively in
this direction. In his working paper *A New Vision of the OAS*, released
in April 1995, Gaviria proposes that the UPD could provide the OAS
with an ideal instrument for anticipating and preventing "the causes
of problems undermining the democratic system." In other words, the
UPD would operate an early warning system on threats to democracy
within the hemisphere.

That the OAS, as a whole, should be moving toward this goal is
laudable and the shift is strongly supported by the Canadian
Government. However, assigning such a sensitive task to the UPD in
this early and still precarious stage of its development is something
else. Apart from electoral observation and electoral support, the
UPD's primary task is to provide support for member countries in the
general area of governance. Under OAS rules, this assistance can only

be provided upon the request of the member state in which the activity is to take place. The UPD's ability to provide democratic support services will depend in large part on maintaining a strictly apolitical, professional track record. (It will also depend, of course, on funding and staffing—more on this later.) Moving into the conflict resolution and "early warning" areas too rapidly and mixing highly political decision-making with governance programs is likely to be counterproductive for the UPD and for the OAS as a whole. These "political" activities should remain within the office of the Secretary-General. For its part, as architect of the UPD, Canada should be directing its influence towards ensuring that the Unit does not set forth on well-meaning, but hazardous, missions inappropriate to its function. At the same time the Canadian Missions to the OAS should be seeking to cut back the extravagant list of objectives assigned to the Unit by the *Vision* paper—such as judicial reforms, constitutional strengthening, enhancing the executive process, improving the function of political parties—so that its very modest resources can be used to meet a more realistic set of priority goals.

The Secretary-General's *Vision of the OAS* is his response to an enormously increased mandate bestowed upon the Organization in December 1994 by collective decision of all the heads of state and heads of government assembled at the hemispheric Summit in Miami.

THE MIAMI SUMMIT

The Miami Summit was the first hemispheric meeting at this level attended by Canada. As a non-member of the OAS, and perhaps in Latin American eyes as a non-member of the hemisphere, Canada did not attend the previous high-level summit in Uruguay 27 years before. Unlike its predecessor, whose agenda was shaped by the Cold War, this was not a conference about debt forgiveness and development assistance. The Summit was concerned primarily with helping the engines of trade to help everybody (or as many as possible) and became the symbolic acceptance by the members of the inter-American community of the neo-liberal thesis in favour of expanding trade by dismantling protective barriers. For those watching the conference unfold, Prime Minister Chrétien's profile emerged briefly above those of his peers when, on inviting Chile to apply for NAFTA membership, CNN recorded his aphorism that "the three amigos have now become the four amigos." However, both Chrétien and

Trade Minister McLaren deserved better. If they had not beaten back attempts by Mexico and the United States to take more time over the initiation of the Chilean process, this announcement, that seemed at the time to cap the Summit's achievements, would not have been made. Moreover, by taking an aggressive role and engaging in policy design at the outset, Canada was attempting to prevent the emergence of a "hub and spokes" trade configuration.

But the expectations for the Four Amigos, like many others that glowed briefly over the Miami skyline as the Summit closed, have not been fulfilled. The route to membership in the new Free Trade Association of the Americas must pass through the U.S. Congress. Procedurally this requires "fast track" authority which a Republican Congress has denied. With the multilateral lane temporarily shut down and the deadline of 2005, set by the Summit for the completion of hemispheric free trade, looking less realistic, McLaren prudently did an end run and opened negotiations for bilateral free trade arrangements with Chile.

Of course, nothing tore away the gleaming facade of the Miami Summit as much or as quickly as the Mexican financial crisis, the early evidence of which the Mexican government kept hidden from the conference and from those nations considering the candidacy of former President Salinas for Secretary-General of the World Trade Organization—the successor to the General Agreement on Tariffs and Trade (GATT).

Inevitably, there were other problems with good intentions moving too far out in front of realistic implementation. While a broad share of responsibility for implementation falls upon individual governments, the appendix to the final Summit document designates the OAS as having "a paramount role in following up the various decisions of this Summit meeting." Democracy, human rights, corruption, free trade, confidence building, terrorism, drugs, women's issues, culture, science, the environment, and telecommunications, as well as the management of a number of conferences related to these issues, are singled out for special action by the OAS. And yet no member state contributed additional funds or proposed a higher scale of assessments to accomplish these goals.

Gaviria has undertaken to reorganize the OAS Secretariat so that its structure and resource allocations would reflect the new responsibilities and priorities. While pruning, shuffling, and reclassifying will allow him to shift funds and personnel (he has doubled the funding for the UPD), it is unlikely that the changes that he may be able to wring from the system will enable the OAS to effectively respond to its new responsibilities without a fresh infusion of funds from member states. In its turn, this scenario begs a serious question. The U.S. pays 59.47 percent of the total OAS budget (Canada is second with 12.36 percent). At the present time there is virtually no prospect of either government increasing its contributions. USAID is facing massive cutbacks and the Canadian government is undergoing serious, if less Draconian, surgery. It is most improbable that the other states would pitch in without a lead from the United States and this would have to be a real lead, not smoke and mirrors. In February, 1995, the U.S. Ambassador to the OAS, Harriet Babbitt, announced that the U.S. was committing one million U.S. dollars to democratic initiatives as its pledge in the spirit of the Miami Summit. However, this appears to be the same million that was pledged to the UPD, but not received, in April of 1994.

A SWITCHBACK ROAD TO REFORM

In effect, the Presidents and Prime Ministers have produced a prescription for corporate schizophrenia. Not surprisingly, the first OAS response to its newly swollen mandate provides some evidence of this condition. The first eight chapters of the *Vision* paper are packed with analyses of how, with increased resources, the new priorities and parameters conferred by the Summit can be accommodated. The final chapters, particularly on technical assistance and administration, offer remarkably refreshing counterpoint. "Resources in real terms have declined as the number of priorities has grown." In 1995 these resources are valued at 48 percent of the amount available in 1970.[4] Yet "the accumulation of priorities, in which, paradoxically, all of them have continued to hold priority rating... is maintained by the OAS." "Operating expenses absorb a disproportionate share of the total resources, leaving even smaller amounts available for programs and projects." (About one third remains for projects). With scorching candour, the Secretariat paper notes "that the Organization is...unable to raise its efficacy and efficiency ... because it lacks sufficient revenue to do so; it is unable to attract more revenue because its effectiveness is too low, thus repelling potential sources of financing which might be interested in collaborating if the OAS indicators were better."

Unlike his predecessor, Baena Soares, who compounded many of these problems, Gaviria is digging at the roots of some of the

Organization's fundamental problems. Unfortunately, he has limited room to manoeuvre. A case in point was the Secretary-General's proposal to close down all field offices of the OAS in member countries so that funds could be redistributed to priority areas. However, at the same Council meeting at which this point was made, the OAS Permanent Representatives agreed to open a new field office in Belize. It is hard to win games when you have thirty-four owners directing management decisions.

Almost all countries, but most particularly the small ones, have a host of vested interests in particular programs and personal appointments. Here lies one of the most difficult tests of the Secretary-General's stamina and diplomacy. So far (January, 1996) the signals from his office are not encouraging. It has been eight months since he tabled his draft and undertook to report to the OAS Council with revisions. Canada, which has pushed for major reform since joining, is lobbying to help keep this process on track.

However, the Secretary-General is not a very accessible person. His communications with his senior staff are inadequate and Permanent Representatives of member states find themselves "distanced." In the interest of keeping Gaviria constructively engaged in fundamental reform Canada proposed the establishment of a "Group of Friends of the Secretary-General." To launch this initiative, Gaviria and a group of key OAS Ambassadors were invited to explore the idea. One of the goals was to improve communications, particularly on these issues, between Gaviria and the representatives of member states. So far the Secretary-General has shown no interest in following up this initiative. Persistent pressure from the Canadian mission, supported from time to time by interventions from the Foreign Minister, along with lobbying from other equally concerned member countries, will be necessary to ensure that the Secretary-General's will to reform does not follow that of his predecessors into the warm mud of collective, vested self-interest at the OAS.

CUBA

The Secretary-General's headquarters on Constitution Avenue lie almost literally in the shadow of the White House. The juxtaposition was not accidental, and although the United States no longer controls all of the policy directions of the OAS it remains a powerful and often intimidating presence. The place of Cuba on the OAS agenda is usually instructive in this regard. Most Latin American and Caribbean countries would welcome the reintegration of Cuba, no longer a threat or source of instability to its neighbours, into the inter-American system.[5] Gaviria, when still President of Colombia, and as recently as last June at the General Assembly in Haiti, lamented the absence of Cuba from the inter-American family. But there has been no follow-up, and indeed Cuba has not been tabled for discussion at the OAS in recent memory. Given the decision by the Canadian Government in June 1994 to restore some CIDA programs to Cuba, the remarks at the Miami Summit by Prime Minister Chrétien and the Secretary of State for Latin America and Africa, Christine Stewart, about the desirability of returning Cuba to the OAS, and also the pressures from Canadian NGOs, expectations grew that Canada would place the issue before the Permanent Council. This has not happened.

On the one hand, the Canadian Government is anxious to see the absurd isolation of Cuba brought to an end. On the other, it would be inconsistent for Canada as a champion of democratization and of Resolution 1080 to press for Cuba's readmission to the Organization without real evidence that the island is moving to constitutional democracy. So far such evidence does not exist. But what is to stop the Canadian mission to the OAS, in the company of some like-minded Latin American and Caribbean members, from proposing bridge-building exercises short of reintegration. Such measures could include a small specialized OAS office in Havana to open dialogue. A mission from the Unit for the Promotion of Democracy (UPD) is likely to be rejected by the Cubans as patronizing, but a technical mission could be a start at window opening. Perhaps there is nervousness in Ottawa about tweaking the eagle's tail when some of its feathers are attached to Jesse Helms and his legislation entitled "the Cuban Liberty and Democracy Solidarity Act," intended to tighten the sanctions on Cuba and impose extraterritorial penalties on Canadians doing business with Cuba. This stems not necessarily from lack of courage, but possibly a prudent concern not to antagonize key congressional votes when there was a chance that the Helms legislation would fail. It did not and the issue moved to the forefront of bilateral relations.

IN A NEW BED WITH THE NEXT-DOOR NEIGHBOUR

Managing the relationship with the United States remains, of course, a key dimension of Canada's involvement with the OAS. Canada belongs to no other important multilateral organization as unbalanced in terms of power as this one. The Clinton administration, like its predecessors, will use (or not use) the Organization as it considers expedient in the light of international and/or domestic circumstances. Coping with this challenge is Terra a little less Incognita for Canadians.

As noted earlier, Canada has played a major role in promoting hemispheric free trade (The Free Trade Area of the Americas) to the position of centrepiece of the Miami Summit. President Clinton became enthusiastic and the U.S. delegation successfully orchestrated a twenty-three point action plan which included assigning major coordinating responsibility for free trade follow-up to the OAS. Subsequently the U.S. trade negotiators removed the OAS from this role. Although it has been providing useful support for trade discussions, especially at Denver, the *raison d'être* of the new OAS Trade Unit has been made to look hollow.

The Summit offers another vivid example of how easily even major players can be eclipsed when trying to do business on the super-power's front lawn. The Summit was a very significant occasion—the first hemispheric conference in twenty-seven years and the first that was truly *hemispheric*, with the inclusion of Canada and most of the Caribbean. It was the sort of event that magnifies signals which the participants, and particularly the host, may wish to transmit. Although committed to revitalizing the OAS and, having virtually selected Gaviria for that purpose and charged the OAS with the most onerous follow-up of the Summit decisions, the host placed Gaviria below the salt, and indeed out of the room on a number of key Summit occasions. Given the purposes of the conference, it would have been appropriate for the Secretary-General to have been co-chair or deputy chair so that he would have had an assigned seat at all the in camera sessions of heads of government. Only at the closing session was he formally included in the agenda. He and the Inter-American Development Bank (IDB) President, Enrique Iglesias, shared a platform with six other speakers.

THE INTER-AMERICAN DEVELOPMENT BANK—AN IMPORTANT PLAYER

The IDB is the other big multilateral player in the inter-American system. It is a much larger and much more amply funded organization than the OAS. Like most institutional behemoths, it cannot turn within its own length, but it is an increasingly effective organization. Canada began contributing to the IDB in 1964 and became a full member in 1972. The Summit leaders charged the IDB and the OAS with supporting member governments in the implementation of anti-corruption initiatives. This was the result of pressure by Chile, Ecuador and Venezuela to have the inter-American system address the culture of corruption. Gossip at the Summit suggested that the motive of Rafael Caldera, the President of Venezuela, was to find another stick with which to beat his favourite scapegoat, former President Carlos Andrés Pérez. Whatever the motivation, this was a promising change and one supported by Canada.

Under the previous OAS administration the word corruption was struck out of drafts as politically incorrect. That this major issue was high on the Summit agenda owes much to the importance attached to governance by Enrique Iglesias. Two years before the Summit, Iglesias was pointing out that the greater part of the enormous investment in structural adjustment is wasted without parallel reform in the area of governance. The subject now forms a chapter, "Combating Corruption and Modernizing the State" in the OAS draft *Vision* paper. The chapter is a nebulous recital of good intentions, but the subject is becoming a permanent part of the inter-American agenda.

ELECTORAL OBSERVATIONS

As with most public institutions, there is seldom public awareness of OAS failings or achievements in essential but mundane areas of cost-effective program delivery, financial management or even governance projects and anti-corruption campaigns. When there is awareness it is usually the negative image of cumulative miasma that is transmitted. At the political level, because governments operate with normal antennae, judgements tend to be made on the basis of newsworthy developments—good or bad. On this level the record of the OAS since Canada joined five years ago has been mixed, but on the whole fairly good. A recent success was the November 1995

Santiago meeting on Confidence and Security Building Measures, effectively orchestrated by Canada and Brazil. However, the Organization's most consistently visible activity over this period has been electoral observation.

The OAS has observed elections in one third of its member countries. The most challenging have been: transitional elections from authoritarian regimes to the beginnings of democracy (e.g. Paraguay, 1993; Haiti, 1990; Nicaragua, 1990); elections where political, economic or social issues and threats from the military are liable to overturn the electoral process (Venezuela 1993); and elections where international observation is a safeguard against significant irregularities arising as a result of intention or incompetence (e.g. the Dominican Republic 1994). The overall success of the OAS electoral missions has contributed more than any other part of its operations to the shedding of some of its somnambulant, self-indulgent image.

Success in this field has required the development of an experienced, competent cadre of observers with the appropriate language skills. In most cases the OAS teams are sent in advance of the election date to ensure familiarity with the process, its idiosyncrasies and its personnel. Over this period, which can stretch to several months, the observers often perform technical assistance or problem-solving roles. They are recruited from member countries but also, from time to time, from nations with observer status at the OAS that are contributing to the cost of the election. Paradoxically, Canada has the reputation at the OAS of being the most difficult participant in the observer process. The former Minister of Foreign Affairs, André Ouellet, insisted on vetting and often naming Canadian observers and his selection standards often related as much to political or constituency factors as to those relevant to the country being observed.

PRESERVING DEMOCRACY

The other sector of OAS activities in which the reputation and credibility of the Organization are openly on the line, is concerned with action to forestall threats to democracy or to restore democracy. As was seen with Resolution 1080, Canada has been an advocate of vigorous OAS engagement in this area. Three studies of cases of which the author has direct experience[6] offer some indication of how the OAS has fared in this area and of the Canadian government's policy performance.

Guatemala

Contributing to the solution of the Guatemalan crisis of May 1993 put a bright feather in the OAS cap. The constitutionally elected President, Jorge Serrano, had staged an "autogolpe" or self-serve coup. He suppressed the Supreme Court, and suspended Congress and constitutional guarantees in order, he said, to secure the more effective government that, allegedly, the Guatemalan people were clamouring for. Serrano miscalculated both international and domestic reactions. The United States, in particular, strongly condemned his action. So did Canada and most of Latin America. Serrano miscalculated again. Realizing that he had gone too far, he attempted to recruit the Secretary-General of the OAS to his side, inviting him to Guatemala to help smooth things out and provide a means of ensuring that his presidency survived.

With the approval of the OAS Permanent Council, the Secretary-General left almost immediately for Guatemala with a small team from headquarters and the Foreign Ministers of Nicaragua and the Bahamas. The OAS presence had a catalytic effect on the growing but still inhibited opposition to the autogolpe. As the invitation to the Secretary-General had come from the President, leaders of virtually all major sectors of society—business groups, conservative politicians, unions, journalists, human rights associations, and indigenous groups (led by Nobel peace prize winner Rigoberta Menchu)—felt they might safely venture out in the capital to complain to the OAS. This produced a ripple effect, as more and more sections of society realized that they stood on common ground in opposition to the autogolpe. The process was carefully monitored by the Guatemalan military (which had supported Serrano's tactic and whose guns were expected to ensure the submission of the populace). Eventually the head of the army came too. As the military withdrew its support from Serrano, the crisis ended. Serrano was forced into exile and surprisingly, for Guatemala, no blood was shed.

The OAS deservedly received some of the credit and the Secretary-General (Baena Soares) received a warm letter of thanks from President Clinton. But this case study does not offer a very serviceable model for dealing with *coups d'état* or attempts at autogolpes in general. How likely is it that the next blundering tyrant will invite the Secretary-General to extricate him (or her) from a self-inflicted mess? Nevertheless it is a fine example of what the OAS can do if it responds rapidly and skilfully to an opportunity—something the OAS is more likely to do if it knows that fast action of this kind can count on the support of the hemispheric community.

Dominican Republic

The OAS involvement in the elections and the post-election crisis in the Dominican Republic provides another example of the ad hoc or idiosyncratic approach to crisis management.

While the Dominican Republic has the distinction of having the third longest unbroken record of constitutional democracy in Latin America, democratic traditions have not fully emerged from the long shadow of the Trujillo dictatorship. Election day, May 16, 1994, began deceptively well. An unprecedented 87 percent of the electorate came out to vote. However, civic dedication was thwarted by a high level of irregularities. By mid-morning a discernible pattern of irregularities was emerging which appeared to be penalizing the principal opposition party. The OAS team and two NGO teams protested to the Dominican electoral tribunal. Preliminary returns indicated that there was an approximately 1 percent or 30,000-vote advantage for President Balaguer over his principal challenger, Dr. Peña Gomez. This election was the first occasion in the history of OAS election observation on which the number of irregularities exceeded the margin of victory by a presidential candidate. For the first time the OAS could not endorse the results and issued a communiqué to this effect. It was subsequently confirmed that approximately 45,000 citizens with valid credentials were denied the right to vote. Balaguer's side claimed victory. The opposition charged fraud. Tension and the prospect of violent destabilization re-emerged. The situation was exacerbated by the Electoral Tribunal which proclaimed Balaguer the winner without any reference to the results of investigation by a special commission (recommended by the local Catholic church authorities, the OAS and others) which had pointed to the likelihood of large-scale fraud.

As the post-electoral crisis deepened, the OAS observer mission was gradually transformed into a mediation body which enjoyed the full support of the President and the Opposition leaders. This mediation phase took place without any specific mandate from the OAS Council or Foreign Ministers. Had such a mandate been formally sought, the Dominican Government would have almost certainly turned it down as an intrusion into their sovereignty. The OAS mediator, a Canadian, in partnership with a Dominican Bishop, was able to broker a solution eventually accepted by all parties. Key provisions were that fresh elections would be held in two years, instead of four, and that a President could not be re-elected to a consecutive term.

The cost of the observation and the mediation were borne by special contributions from the United States and Germany, with the Americans providing almost 80 percent of the total. As mediation stretched on (three months), more funds were required and, given the delicacy of the situation, it would have been prudent to appear less dependent on the United States. Canada was asked to help. Although the Canadian Consulate in Santo Domingo was helpful and the Canadian mission to the OAS was supportive, funds were not forthcoming.

Haiti

On the other side of the island, the overthrow of President Aristide provided a more structured example of OAS response to a major crisis in a member country. The legitimate government had been violently cast out and the recently created supranational mechanism, Resolution 1080, was invoked. OAS Foreign Ministers met in emergency session. The illegal government was condemned and eventually sanctions were imposed. The most vigorous players in directing international heat on to Haiti in the early stages were Canada and Venezuela. The United States was also an essential player, but its actions were sometimes tempered by countervailing pressures—for example, from the tax-free industrial zones of Haiti that faced bankruptcy. As the long saga unfolded Canada's record of positive intervention was also looking bruised.

In collaboration with the UN, the OAS established a civilian human rights monitoring force (MICIVIH).[7] Despite the restrictions and harassment imposed by the de facto government, the presence of this group restricted the barbarities of the Haitian military and the civilian thugs of *Le Front Révolutionaire pour l'Avancement et le Progrès en Haiti* (FRAPH).[8] When the U.S. naval vessel, *Harland County*, with its cargo of U.S. specialist troops and RCMP officers was inexplicably repelled by a ragged FRAPH demonstration on the Haitian waterfront, the OAS and the UN withdrew their human rights monitors across the border to the Dominican Republic. The Canadian government concurred with this decision and in addition evacuated RCMP officers who had previously arrived in Port-au-Prince.

This was a low point. The risks to the RCMP and particularly to the monitors had increased but the population felt betrayed by their departure and by the impotence of the international community. The next step by the international community was to impose UN-wide sanctions and tighten the enforcement of the economic squeeze with U.S., Canadian and other warships.

The sanctions did not achieve their political purpose. The end of the de facto government was only obtained by the shrewd negotiations of Jimmy Carter, Colin Powell and Sam Nunn, backed up by the imminent threat of an American invasion. In fact, the sanction route had been a disaster. Commenting on the very pertinent account of the OAS and the Haitian crisis by CAPA,[9] Ian Martin, former deputy head of the UN/OAS monitoring team, described the turmoil of haphazard and inadequately targeted application of sanctions as "mangled multilateralism."[10] In time the sanctions were biting hard, but mostly they were biting the wrong people.

It is difficult to exaggerate the appalling impact of three years of sanctions on almost every segment of Haitian society. When President Aristide and his government returned, the task they faced had been made many times more formidable by the economic, social, political and agricultural devastation, which OAS sanctions had caused and UN sanctions had multiplied. Investment confidence has not returned. The economic and administrative infrastructure is in more serious disarray than it was before the coup. Unemployment and underemployment remain potentially destabilizing factors and the small professional class from which the new managers, civic leaders and technicians must be recruited has been seriously depleted by violence and exile.

Against this wreckage must be placed the gains. Civil society has been refreshed by the return of constitutional government, the dismantling of the army, the significant reduction of human rights abuses and the lowering of tensions. Notwithstanding major problems of incompetence and obstruction, particularly at the beginning, the election process of the past eight months has gone reasonably well. The OAS observation of the election was effective. It would have been more effective if the respective headquarters of the UN and the OAS had not insisted that the OAS/UN human rights monitoring teams, with their unique familiarity with the country and their knowledge of Creole, be relegated to a limited support role for the electoral process. Separate new OAS administrative machinery had to be put in place to manage the electoral observation. However, the OAS presence and most especially that of UN troops acted as a deterrent to those who may have contemplated large-scale electoral fraud.

But any close look at the Haitian balance sheet raises questions about what should have or could have been done to achieve the positive results without paying the colossal price of three years of human, institutional and material devastation. By early 1994 many persons, "including people connected to the human rights community ... [concluded] that there was no alternative to humanitarian (military) intervention."[11]

Somalia was still spooking Congress and through the spring and summer domestic opposition to an invasion kept the Clinton administration tied to the disastrously futile sanctions policy. However, President Clinton too came to the conclusion that there was no choice short of military intervention. He urged Mr. Chrétien to join him and commit some elements of the Canadian military to this enterprise. The same narrowing of options, reinforced by the special responsibility that Canada had assumed and loudly proclaimed in respect of Haiti, should have led the Canadian government to the same conclusion. However, Mr. Chrétien turned down Mr. Clinton, indicating that he would support the post-invasion phase—the policing of Haiti.

Since 1990, the OAS has also been involved in conflict resolution in Peru (the autogolpe of Fujimori) and in Nicaragua (a political reconciliation program following the election of Violetta Chamorro) and is co-ordinating de-mining programs throughout Central America. Although activities in Peru and Nicaragua generated controversy they were responsible undertakings to address major problems. However, there is by no means an automatic reflex in Latin America that calls on the OAS whenever external mediation is required. Neither Ecuador nor Peru sought OAS assistance to settle their border conflict in 1995. In El Salvador, both government and rebels bypassed the OAS when the United Nations was invited to broker deals and coordinate arrangements that led to a peaceful settlement. While it had played a key role in the resolution of the Serrano autogolpe in 1993, the OAS subsequently antagonized the Guatemalans, with the result that the UN was called in to facilitate negotiations between the government and the rebels.

HUMAN RIGHTS

The Inter-American Commission on Human Rights and the Inter-American Human Rights Court represent another very important sector where results lag seriously behind expectations. Both suffer from organizational deficiencies and major shortages of human and financial resources. What is more critical is that they receive very inadequate cooperation from member governments, which more often than not makes a sham out of enforcement. In the case of the Inter-American Court there is very little that the Canadian government can do, as it has neither accepted the jurisdiction of the Court, nor signed the Inter-American Convention on Human Rights, and cannot do so until it submits a number of reservations acceptable to provincial governments. In these circumstances it is hardly surprising that the Canadian government's nomination in 1991 of an excellent candidate for appointment to the court, Judge Bertha Wilson, failed to secure the necessary votes.

WHERE TO FROM HERE?

It is much easier, and more devastating, to count the shortcomings and failures than it is to measure the successes of the OAS. Nevertheless, the OAS record is better than its caricature. The relatively minor Canadian subscription has been a useful investment. And even if the returns are not sufficiently visible in OAS-managed achievements, the membership fee is a small price to pay for being seen as a full participant in the Pan-American system by member states that are becoming an increasingly important part of Canada's international trading and political strategy. As Peter McKenna has written, "if Canada hoped to play a larger role in the hemisphere ... it would have to join [its] principal institutional entity."[12]

If the OAS image has shown improvement, what has happened to the Canadian image in the OAS? On the whole, Canada has been regarded as vigorous and professional, but there is some disappointment that it has not provided more funding and that Canada's Latin American policy is not more distinct from that of the U.S. Distinctions and abrasions were more apparent in the 1980s: differing Cold War strategies and their application in such cases as Grenada and Central America and of course, Cuba. Cuba remains, but then, Fidel Castro, Jesse Helms, Mas Canosa, and other players walk on a smaller stage.

Where to from here?[13] It is vital that more pressure be exerted on the Secretary-General to thoroughly overhaul the management and professional standards of the Organization and to dramatically improve vertical and horizontal communication. In his own *Vision* paper Gaviria has acknowledged that "the OAS must recover the political legitimacy and technical credibility it has lost." It should be equally important for the Chrétien government to give once more to democratization and governance the high priority it now gives to trade and to recognizè that, in Latin America and the Caribbean, the two are increasingly inseparable.

NOTES

1   For the most comprehensive account of Canada's relationship with the Pan-American system and the background to the decision to join the OAS see Peter McKenna, *Canada and the OAS* (Ottawa: Carleton University Press, 1995).

2   Known as the Washington Protocol. For a set of pertinent recommendations about reform of the OAS in the areas of human rights and democracy, see *Special Report of the Inter-American Dialogue on the OAS*, Inter-American Dialogue, Washington, D.C., August 1994, 11-14.

3   This approach to issues touching on sovereignty is known in Mexico as the Estrada doctrine.

4   *A New Vision of the OAS*, draft OAS paper, Organization of American States, Washington, D.C., 51.

5   President Menem of Argentina is a strong opponent of the reintegration of Cuba into the OAS.

6   I was a member of the Secretary-General's mission to Guatemala, head of the OAS observation/mediation mission in the Dominican Republic, and in the spring of 1995 led an electoral support mission of the International Foundation for Electoral Systems (IFES) to Haiti.

7   MICIVIH: The United Nations/Organization of American States International Mission in Haiti.

8   FRAPH embodies a deliberate play on words: "frappe" means "hit."

9   Canada-Americas Policy Alternatives (CAPA), *Report on Canada's Fifth Year in the OAS* (Toronto: CAPA, 1995).

10   Ian Martin, "Haiti: Mangled Multilateralism," *Foreign Policy*, 95, (Summer 1994), 72-89.

11   Thomas G. Weiss, "Triage: Humanitarianism Intervention," *World Policy Journal* XI, no. 1 (Spring 1994), 59-68.

12   McKenna, *Canada and the OAS*, 117.

13   Viron P. Vaky and Heraldo Muñoz, *The Future of the Organization of American States*, (New York: Twentieth Century Fund Press, 1993), 72.

ACRONYMS

A&E	Arts and Entertainment Channel
AfDB	African Development Bank
AsDB	Asian Development Bank
AFSOUTH	Allied Forces South (NATO)
AIDS	Acquired Immuno-deficiency Syndrome
ANWAR	Arctic National Wildlife Refuge (Alaska)
APEC	Asia Pacific Economic Cooperation Forum
ASEAN	Association of South East Asian Nations
BIS	Bank for International Settlements
BMD	Ballistic Missile Defence
BQ	Bloc Québécois
CAPA	Canada-Americas Policy Alternatives
CBC	Canadian Broadcasting Corporation
CCIC	Canadian Council for International Co-operation
CCSR	Centre for Complex Systems Research
CF	Canadian Forces
CFB	Canadian Forces Base
CIDA	Canadian International Development Agency
CIIPS	Canadian Institute for International Peace and Security
CINCNORAD	Commander-in-Chief, NORAD
CIORU	Carleton Industrial Organization Research Unit
CMAC	Cambodian Mine Action Centre
CMT	Country Music Television
CNN	Cable News Network
COSICS	Canadian Online Secure Information and Communications System (DFAIT)
CRTC	Canadian Radio-Television and Telecommunications Commission
CUSO	Canadian University Services Overseas
CWB	Chemical Weapons Ban
DAC	Development Assistance Committee (OECD)
DFAIT	Department of Foreign Affairs and International Trade (Canada)
DND	Department of National Defence (Canada)
DPKO	Department of Peacekeeping Operations (DFAIT)
EBRD	European Bank for Reconstruction and Development

EC	European Community
ECOSOC	The Economic and Social Council (UN)
EPA	Environmental Protection Agency (U.S.)
ESPN	Entertainment and Sports Network
EU	European Union
FOL	Forward Operating Location
FRAPH	Revolutionary Front for the Advancement and Progress of Haiti
FTA	Canada-United States Free Trade Agreement
FXE	Foreign Currency Exchange
GA	General Assembly (UN)
GAB	General Agreements to Borrow
GAR	General Assembly Resolution (UN)
GATS	General Agreement on Trade in Services
GATT	General Agreement on Tariffs and Trade
GDP	Gross Domestic Product
GM	General Motors
GNP	Gross National Product
GOP	Grand Old Party (U.S.)
G-7	Group of Seven (Canada, France, Germany, Great Britain, Italy, Japan, United States)
G-77	Group of Seventy-Seven (non-aligned states coalition at the UN)
G-10	Group of Ten (G-7 states & Belgium, the Netherlands, Sweden, and Switzerland)
G-3	Group of Three (European Union, Japan, United States)
G-24	Group of Twenty-Four (developing states coalition at the IMF/World Bank Forum)
HBO	Home Box Office
ICJ	International Court of Justice
ICRC	International Committee of the Red Cross
IDA	International Development Association
IDB	Inter-American Development Bank
IDRC	International Development Research Centre
IFC	International Finance Corporation
IFES	International Foundation for Electoral Systems
IFI	International Financial Institution
IFOR	Implementation Force (NATO)
ILO	International Labour Organization

IMF	International Monetary Fund
INGO	International Non-governmental Organization
IO	International Organization
IT	Information Technology
ITAC	International Trade Advisory Committee (DFAIT)
JNA	Yugoslav National Army
MCA	Music Corporation of America
MCCC	Mennonite Central Committee Canada
MDB	Multilateral Development Bank
MICIVIH	United Nations/Organization of American States International Mission in Haiti
MNF	Multi-National Force (Lebanon)
MP	Member of Parliament
NAFTA	North American Free Trade Agreement
NATO	North Atlantic Treaty Organization
NCN	New Country Network
NCO	Non-commissioned Officer
NGO	Non-governmental Organization
NORAD	North American Aerospace Defence Command
NPT	Non-Proliferation Treaty
NWS	North Warning System (NORAD)
OAS	Organization of American States
OAU	Organization for African Unity
ODA	Official Development Assistance
OECD	Organization for Economic Cooperation and Development
OSCE	Organization for Security and Cooperation in Europe
PACE	Protestant and Catholic Encounter (Northern Ireland)
PCO	Privy Council Office
P-8	Political-Eight (G-7 & the Russian Federation)
PK	Peacekeeping
PLO	Palestinian Liberation Organization
PQ	Parti Québécois
PTSD	Post-traumatic Stress Syndrome
RCMP	Royal Canadian Mounted Police
SAGIT	Sector Advisory Groups on International Trade (DFAIT)
SAP	South Asia Partnership
SC	Security Council (UN)

SCF	Save the Children Fund
SCR	Security Council Resolution (UN)
SDR	Special Drawing Right
SDS	Serbian Democratic Party
SG	Secretary-General (UN)
SIGNET	Secure Integrated Global Network (DFAIT)
SLCDF	Sri Lanka-Canada Development Fund
SNF	Somali National Front
SNM	Somali National Movement
SPM	Somali Patriotic Movement
SPS	Serbian Socialist Party (Federal Republic of Yugoslavia)
SSDF	Somali Salvation Democratic Front
SSEA	Secretary of State for External Affairs (Canada)
TCC	Troop Contributing Country
TMD	Theatre Missile Defences
UPD	Unit for the Promotion of Democracy (OAS)
UK	United Kingdom
UN	United Nations
UNA	United Nations Association
UNAMIR	United Nations Mission in Rwanda
UNCED	United Nations Conference on the Environment and Development
UNDP	United Nations Development Programme
UNDPI	United Nations Department of Public Information
UNEF	United Nations Emergency Force
UNEP	United Nations Environmental Programme
UNESCO	United Nations Educational, Scientific, and Cultural Organization
UNFPA	United Nations Fund for Population Activities
UNHCR	United Nations High Commission for Refugees
UNICEF	United Nations Children's Fund
UNIDO	United Nations Industrial Development Organization
UNITAF	Unified Task Force (Somalia)
UNOSOM II	United Nations Operation in Somalia II
UNPREDEP	United Nations Preventative Deployment (Former Yugoslav Republic of Macedonia)
UNPROFOR	United Nations Protection Force (former Yugoslavia)
UNTAC	United Nations Transitional Authority in Cambodia
U.S.	United States

USAF	United States' Air Force
USAID	United States Agency for International Development
USC	United Somali Congress
USSR	Union of Soviet Socialist Republics
USTR	United States Trade Representative
VCR	Video Cassette Recorder
WB	World Bank
WEOG	West European and Other Group (UN)
WEU	Western European Union
WFP	World Food Programme (UN)
WTO	World Trade Organization
WUSC	World University Service of Canada
YM/YWCA	Young Men's/Young Women's Christian Association

The **Canada Among Nations** series is available from
Carleton University Press, Suite 1400, CTTC,
1125 Colonel By Drive, Ottawa Ontario K1S 5B6

Canada Among Nations 1995: Democracy and Foreign Policy
  edited by Maureen Appel Molot
  ISBN 0-88629-261-1 pbk. $22.95

Canada Among Nations 1994: A Part of the Peace
  edited by Maureen Appel Molot and Harald von Riekhoff
  ISBN 0-88629-227-1 pbk. $22.95

Canada Among Nations 1993-94: Global Jeopardy
  edited by Fen Osler Hampson and Christopher J. Maule
  ISBN 0-88629-203-4 pbk. $22.95

Canada Among Nations 1992-93: A New World Order
  edited by Fen Osler Hampson and Christopher J. Maule
  ISBN 0-88629-167-4 pbk. $21.95

Canada Among Nations 1990-91: After the Cold War
  edited by Fen Osler Hampson and Christopher J. Maule
  ISBN 0-88629-144-3 pbk. $21.95

Canada Among Nations 1989: The Challenge of Change
  edited by Maureen Appel Molot and Fen Osler Hampson
  ISBN 0-88629-106-2 pbk. $19.95

Order by phone (613) 520-3740 or by fax (613) 520-2893
(email orders: jsloan@ccs.carleton.ca)